A History of American Literary Journalism

D1506255

JOHN C. HARTSOCK

A History
of American
Literary
Journalism

*The Emergence
of a Modern
Narrative Form*

UNIVERSITY OF MASSACHUSETTS PRESS
AMHERST

Printed in the United States of America
LC 00-030279
ISBN 1-55849-251-8 (cloth); 252-6 (paper)

Designed by Dennis Anderson
Set in New Baskerville by Graphic Composition, Inc.
Printed and bound by Sheridan Books, Inc.

Library of Congress Cataloging-in-Publication Data

Hartsock, John C., 1951–
  A history of American literary journalism : the emergence of a modern narrative form/
  John C. Hartsock.
     p. cm.
  Includes bibliographical references (p.) and index.
  ISBN 1-55849-251-8 (cloth : alk. paper) — ISBN 1-55849-252-6 (pbk. : alk. paper)
  1. Reportage literature, American—History and criticism. 2. Journalism—United
States—History—20th century. 3. American prose literature—History and criticism.
  4. Narration (Rhetoric) I. Title.

PS366.R44 H37 2000
071'.3—dc21

                                                                    00-030279

British Library Cataloguing in Publication data are available.

For my wife, Linda, and son, Peter,
and my parents, John and Lydia

Contents

Preface

SEVERAL YEARS ago, when I began to engage in the scholarship of literary journalism, I took what seemed to me a reasonable path of inquiry and sought out a history of the form. After all, what could be more reasonable than to review a literary history—no matter how biased and incomplete histories must inevitably prove—in order to acquire a broad overview of my subject? Whatever the shortcomings of any history, it can still provide the beginnings of a critical contextualization of the past. Imagine my dismay, then, when I discovered that there was no history of the form. It seemed to me there were two ways to approach such a dilemma. The first was to put off the project and move on to other more fully examined scholarly themes that would not be so taxing. The second was to see the absence of a history as a scholarly opportunity. I confess that initially I was put off, intimidated by the prospect of writing a history of a form for which there was little historiographic perspective. But in time, I began to see the opportunity, perhaps much the way Huck Finn saw the Oklahoma Territory as an opportunity. From such a relatively unfettered freedom I found I had the luxury of ranging widely and at will. Such a circumstance proved one of the most critical factors in seeing this book to completion.

As for my approach to the material, I am one of those lovers of literature with one foot in the "old" "new criticism." Thus I still appreciate the "canon." But another foot is clearly planted in the more recent poststructural and postmodern critical currents. As a consequence, my approach may be more theoretical than some historians care for because I am one of those who believe that history is, indeed, highly theoretical and subjective. One consequence is that I write in the first person, thus consciously eschewing the pose of historical limited omniscience. My reason for doing so can be found in *Let Us Now Praise Famous Men*, when James Agee observes of one of the sharecroppers of

ix

whom he writes: "George Gudger is a man, et cetera. But obviously, in the effort to tell of him (by example) as truthfully as I can, I am limited. I know him only so far as I know him, and only in those terms in which I know him; and all of that depends as fully on who I am as on who he is" (239). The same could be said of the historian's relationship to history, and I readily acknowledge those inherent limitations. This does not mean that I do not work within certain historiographical constraints and methodologies. But it does mean that I recognize that my history is, like all histories, an interpretation of the moment, one that not only attempts to reflect (no matter how imperfectly) past eras but also undoubtedly reflects our current period as well.

My audience for the book is threefold. First, I have in mind scholars and teachers in English, journalism, mass communication, and American studies who wish to begin developing their own contextualization of the form—no matter how imperfect a history my book must prove. Such a wide audience will account for why at times I must seem to indulge the commonplaces of literary or journalistic history: they may not be so commonplace to some members of the academy. Second, I have in mind graduate students and perhaps even upper-level undergraduates who seek to explore the form more fully. Again, this may account for why, to the first group, I at times seem to indulge in commonplaces of history. I can only beg that they bear with me in the interests of our students. Third, I have in mind practitioners of the form and professional journalists, if only they will excuse what might seem to them an obtuse critical language, which the academy is notorious for out in the "real" world. In my defense all I can say is that nowhere is it writ that understanding must be simple. Indeed, the risk of such an approach—"Write it simply and to the point"—is to fail to acknowledge the paradoxical complexities of the ontological and epistemological worlds. But if this last group is patient, I hope they will discover that literary journalism is part of an ancient enterprise as venerable as poetry and drama. Indeed, the roots of literary journalism extend back at least to the classical period in the Western tradition.

I should probably elaborate on my approach toward ideology. Underlying my examination, on the one hand, is the critical assumption that ideology can never be *entirely* escaped. On the other is implicit the view that there is always the possibility of some degree of resistance, linguistically, consciously, culturally, or some combination of the three, against *social* ideology. As the eminent teacher of philosophy William Barrett remarked: "The essential freedom, the ultimate and final freedom that cannot be taken from a man, is to say No" (241). Barrett is responding to Jean Paul Sartre's recollection of the French Resistance when the latter observed: "We were never more free than during the German occupation." Barrett continues: "Freedom is in its very essence negative, though this negativity is also creative. At a certain moment, perhaps, the drug or the pain inflicted by the torturer may make the victim lose consciousness, and he will confess. But so long as he retains the lucidity of consciousness, however tiny the area of action possible for him, he can still say in his own mind: No. Consciousness and freedom are thus given together." Such a circumstance (in the silence of consciousness, whether linguistically articulated or not), Barrett adds, "affords man his final dignity." Thus, I see *social* ideology and freedom always engaged in some degree of negotiation. Freedom may always be colored by social ideology, but it can also resist it. I do not deny that such acts can be co-opted, reinscribed, and otherwise made to reflect social ideology. But at the same time we must bear in mind that such acts of resistance are still possible, "however tiny the area of action." My explanation should help to account for the dissatisfaction of those who will take the position that social ideology is all-encompassing. Such a freedom is one that the slippage between figure and presence alone assures cannot be brought to closure.

Such a "slippage," as Linda Orr has expressed it (13), is the terrain where this history takes place, exploring what has elapsed between figure and presence. That said, I was guided by a number of critical considerations. Foremost, I realized the impossibility of writing a "comprehensive" history given that in historiography something must always be excluded or silenced. Once that was acknowledged, I was free of the critical straitjacket of thinking I had to be "comprehensive." I had more room for movement in theorizing the form. I must emphasize that this history is hardly the final word on the matter. It is only "a" history, not "the" history of the form. But then from my critical position, no comprehensive history enclosed by the definite article is possible. Instead, mine is just one interpretation, and I look forward with excitement to other interpretations in the future. Ultimately, the story of the "history" of literary journalism is an unfolding one if for no other reason than because of an issue I explore in chapter 2, critic Mikhail Bakhtin's "inconclusive present." I look forward to those future findings and the critical site they continue to establish even if the form's boundaries, to borrow from John Keats, forever "tease us out of thought."

PORTIONS OF chapter 6 derive from my article "The Critical Marginalization of American Literary Journalism," *Critical Studies in Mass Communication* 15.1 (March 1998): 61–84; this material is used by kind permission of the National Communication Association.

JOHN C. HARTSOCK

Acknowledgments

THERE ARE many to whom I must acknowledge my debt in the writing of the book. First, it would not have been possible without the work of pioneers in this field of scholarship. While *A History of American Literary Journalism: The Emergence of a Modern Narrative Form* is very much a scholarship of discovery, it is also, as any history must prove, a scholarship of synthesis—to borrow from the late Ernest L. Boyer—that must negotiate with those who preceded. In particular, I single out those who introduced me to the form and to the scholarship of the form. They include Norman Sims, who, as he did for many other teachers, scholars, and other devotees of literary journalism, provided my introduction to the form in his *Literary Journalists* and to the scholarship in his collection *Literary Journalism in the Twentieth Century*. Then there is the scholarship of Thomas Berner, Thomas B. Connery, David Eason, Barbara Lounsberry, John J. Pauly, Sam G. Riley, and Ronald Weber, among others. Now that my book is complete, I see more fully just how much they were willing to take critical plunges into what had been largely a scholarly void. That took guts. I view them (although I must emphasize that such a list is not exhaustive) as the first generation of scholars who approached the form with a *sustained* interest.

Moreover, as I worked the conference circuit, my enthusiasm for literary journalism was revived by meeting those who shared my interest. The shared enthusiasm was crucial when my interest and energies flagged during the five-year effort to write this book, sandwiched as it was between getting married, changing jobs, and the birth of my son (my wife might suggest that those events were sandwiched between the book). Those in particular who helped to rekindle my enthusiasm when it wavered include Tom Connery, Sam G. Riley, Michael Robertson, and Jan Whitt.

I also thank William Seibenschuh, who helped me through a difficult problem of Boswellian scholarship on short notice and amid the holiday season.

Furthermore, this book would not have been possible without the untiring efforts of my editors at the University of Massachusetts Press, Carol Betsch and Clark Dougan, as well as my copy editor, Anne R. Gibbons. They were always patient and encouraging when I indulged in my excesses, especially regarding last-minute corrections.

In addition, I owe a debt to three individuals who never hesitated to encourage me "to push the envelope" as I was laying the groundwork for this book during my doctoral studies at the State University of New York at Albany: Jeff Berman, Ron Bosco, and Steve North. They took a chance on an unknown quantity, me, when I embarked into parts equally unknown, and I can only hope that this book amply rewards them for their risk.

Finally, I acknowledge the unwavering support of my wife, Linda, and my family. Their love provided the most critical ingredient.

J. C. H.

A History
of American
Literary
Journalism

Introduction

IN A MOMENT inspired with and hopeful for the history of his art, the journalist Hutchins Hapgood in his 1939 autobiography recalled his years as a reporter at the old *New York Commercial Advertiser,* where he had been a practitioner of what some scholars today call "literary journalism": "and it is not indulging too much in the natural tendency to exaggerate in memory a significant and pleasurable experience, to say that many bits of living writing, by a number of different persons, could be discovered by some future historian, by looking through the files of the paper—articles mostly unsigned, sometimes bits in the news, sometimes fillers in the Saturday supplement, or short stories full of color" (*Victorian* 146). Thus Hapgood sensed that something memorable—of historical literary import—had occurred in journalism practice during the fin de siècle. Yet despite Hapgood's fond hopes, few attempts have been made to historicize the last century or so of American literary journalism, or what might be characterized more definitively as "narrative" literary journalism because the form fundamentally works in a narrative mode.

The consequences of this lack of examination are perhaps predictable. For the scholar or teacher who sees value to the form and is eager to explore it individually or in the classroom, a large void exists which makes it difficult to contextualize a body of writing that, to provide a working definition, reads like a novel or short story except that it is true or makes a truth claim to phenomenal experience. Such a literary journalism, then, is a kind of literary "faction," on the one hand acknowledging its relationship to fiction—as we conventionally understand the meaning of fiction—while on the other making a claim to reflecting a world of "fact."

Another consequence is perhaps more ominous for the current state of contemporary American literature. As Barbara Lounsberry notes in *The Art of Fact,* the most widely circulated book review in the

1

country, the *New York Times Book Review*, reviews nonfiction over fiction
by almost three to one (xi). This is not to suggest that all such works
are the kind of narrative "literary journalism" under consideration
here given that the reviews include autobiography, history, sociological
examinations, and so forth. But they also include such works as Jonathan Harr's *Civil Action*, a "masterly treatment," the reviewer notes, of
the impact of toxic pollution on the lives of residents of Woburn, Massachusetts. The reviewer writes that Harr "employs a mild version of
the novelized you-are-there format. . . . This should strike readers as a
reasonable use of the disputed novelization technique, because apparently Mr. Harr has not taken liberty with the reconstituted quotations"
(Easterbrook 13). To cite still another example, how can a scholar and
teacher critically contextualize a work when its publisher characterizes
a writer as "award-winning literary journalist Mark Bowden" in the recently published *Black Hawk Down* (Bowden, dust cover notes)?

What begins to emerge then is a paradox: a contemporary body of
work is going largely unexamined by the academy. Yet any attempt to
engage in such an examination and to do so historically must confront
the frustration of realizing that there is only limited scholarship on the
form and even less that specifically historicizes it as a literary form.
Given that historicizing provides one important context for examining
any material critically, one from which other critical examinations can
depart, such an inquiry is long overdue. One measure of the need is the
passage of a half century between Hapgood's 1939 and Lounsberry's
1990 remarks.

My purpose, then, is to explore several related historical issues that
will help contextualize the form. They are

1. the evidence of the emergence of a "modern" American literary
   journalism, narrative in modal disposition, during the post–Civil
   War period;
2. reasons for the form's emergence and the form's epistemological
   consequences;
3. antecedents to the form;
4. how to distinguish the form from other nonfiction forms such as
   the discursive essay, muckraking, and sensational journalism;
5. post–fin de siècle evidence of the form up to the so-called new jour-

nalism of the 1960s with the reasons for its initial emergence providing a continuing historical modus; and

6. reasons for the form's critical marginalization, which further historically contextualizes it by the "literary" presence it was not permitted
to have.

Perhaps critical usage will eventually characterize such texts as a
"genre" but for the moment, I adopt the more conservative usage of
"form" by scholar Thomas B. Connery as an acknowledgment that our
understanding of it is still very much emerging ("Third Way" 6). In
writing a history of the form, I take a largely thematic approach, as
opposed to a perhaps more traditional chronological approach, in order to highlight what I believe are the major critical issues weaving
their way through such a history. I do so because such an approach
helps to provide sharper critical definitions of the historical subject. In
addition, the appendix presents an overview of recent nonhistorical
scholarship of the form because it may as yet be unfamiliar to many
readers.

I do not suggest, however, that this effort provides a comprehensive
history. Undoubtedly, I have left out someone's "favorite" author. Instead, this is a fluid critical history through which I examine basic issues
at the intersection of epistemology and ontology, those of language
and consciousness on the one hand, and external culture on the other.
Much excavation of the subject remains to be done. Still, enough scholarship has accumulated that we can begin to see the broad critical outlines of a literary history long neglected.

Before embarking on an examination of the historical issues I have
identified, three important considerations remain in order to provide
broad context. The first is the problematic nature of the form's name.
The second is the relationship of travelogue, sports narrative, and
crime narrative to the form. The third is a review of the limited scholarship that specifically historicizes the form.

"LITERARY JOURNALISM" is by no means the universal designation
for the form. An electronic search of the *MLA Bibliography* reveals the
nature of the problem. Scholarship on the kind of narrative under consideration here is listed as "literary journalism" only about twenty-five

times (some are borderline) from 1963 through the end of the twentieth century. The nearest competitor, "literary nonfiction," fared better,
with thirty-eight listings. That would seem to favor the latter usage if
frequency alone were the measure for determining a form's identity.
But such a conclusion is problematic for two reasons. First, only about
fifteen of those listed as "literary nonfiction" would qualify as scholarship examining the kind of narrative discussed here. Second, and perhaps more important, the *MLA Bibliography* privileges scholarship that
derives from English studies and cannot be definitive in accounting for
scholarship on the form that comes out of other disciplines such as
journalism, mass communication, and American studies. For example,
the *MLA Bibliography* fails to acknowledge the 1992 *Sourcebook of American Literary Journalism: Portrait of an Emerging Genre,* edited by Connery,
or the 1990 *Literary Journalism in the Twentieth Century,* edited by Norman Sims. Connery teaches journalism at the University of St. Thomas
in St. Paul; Sims teaches journalism at the University of Massachusetts
in Amherst. The scholarly allegiances of both belong to the Association
for Education in Journalism and Mass Communication (the AEJMC)
and not the MLA (McGill 140, 278).

It should also be noted that of the thirty-eight MLA listings in "literary nonfiction," seventeen belong to one collection edited by Chris
Anderson, the 1989 *Literary Nonfiction: Theory, Criticism, Pedagogy.* In
addition, that collection does not distinguish between fundamentally
discursive and narrative forms. If the Connery and Sims collections of
scholarship on the form were included in the *MLA Bibliography,* usage
of the term "literary journalism" would far outweigh, in numbers
alone, usage of "literary nonfiction": Connery's text contains thirty-six
critical articles; Sims's contains twelve.

Such an approach, however, amounts to little more than bean counting and perhaps has no more utility than that it reveals the problematic
nature of identifying the form. Matters are further muddied when one
considers that "literary journalism" and "literary nonfiction" are not
the only terminologies for designating the form. They appear to be the
two most widely used, but others include "art-journalism, nonfiction
novel, essay-fiction, factual fiction, journalit, . . . journalistic nonfiction, . . . nonfiction reportage, . . . [and] New Journalism" (Weber, *Literature of Fact* 1). In 1993 *Creative Nonfiction* began publication. Initially,

it was published biannually by the Department of English at the University of Pittsburgh and then triquarterly by the Creative Nonfiction Foundation. The literary journal is dedicated to running narrative literary journalism, and other nonfiction forms, as characterized by the journal's title (1:ii, 13:iv). Meanwhile, in 1999 an Associated Press book review cited "narrative nonfiction" (Anthony 16). Still other possibilities include "lyrics in prose," "the confession," "the nature meditation," "literature of fact," and "non-imaginative literature" (Winterowd ix). W. Ross Winterowd acknowledges that the "greatest problem, perhaps, is finding a term that covers the texts I deal with." Finally, in a fit of critical frustration, he says "I have decided merely to surrender" and calls the texts under consideration the "other" literature (ix). They are, indeed, a kind of literary "faction" given their factionalized status. Moreover, matters are confused still again when one considers that if examples of literary journalism/nonfiction other scholars cite are any indication, the form can include more traditional generic and subgeneric categories such as "personal essay," "travelogue," "memoir," "biography" and "autobiography" (Paterson).

Connery, who has taken the lead in defense of "literary journalism," acknowledges the difficulty of the form's identity when he cites the need for a justification for the name in his *Sourcebook of American Literary Journalism* (xiv): "Use of the word 'journalism' is preferred over 'nonfiction' because the works assigned to this literary form are neither essays nor commentary. It is also preferred because much of the content of the works comes from traditional means of news gathering or reporting" (15). But that Connery must look for a justification at all clearly reflects the extant critical discomfort with the form's identity. The use of "literary nonfiction" is equally discomfiting, however. Lounsberry, for example, says "we can proceed to study these works without a term for this discourse" (xiii), but only after she notes without reservations, "I will call [the form] artful literary nonfiction" (xi). Given that *both* Lounsberry and Winterowd are associated with the English academy, her "artful literary nonfiction" poses, of course, a striking contrast to Winterowd's "non-imaginative literature." Can what is "artful" be "non-imaginative"? Can what is "non-imaginative" be "artful"?

What is the cause of this uncertainty surrounding the identity of the form? It can be traced in part to the critical furor surrounding the new journalism of the 1960s, which includes such classics of the form as Truman Capote's *In Cold Blood* and Tom Wolfe's *Electric Kool-Aid Acid Test*. Critics soon noted that there was nothing "new" about this kind of impressionistic journalism. Nonetheless, the new journalism *aka* literary journalism *aka* literary nonfiction did attract considerable critical scrutiny. What scholars found was that whatever the form was called, it was ill-defined. Ronald Weber, for one, acknowledged this in his 1980 *Literature of Fact*. One of the early attempts to account for the new journalism, his study notes that "needless to say, this category of serious writing is not well defined, and the many terms used to describe it . . . have done nothing to clarify matters" (1). Some seventeen years later, not much had changed, as Ben Yagoda notes in *The Art of Fact* when he characterizes "literary journalism" as "a profoundly fuzzy term" (13).

The problem of identification is also political, reflecting as it does a rough but not definitive split between journalism and English studies. Anderson and Lounsberry, who are affiliated with English studies, prefer "literary nonfiction." Connery and Sims, affiliated with journalism studies, prefer "literary journalism." But the bifurcation should not come as a surprise given the politics in the academy that surrounds a loaded term such as "journalism." Simply, there long has been a bias against "journalism" by English studies, an issue I explore in the last chapter when I discuss the form's critical marginalization. Thus when Winterowd characterizes the form as the "other" literature, he tacitly reinscribes the marginalized status of a form of writing that could be construed as a "journalism": in his probing search for a terminology, testing different nomenclatures, not once does he consider the possibility that the form could be considered a "journalism" (ix). Yet a reverse kind of marginalization, or discrimination, also occurs in the journalism and mass communication academies when it comes to the possibility that journalism could have "literary" merit, an issue I explore later.

There is evidence that such an academic split may be beginning to break down with the 1997 publication of the historical anthology *The Art of Fact* edited by Yagoda and Kevin Kerrane. Both are on the English faculty of the University of Delaware and both use the terminology "literary journalism." (Their *Art of Fact* should not be confused with Lounsberry's 1990 title of the same name.) It is perhaps also significant that their anthology has been published by a major publishing house, Scribner, thus giving "literary journalism" mainstream publishing cachet, one reinforced by Ballantine's publication in 1984 of the anthology *The Literary Journalists,* edited by Sims, and publication in 1995 of a newer anthology, *Literary Journalism,* coedited by Sims and "literary journalist" Mark Kramer. And perhaps the mood is catching because the Atlantic Monthly Press characterizes Mark Bowden, author of the 1999 *Black Hawk Down,* as a "literary journalist."

Still another problem is the way the form is cataloged: generally it isn't, thus leaving much of what might be considered narrative literary journalism homeless in library science. While the canonical fictional novel and poetry have their own classifications under the Library of Congress system, works identified as narrative literary journalism are generally cataloged topically. It is true that the Library of Congress has designated a category for the form, labeling it as "reportage literature": "Here are entered works on a narrative style of literature that features the personal presence and involvement of a human witness" (Library 4944). "Reportage" as a terminology applying to narrative literary journalism dates from the 1930s (North 121; Kazin, *Native Grounds* 491). However, since then, as any contemporary standard dictionary definition will indicate, "reportage" has come to apply to all journalism. The consequences for a narrative literary journalism are that it has found itself dispersed throughout the library. Thus John McPhee's account of basketball star Bill Bradley, *A Sense of Where You Are,* can be cataloged under sports, while his *Basin and Range* can be found in geology. The collection of Lafcadio Hearn's sketches of levee life in Cincinnati during the early 1870s, *Children of the Levee,* can be cataloged under ethnographic studies, while Tom Wolfe's *The Kandy-Kolored Tangerine-Flake Streamline Baby* can be cataloged under American society and culture, and *The Right Stuff* under aerospace. Meanwhile, Truman Capote's *In Cold Blood* can be cataloged under criminology, and John Hersey's *Hiroshima* under physics and atomic energy. The consequence is that narrative literary journalism does not fit into the discrete categories librarians invent. As Alberto Manguel observes, "Every library is a library of preferences, and every chosen category implies an exclusion" (198). It is those exclusions that are being recovered here. For, as Manguel adds, "Whatever classifications have been chosen, every library tyrannizes the act of reading, and forces the reader—the curious reader, the alert reader—to rescue the book from the category to which it has been condemned" (199).

If naming the form is problematic now, it can only be sobering to recognize that nonfiction in general was in a similar state in 1952 when the editors of *American Non-Fiction, 1900–1950* brought out their survey of the form as they perceived it: "Despite difficulties of definition, poetry, fiction, criticism, and drama can be analyzed as literary forms or at least discussed in literary terms. Non-fiction, especially in our time, is another matter. There is a tremendous mass of such writing. Much of it is done with little or no cognizance of the formal patterns of a work of literature. Much of it is ephemeral" (O'Connor and Hoffman v). The formalist and New Critical bias is evident in the essentializing of the inquiry, namely that there is a perceived lack of "formal patterns" and that in the form's ephemerality there is little of it that like the Grecian urn might prove lasting or eternal. (Nor would the Grecian urn if some angry postmodernist smashed it against a rock!)

Thus the vast textual region of "nonfiction" was as problematic then as now, nearly half a century later, and the New Critical rhetoric in the 1952 study veils some of the same vexing problems scholars of the form are attempting to address today. Chris Anderson, among others, attempts to justify "literary nonfiction" as the preferred usage when he appeals to origins. He cites *The Literature of Fact*, noting that Weber "coined" the terminology (ix). By doing so, however, Anderson grants the terminology a critical "legal tender" when he reifies Weber's meaning. Weber offers "literary nonfiction" as the designation for the form only tentatively when he says, "Here I shall be using a simple descriptive term: literary nonfiction." This, after he has just admonished readers (including, presumably, Anderson) that "needless to say, this category of serious writing is not well defined, and the many terms used to describe it . . . have done nothing to clarify matters" (1).

If origins are the basis for what the form should be called, then "literary journalism" has its own pedigree. Sims offers "literary journalism" in his 1984 anthology *The Literary Journalists*, when he notes without further explanation in his prefatory critical examination of the form that "unlike standard journalism, *literary journalism* demands immersion in complex, difficult subjects" (3, emphasis added). In offering "literary journalism" as a terminology, however, he resuscitates an older usage. In 1907 the *Bookman,* a prominent literary review, published "Confessions of 'a Literary Journalist,'" in which the anonymous author examines his own efforts to write stories as opposed to news, or "just telling the story as it appealed to me" (371), drawing on the one hand from his opportunities to be "close to life" and on the other from "subjective imagination" (376). Hutchins Hapgood, whose quote opens this chapter, espoused the cause of what was fundamentally a literary journalism in a *Bookman* article in 1905. Hapgood did not use the term at the time, but in his 1939 autobiography he acknowledged that he was attracted to editor Lincoln "Steffens's idea of a literary journalism" in the late 1890s (*Victorian* 140). Steffens was editor of the old *New York Commercial Advertiser* and at the turn of century was an important proponent of the form today called literary journalism. The term also gained more currency with the publication in 1937 of Edwin H. Ford's *Bibliography of Literary Journalism in America,* perhaps the earliest scholarly attempt to characterize the form as "literary journalism."

The problem of what to call Winterowd's "other" literature might be remedied relatively easily if one form were subsumed or classified under the other, and perhaps most obviously if literary journalism were a subform of a broader literary nonfiction. Tentatively, for my purposes here, I adopt such a critical posture. But such a situating of the two terms raises additional problems when one considers delineating the form, or forms if they are indeed different, of what they consist. The scholars of the form can perhaps be divided into two groups, those like Connery who take a more narrow view as to *whom* they will permit to be practitioners, which determines *what* will be literary journalism, and others like Anderson and Judith Paterson who take a broad view and tend to include most literary "nonfiction" texts as part of one overall form or genre. In the case of Connery's *Sourcebook,* all the writers examined were primarily writers who had careers as newspaper or magazine journalists or both. By implication then, a prerequisite for inclusion in the narrative form "literary journalism" appears to have been the professional practice of journalism. The matter becomes complicated however when Paterson lists Annie Dillard's *Pilgrim at Tinker Creek* as one of "literary journalism's twelve best" in an article of the same name. That would seem to argue in favor of the personal essay or nature meditation as subcategories of the form, which undoubtedly will trouble advocates of literary nonfiction. Paterson complicates matters when she includes M. F. K. Fisher's culinary essays *How to Cook a Wolf,* Andrea Lee's memoir *Russian Journal,* and Art Spiegelman's comic book *Maus: A Survivor's Tale,* a biographical tale based on the author's father's survival of the Holocaust. Paterson is a faculty member at the University of Maryland's prestigious College of Journalism.

Thus the range of what can be considered texts of a "literary journalism" or "literary nonfiction" varies greatly among scholars. Nor is it always clear whether such texts include fundamentally discursive examples or are largely narrative in mode. Phyllis Frus in her interpretation of literary journalism, *The Politics and Poetics of Journalistic Narrative,* takes Connery to task for excluding essay and commentary from his variety of literary journalism. At the same time, she further problematizes the matter by refusing to acknowledge that there can be a literary journalism at all: "I cannot accept the valuation that results from separating some examples of journalistic narrative from general coverage of current events and issues. Designating narratives as 'literary' places them within an objectivist and essentialist framework . . . [which] tends to remove the text from historical or political analysis" (x). By definition, such a journalism could include those writers of literary nonfiction in Anderson's collection who write on "current events and issues." We have come full circle, and the question is not which came first, the chicken or the egg, but which is the chicken and which is the egg? Even Connery, ultimately, has difficulty with his narrower critical view when he attempts to define the form: "Literary journalism can briefly be defined as nonfiction printed prose whose verifiable content is shaped and transformed into a story or sketch by use of narrative and rhetorical techniques generally associated with fiction" (*Sourcebook* xiv). Such a definition can include Lee's memoir, *Russian Journal,* and arguably, Henry Adams's autobiography, *The Education of Henry Adams.*

Amid such critical uncertainty it is perhaps no wonder that the form has been so little acknowledged by the academy as a significant literary discourse in our century, and it would be easy to conclude here with scholarly defeat. That, however, would do little justice to the fact that texts of a narrative literary journalism, or whatever it may eventually be called, are being produced and are being reviewed as among our most compelling contemporary commentary. In order for scholarly consideration to move forward in the examination of this body of work, a critical leap of faith is required when it comes to the nomenclature by which the form will be characterized. I do so by favoring for now "literary journalism" in which it is understood that it is written largely (but not exclusively) in a narrative mode. If nothing else, what this discussion about different nomenclatures should demonstrate is that there is a critical site of competing claims, which itself is evidence of the form.

Understanding that the form works largely in a narrative mode is important because there is no reason why the essay or newspaper commentary cannot be viewed equally as a kind of literary journalism. Additionally, the appellation of "literary" alone to journalism is, at best, fraught with problems, not the least of which is what constitutes "literature." For this reason, I prefer "narrative journalism" as a simple descriptive term, or "narrative literary journalism" since such works are fundamentally narrative rather than discursive. Given that the first has no current critical cachet, and given that the piling on of adjectives in the second is considered bad style, I have decided to stay with "literary journalism" with the understanding that the texts under consideration are narrative in mode. Future discussions among scholars will have to culturally construct any final nomenclature, if such a nomenclature is possible.

Moreover, there are reasons for continuing to characterize the form as "literary," Frus's able and valuable arguments notwithstanding. One is that such a form borrows techniques often associated with the realistic novel and short story, thus giving such texts a literary context detected by scholars such as Ford, Sims, Connery, and Yagoda, among others. Second, there has long been a critical consciousness that such texts have the potential for being literary even if what constitutes "literature" is open to considerable debate in our postmodern era. At the heart of the issue is the perception among scholars, critics, and writers that a work is "literary" as opposed to its being some kind of demonstrably transcendent "literature." Third, such texts are literary in the sense that as social allegories they eschew a rhetorical literalness for a figurativeness or literary resonance reflected in a host of interpretive possibilities, including ethical, existential, philosophical, and cultural, as well as in the full range of more traditional figures of speech and the techniques associated with the traditional fictional novel. Such texts then are more than the sum of their critical parts, and all we can attempt to do is deepen our understanding of the form while avoiding privileging any one critical perspective as politically correct in our current age of disarray on literary and cultural fronts.

But perhaps more important, such a literary resonance fulfills Mark Edmundson's implied definition of literature as a discourse that ultimately escapes critical theory because, as he says, it "resists being explained away" (31). As the poet John Keats so well understood, literature does forever "tease us out of thought" or interpretation when we administer our different critical parameters (295). No doubt the linear-thinking empiricist with his eviscerating calipers will be dissatisfied with such an approach, as will the litterateur subscribing to the warm fuzzy feel of a transcendental literary essence. My purpose is to deepen understanding, not to arrive at totalized truth. I make no claim to establishing first causes.

Finally, I prefer "journalism" as the last element for three reasons. First, to define the form as a "nonfiction" reinscribes its status as a "nought," thus reenacting an elitist literary conceit that has long consigned such writing as a "non" "essential" literature. Second, the writers I discuss were and are professional journalists. Third, journalism, as both a journey and the passage of the *diurnal* from which, etymologically, it derives, provides a challenge to literary conceit making, or literary resonance. I am only suggesting that literary conceit making is not privileged in its relationship to what continues to have a phenomenalist status. Rather, there is a dynamic pull established between the two that helps to distinguish the form from more traditional and canonical fictions.

But in adopting for now a narrative "literary journalism" as my usage it is not my intention to solve what may ultimately prove to be irresolvable. My purpose rather is to contribute toward establishing a critical site by acknowledging the problematic nature of the nomenclature and then to move ahead to examine the evidence of its historical presence. That said, I approach the usage of a narrative literary journalism conservatively by sidestepping much of the issue of what to call the form. Instead, I adopt a narrow definition implied in the contents of Connery's *Sourcebook*. The contents suggest that from its emergence in the late nineteenth century and up until at least the new journalism of the 1960s and early 1970s the narrative literary journalism under consideration here has been composed of texts written largely by professional journalists or those writers whose industrial means of production is to be found in the newspaper and magazine press, thus making them at least for the interim de facto journalists. As a result, I include such writers as Sherwood Anderson who, although he may be remembered primarily as a fiction writer, wrote the sketches for his 1935 *Puzzled America* as columns first for a weekly news magazine. Moreover, to take this approach consciously foregrounds the problem of a professional class as makers of literature that historically has been marginalized by English studies.

Another problem that arises is how a narrative literary journalism differs from and is similar to such forms as travel, crime, and sports narratives, among some of the more prominently delineated topical forms. For example, an effort has already been made to separate travelogue from narrative literary journalism as two different forms or genres (Yagoda 14). No such effort is entirely successful, however. Ultimately, the problem is one of attempting to force both into a discrete Linnaean classification scheme, when both in reality belong to different kinds of forms or genres that are not mutually exclusive. Travel narratives, on their face, belong to a topical genre. The kind of literary journalism under discussion here, on the other hand, is fundamentally a modal genre, that of narrative. But travelogue clearly can be in the form of narrative as well; thus boundaries can disappear between travelogue and narrative literary journalism. It depends upon if they are approached as topical or modal genres. There may, however, be compelling reasons to set travelogues aside as a separate grouping if only because their sheer volume can overwhelm other topical narrative literary journalism. That is the approach taken here, where the examples of narrative literary journalism are generally those that engage in a broader social portraiture that is more difficult to define topically. The same can be said of crime and sports narratives. One example is Truman Capote's *In Cold Blood,* which has achieved all but canonical status as narrative literary journalism despite fictional invention of which Capote has been accused. In any event, such an overlap is particularly important to acknowledge when examining the presence of the form in the first three-quarters of the twentieth century up to the new journalism of the 1960s and 1970s. When narrative literary journalism went into a kind of remission, particularly in the teens, the twenties, the late forties, and the fifties, it survived at least in part through vigorous travel, crime, and sports narratives.

Not many attempts have been made to historicize a century of modern narrative literary journalism in the American experience, and only six relatively recent—and brief—efforts do so broadly. The first and most important for the purposes of this history is a brief description by Connery of three major periods of the form, the first around the turn of the century, the second from the 1930s and into the 1940s, and the third the new journalism of the 1960s and early 1970s (preface xii–xiii). Connery's historiography assumes the 1890s as the beginning of American literary journalism in a fundamentally narrative mode, noting that it was "partially fueled by a cultural need to know and understand a rapidly changing world, and by a staunch faith that reality was comprehensible through printed prose" ("Third Way" 4). But further examination is also needed, as Connery suggests, as to why "a rapidly changing world" and "a staunch faith that reality was comprehensible through printed prose" would result in a literary journalism (preface xv). Clearly, periods of rapid change have occurred throughout history, but they did not necessarily result in a literary journalism. Moreover, writers have often expressed their faith that reality was comprehensible by means of printed prose, at least as far back as Cicero when in the first century B.C.E. he was kept informed of events in Rome by letters from his friend Caelius (Stephens 51, 61–62).

Nonetheless, Connery deserves his due. One reason is that my examination uses as a point of embarkation his suggested historiographic template of three major periods, as well as some of the once-obscure primary sources he has uncovered as a pioneer scholar of the form. That said, I attempt to recast that material in a conceptualization of the history of the form that incorporates but also moves beyond what Paul Many calls the "biographical-institutional approach to journalism history" (561). This is fundamentally the point of departure taken by Connery on the emergence of a narrative literary journalism in the 1890s when he discusses Stephen Crane, Lincoln Steffens and the

Commercial Advertiser, and Hutchins Hapgood in that "biographical-institutional" order ("A Third Way" 3–20).

A second reason why Connery deserves his due is that his *Sourcebook of American Literary Journalism* is a pioneering effort in its presentation of critical articles on thirty-five authors. Moreover, as much as any scholar today he has been a vigorous voice calling for examination of the form from different critical perspectives, welcoming investigations from such diverse sectors of the academy as mass communication, English, and American studies. This examination accepts that invitation and adopts the brief outline of his historical template. But ultimately my approach to historicizing leads me to the conclusion that narrative literary journalism is at least as much a response to an epistemological crisis, thus reversing the tendency in Connery's approach that the form is "distinguishable . . . by virtue of *what* was conveyed, not just by *how* it was conveyed" (preface xiii–xiv). I examine not only *what* we believe we can know about our phenomenal world but *how* such attempts to know it were prompted by an epistemological crisis. Ultimately then, we can arrive at a better understanding of *why* journalists took up the form in defiance of mainstream journalistic practice. Once we can identify the *why*, we can determine the *what* that matters and not taken-for-granted assumptions that narrative literary journalists and their readers were simply observing external cultural artifacts. If anything, narrative literary journalism has been a consistent voice for challenging taken-for-granted assumptions, including critical assumptions. Ultimately, I propose that something far more profound and existentially dignifying was taking place in what Hapgood characterized as "living writing."

A second effort to historicize the form is Paul Many's "Toward a History of Literary Journalism." Many approaches the form from the direction of conventional journalism historiography, or the "biographical-institutional approach to journalism history." Specifically, he ties the form's emergence to the development of American journalism practice at large during five historical periods, the Colonial, Penny Press, Populist-Progressive, Modern, and Contemporary periods (561). Two problems can be detected in Many's argument, however. First, when he suggests "it might be possible to begin the outline of a history of literary journalism in this country" by tying it to the five historical periods, he implies that literary journalism had a presence during each period. But as he develops his argument he reverses his position and excludes the first two periods as times when a fully formed literary journalism was practiced. In rough correspondence with Connery, he suggests instead that the Populist era from 1870 to 1914 heralded "the true beginning of 'literary journalism'" (565).

The second and perhaps larger problem in Many's argument is that by attaching it to conventional journalism historiography he has attempted to make the form under discussion fit an already-determined historical mold. As the physicist Werner Heisenberg so well understood, any critical approach determines and shapes our view of the world at the exclusion of other views so that evidence may be ignored for lack of recognizing it because of the critical straitjacket imposed on the material (55). The unfortunate consequence of Many's critical straitjacket is that he ignores altogether the very active narrative literary journalism practiced in the 1930s and early 1940s. Indeed, Many characterizes such a literary journalism during the period from 1915 to 1960—what he calls the Modern period—as the exception rather than the rule when he cites the example of Ernest Hemingway. What he fails to note is that while Hemingway did indeed engage in narrative literary journalistic practice during the 1920s when the form was in remission, he was also very much a participant in what could be called a second Populist or Progressive Era during the 1930s and 1940s that included such luminaries as Sherwood Anderson, Erskine Caldwell, Edmund Wilson, James Agee, and John Hersey. Connery cautions against falling into just such a trap when he says the form should not be judged by just the standards "of either conventional journalism or realistic fiction" (preface xv). Ultimately, what Many fails to perceive is that there are political reasons for why conventional journalism historiography (as well as traditional literary studies) has excluded narrative literary journalism from serious scholarly consideration, reasons that justify the application of "Modern" to both mainstream journalistic practice of the period and belletristic practice during this time as a hegemonic appellation that marginalized narrative literary journalism.

Nonetheless, to Many's credit he does note that such an American literary journalism arose out of a "rift" that occurred between literature and journalism as the two developed different identities (562–65). I contend not only that a rift occurred between literature and journalism but also that a rift occurred *within* journalism as a result of the objectification of news to which narrative literary journalism would prove a reaction.

This "objectification" of news is central to demonstrating a modus by which I suggest narrative literary journalism operates. By the "objectification" of news or journalism I mean disengaged journalisms that objectify the world as something different or alien from the viewing subject, namely either that of author or reader. This applies to the evolution in the late nineteenth century of a factual news style that in the twentieth century came to be called objective journalism, and of sensational yellow journalism, which in its own way also objectifies the experience of the world. Indeed, while objective journalism and yellow sensational journalism are often represented as being in opposition to each other, they share a common epistemological problem.

Many also hints at but does not examine evidence that narrative literary journalism has often (although not exclusively) been associated with Populist and Progressive politics and ideology as reflected in those texts not only from the turn of the century but also from the 1930s and 1940s and the 1960s and 1970s. This can be traced to the epistemological crisis the form, in its ambition, has sought to remedy.

Elsewhere, Yagoda identifies three kinds of historical literary journalism: (1) a "narrative journalism," (2) a more participatory journalism in which the journalist's subjectivity exists in the foreground of the text, and (3) an artfully written literary journalism in which "style" is "substance" (15–16). I differ in that all such texts are fundamentally a narrative journalism; all reflect to some degree, even in the case of a writer like John Hersey, a writing subjectivity; and the line between a literary style and a nonliterary style cannot be detected in such texts— otherwise they cannot be, in sum, a literary journalism (assuming that what we mean by "literary" and "artful" styles amounts to one and the same). Ultimately, Yagoda takes a modernist stance in insisting on old-fashioned classification. Undoubtedly the issues he raises are at work in the form. But I suggest that such issues among others are at work as influences, not categories, and that the form works on a narrative spectrum or continuum that makes it impossible to classify into clear-cut modernist categories. Indeed, I view that as one of the virtues of the form.

Then we come to collections that contribute to historicizing the form. But because they are collections, they lack the continuity of a synthesized historical conceptualization. Still, what they lack formally they fulfill in the breach, and their total effect has been to provide the immediate precursors to a more fully synthesized history as attempted here. Among the most eminent is Norman Sims's *Literary Journalism in the Twentieth Century*, a collection of a dozen scholarly articles treating writers as diverse as Hutchins Hapgood (Connery, "Third Way" 15) and Gloria Anzaldúa (Fishkin 160), and topics as diverse as the plain style (Kenner 183–90) and the new journalism as a form of "cultural politics" and "symbolic confrontation" (Pauly, "Politics" 111). The volume, as Sims observes, "addresses both the history of literary journalism and some of the issues of literary theory surrounding it" (preface vi). It was an important primer for undertaking the history you are reading now.

Edd Applegate's 1996 *Literary Journalism* contains biographies on 180 authors. However, Applegate makes no effort to contextualize a history as such, restricting his prefatory remarks largely to the new journalism of the 1960s and 1970s. The virtue of Applegate's dictionary is that it attempts to be inclusive. But inclusiveness can also be its weakness. For example, it includes biographies on Richard Steele and Joseph Addison. Steele and Addison are problematic largely because they are discursive, not narrative, writers. Similarly, Upton Sinclair is included and his *Jungle* cited as containing examples of literary journalism. But formally *The Jungle* is an open and conspicuous fiction. Occasionally, moreover, there are omissions, such as that of Frank Norris. Yet such problems are, perhaps, to be expected as our understanding of the form continues to be refined. If nothing else, Applegate's effort serves to help in the ongoing critical negotiation of what constitutes the form.

Most recently, there is Arthur J. Kaul's contribution to the Dictionary of Literary Biography series, *American Literary Journalists, 1945–1995*. The first in a planned series, it contains biographies of thirty-six authors from the post–World War II period. But it also propagates the literary myth that somehow narrative literary journalism was a postwar phenomenon, one strongly tied to the new journalism. As Kaul notes: "Critics, scholars, and practitioners of literary journalism have grappled with ways to define *this emerging form of expression* that revitalized post–World War II American writing as it appeared primarily in magazines" (xvi, emphasis added). And: "The rise of literary journalism in the post–World War II era . . ." (xvi). Thus the myth is perpetuated. Nonetheless, Kaul's effort provides an important overview of the fifty-year period from 1945 to 1995.

Earlier attempts have been made to historicize the form, primarily in a spate of articles in the 1970s prompted by the new journalism debate. In 1975 George A. Hough historicized the form largely by means of brief biographical descriptions of seven authors (117/19–119/21). In 1974 Jay Jensen described how the "new journalism" was an old terminology for different kinds of journalistic efforts very different from what today we would call narrative literary journalism (37). In addition, he notes that the techniques of the new journalism of the 1960s did have historical antecedents. In a 1975 article Joseph Webb claimed that the 1960s "new journalism" derived from a "romantic" impulse that could be traced historically (38). His is an interpretation that echoes a not-dissimilar view of Hamlin Garland in the 1890s. Garland may be known more as a fiction writer but he was also a sometime literary journalist and a fan of the form. Webb, however, ignores altogether the abundance of literary journalism in the 1890s and 1930s, reflecting perhaps just how limited were the critical efforts that attempted to account for the history of the form in the immediate aftermath and overwhelming shadow of what was perceived as a new journalism in the 1960s. The assertion of "newness" could only tend to reduce earlier versions to mere antecedents and precursors and not the real thing. Still another early effort is Warren T. Francke's "W. T. Stead: The First New Journalist?" which, as its title suggests, is an attempt at determining origins. As such, it ignores the development of the form as an evolution, a position that challenges any attempt at determining a first cause.

One of the earliest attempts to historicize the form is that of Edwin H. Ford. His 1937 *Bibliography of Literary Journalism in America* historicizes the form by virtue of citing primary sources of and critical articles about literary journalists and their work, extending back to

Benjamin Franklin. In addition, the form is implicitly historicized with a section citing articles of critical response to it, particularly from the first decade of the twentieth century. That critical response is important in locating the modern emergence of the form to the late nineteenth century and the beginning of the twentieth. In addition, Ford historicizes the form in "The Art and Craft of the Literary Journalist" when he briefly describes seven writers as "great names in literary journalism" (307).

Finally, there are periodic brief discussions of the form scattered throughout many sources in different fields of inquiry, such as Larzar Ziff's discussion of the 1890s and Michael Schudson's discussion of the development of American journalistic practice. And one can piece together elements of literary journalistic practice from Sam G. Riley's Dictionary of Literary Biography series, *American Magazine Journalists*. But by and large, efforts to historicize the form have been few because there is no consensus as to what to call it. Also, the form has been marginalized by both belletristic and mainstream journalistic practice, and by the dominant critical stances of the English and mass communication academies in the twentieth century. Moreover, those efforts that do attempt to historicize the form take, as Many observed, a largely "biographical-institutional" approach and as a consequence overlook that the form ultimately was and still is an attempt to deal with an epistemological crisis wrought by the development of modern journalistic practice.

What is needed then, and what I attempt to do, is to seek for evidence that cuts across the collection of biographies and institutions in order to arrive at critical denominators. To do so will, I hope, bring us to a new critical threshold from which we can begin to understand better this compelling discourse that has a larger presence in our time than the academy as yet fully acknowledges or has been able to acknowledge. Perhaps then we can begin to more fully understand why Hapgood so fondly recalled, and longed for a better appreciation of, what he characterized as "living writing."

1 Locating the Emergence of Modern Narrative Literary Journalism

YEARS LATER, when he looked back on his career as a newspaper editor in the 1890s, Lincoln Steffens recalled giving the following advice to reporter, novelist, and editor Abraham Cahan: "Here, Cahan, is a report that a man has murdered his wife, a rather, bloody, hacked-up crime. . . . There's a story in it. That man loved that woman well enough once to marry her, and now he has hated her enough to cut her all to pieces. If you can find out just what happened between that wedding and this murder, you will have a novel for yourself and a short story for me. Go on now, take your time, and get this tragedy, as a tragedy" (*Autobiography* 317). What makes Steffens's advice remarkable is just how much its intention is literary, the end to provide a short story for himself and a novel for Cahan. Steffens, as city editor of the *New York Commercial Advertiser,* was advocating a narrative literary journalism and in doing so reflected a critical consciousness of this form caught somewhere between literature and journalism. That critical consciousness is one of several factors that help to locate the origins of modern American literary journalism, narrative in nature, as having come of age by the 1890s. The issue is no small matter, given that the form, as Thomas B. Connery among others has noted, has been "either ignored, mislabeled or misread" ("Third Way" 6). As Barbara Lounsberry notes, the form remains "the great unexplored territory of contemporary criticism" (xi).

Connery proposes that in response to the developments in journalism and the realistic novel in the late nineteenth century, "two categories of printed prose to depict observed life were not enough, but a

21

third—a literary journalism—was possible and necessary. . . . Despite the enormous cultural pressure to classify and separate prose into creative and noncreative categories, resistance to such sharp demarcations was salient at the turn of the century" ("Third Way" 5). Paul Many simply asserts that the post–Civil War period marks "the true beginning of 'literary journalism'" (565). While both efforts attempt to address the form more broadly, ultimately they do so largely by means of biographical and institutional categories. For example, Connery examines the evidence of the form by noting the specific contributions of Stephen Crane, Hutchins Hapgood, and Steffens as city editor of the *Commercial Advertiser.* Many frankly calls for the application of the "biographical-institutional approach to journalism history" to the form (561). Here I explore the convergence of three specific factors—rhetorical, professional, and literary criticism—in the 1890s and more generally during the post–Civil War period that transcend biographical and institutional boundaries to establish a critical site that locates the emergence of the form. I do not suggest that such a site is the final word on the matter. Undoubtedly, other common factors can and will emerge as scholarship in this area continues to evolve, ultimately adding critical depth and breadth to any historical effort. That said, I fine-tune Connery's and Many's positions and suggest that the post–Civil War period marks not so much the first period of American literary journalism as the first period of *modern* narrative literary journalism in the United States. To do so anticipates the criticism, and a justifiable one, that there has long existed some form of narrative literary journalism.

By way of a preliminary definition of narrative literary journalism, I mean those true-life stories that read like a novel or short story—much as in Steffens's advice to Cahan. Such a definition is of course problematic, and I discuss those problems as they arise. Doing so, however, should further delineate and situate this long-ignored form. In reading like a novel or short story, such texts were more than the sum of their rhetorical techniques long associated with those genres. In addition, the result was often social or cultural allegory, with potential meanings beyond the literal in the broadest sense of allegory's meaning. Largely, although not exclusively, that allegory is about embracing an understanding of the social or cultural Other.

THREE IMMEDIATE factors converging roughly at the same time can be detected in confirming Connery's and Many's positions that a narrative literary journalism came of age during this period. The first and one of the most widely acknowledged was the widespread "adoption" of the techniques commonly associated with realistic fiction—dialogue, scene construction, concrete detail, and showing activity. Many scholars have taken note of the application of these techniques as one of the measures of the form.[1] I suggest "adoption" only tentatively, given that these techniques were long utilized in the writing of narrative journalism. Indeed, their use preceded that of the literary realism of the fictional novel. But it is true that after the Civil War the ascendancy of literary realism in the fictional novel helped refocus the efforts of narrative journalists, as if what they were undertaking was newly discovered. The second factor is that the form was practiced primarily by professional journalists or those who had worked as professional journalists and whose industrial means of production and expression were for the most part the newspaper and magazine press. Finally, and perhaps most important, there was a new and vigorous critical awareness that the form as practiced could be "literary." This was expressed in a critical debate that emerged in the 1890s and intensified in the first decade of the twentieth century.

The attempt to apply the techniques of novel-writing to journalism was not new, and before the 1890s there were examples such as Lafcadio Hearn's portraits of African American life on the Cincinnati levee, Mark Twain's *Life on the Mississippi* and *Innocents Abroad,* and the travelogues of Charles Dudley Warner, the now largely forgotten joint author with Twain of *The Gilded Age.* Still earlier precursors include Henry David Thoreau's Cape Cod sketches, parts of which were serialized in *Putnam's Monthly Magazine* in 1855 and published posthumously in book form as *Cape Cod* in 1865. Another precursor was Augustus Baldwin Longstreet's *Georgia Scenes* of the 1830s, which initially appeared in newspapers. In the eighteenth century, techniques of novel-writing in true-life texts or texts claiming a phenomenalist status were

---

1. See Connery, "Third Way" 6–7; Weber, "Some Sort" 20; Lounsberry xiv–xv; Wolfe, "New Journalism" 31; Berner, "Literary Notions" 3.

reflected in the literary friendship of Samuel Johnson and James Boswell. In a letter Johnson writes to his friend and confidant Hester Thrale, he says that Boswell "has some thoughts of collecting [material about a notable of the time] and making a novel of his life" (*Letters of Johnson* 290). Still elsewhere, in a memoir Boswell published near the end of his life, he quotes a letter from Johnson regarding Boswell's *Account of Corsica,* published in 1768: "You express images which operated strongly upon yourself, and you have impressed them with great force upon your readers. I know not whether I could name any narrative by which curiosity is better excited or better gratified" ("Memoirs" 326). In the true-life "narrative" replete with "images" lies an early form of narrative literary journalism. Boswell acknowledges his attempts at writing true-life accounts in the style of a novel when he notes of the discouragements he faced in life in his *London Journal,* "Let me consider that the hero of a romance or novel must not go uniformly along in bliss, but the story must be chequered with bad fortune" ("Memoirs" 206). In searching for antecedents to the modern American version of narrative literary journalism, Boswell and Johnson recur because of the issues they confronted in attempting to interpret the phenomenal world. In his account of his walking tour of Scotland with Johnson, Boswell acknowledges apologetically his rhetorical intention (as well as that of moral philosopher and early economist Adam Smith's) in using novelistic technique when he describes his traveling companion:

> He wore a full suit of plain brown clothes, with twisted-hair button of the same colour, a large bushy greyish wig, a plain shirt, black worsted stockings, and silver buckles. Upon this tour, when journeying, he wore boots, and a very wide brown cloth greatcoat, with pockets which might have almost held the two volumes of his folio dictionary; and he carried in his hand a large English oak stick. Let me not be censured for mentioning such minute particulars. Every thing relative to so great a man is worth observing. I remember Dr. Adam Smith, in his rhetorical lectures at Glasgow, told us he was glad to know that Milton wore latchets in his shoes, instead of buckles. When I mention the oak stick, it is but letting Hercules have his club. (165)

It is in such descriptive particulars, Boswell adds, that his readers "will attain to a considerable degree of acquaintance" with Johnson (165).

Boswell's intention then is to move beyond rhetorical abstraction in order to provide what Connery calls the "feel" of facts ("Third Way" 6).

What is remarkable about the post–Civil War period leading up to the fin de siècle is just how much those novelistic techniques were drafted for use in the popular press. As Connery notes of Stephen Crane's New York City sketches: "Crane used a host of literary techniques, including contrast, dialogue, concrete description, detailed scene setting, careful word selection that built a repetition of imagery, and irony" ("Third Way" 7). Crane, the novelist, had been a practitioner of a narrative literary journalism since at least 1892 when his first New York City sketches began appearing—human interest stories about daily life in the expanding metropolis, which Crane characterized in a letter to his brother as "some of my best work" ("To William H. Crane"). That eye for daily life in the city ranged considerably. For example, in "A Lovely Jag in a Crowded Car" Crane records the inebriated exploits of a drunk and passengers' reactions to him. Among the novelistic techniques Crane drafts are scene description: "The drunken man put his hands on his knees and beamed about him in absolute unalloyed happiness. . . . The man spent some anxious moments in reflection, calculating carefully upon his fingers. Then he triumphantly ordered one beer and nine Manhattan cocktails of the conductor" (126–27). Similar examples of description, as well as dialogue, can be found in "The Men in the Storm," Crane's sketch of homeless men in a snow storm waiting for a public shelter to open (91–96), and in "When Man Falls a Crowd Gathers," a sketch of a man's apparent epileptic seizure on a New York street that becomes an opportunity to report on the self-serving reactions of the crowd that gathers (102–11).

Nor was Crane alone. Among other practitioners of the art of novelistic color applied to journalism—"factions" in short—was writer and journalist Frank Norris. In one example Norris re-creates a room in which detectives live on the San Francisco wharves while awaiting the arrival of a sailing vessel carrying a man wanted in Australia for murder: "There were four beds made up on the floor of the room, and Conroy was dozing in one, pretending to read 'Phra the Phoenician,' the whiles. The other detectives sat about a gas stove, smoking. They were for the most part big, burly men, with red faces, very jovial and not at all like the sleuths you expected to see" (*Frank Norris* 120).

Still another prolific writer who practiced narrative literary journalism is the now largely forgotten Lafcadio Hearn. In the 1870s Hearn anticipated the narrative literary journalism of the 1890s. Yet he was not a failed mainstream journalist. Like many narrative literary journalists he was also adept at writing mainstream news. Among examples of his conventional mainstream journalism is his formulaic feature of the 1877 Ohio River flood ("The Rising of the Waters"). The account is formulaic because it largely lacks the specificity of concrete detail necessary to the novelistic scene construction of narrative literary journalism and is framed mostly in generic summaries of those scenes. Another example is a conventional obituary feature for *Harper's Weekly* in 1885 on Jean Montanet, a voodoo high priest in New Orleans ("Last of the Voudoos"). Moreover, Hearn was successful at writing fiction, folklore studies, anthropology, and some categories of prose that defy conventional definition. Among the most peculiar are what he called "fantastics," romantic and mystical writings that he characterized in a letter to his friend Henry E. Krehbiel in 1880 as "my impressions of the strange life of New Orleans." Yet he also described them as "dreams of a tropical city" ("To H. E. Krehbiel" 220). For example, "All in White" is a narrator's dialogue recounting how the most beautiful woman he saw on a visit to Havana was sitting in a window—dead (217). Another example is "Y Porque?" which is about a young man who is asked why he will not return to Mexico City, a question he does not answer but for which Hearn provides a speculative answer. What remains unclear is what of the fantastics are phenomenalistic "impressions of the strange life of New Orleans" and what are his "dreams of [the] tropical city." What also remains unclear is where in individual fantastics phenomenalistic impressions leave off and his dreamy speculations or reveries pick up. Provocatively, one technique Hearn often favored was to provide a spatial break in the typography between what could have had a phenomenalistic status—an overheard conversation, say, as is the case in "Y Porque?"—and what is clearly interior monologue or other overtly fictional invention derived from his reveries. Moreover, at this juncture in his life he was the assistant editor at the *New Orleans Item* where the fantastics first appeared. He served in that capacity from mid-1878 through the end of 1881, the period when he created most of the fantastics (Stevenson 88, 102–6). In such a capacity he was in a position to direct how the articles were typeset. Yet the issue remains unresolved.

In any event, such gorgeous and fantastical invention on Hearn's part (echoed a century or so later in the "magical realism" of Latin American writers such as Gabriel Garcia Marquez) might suggest he is only a narrative literary journalist in passing. But such invention is balanced by the fact that his literary journalism at times overlaps with the study of folklore and anthropology. For example, his "Levee Life" from 1876 provides, along with other sketches, "about the only picture we have of Negro life in a border city in the post–Civil War period. They form an invaluable record of the customs, folkways, and family organization of the urban Negro; they form also a case study of the process of acculturation at a vital point in American Negro history" (Ball 8). The same is true of "Voices of Dawn," which captures the linguistic intonation of Creole-flavored English among the street hawkers going from house to house selling fruits and other provisions in the early New Orleans dawn (266–68).

If nothing else, Hearn's versatility as a writer reflects the porosity of the boundaries between narrative literary journalism and other forms. Hearn's reputation declined considerably in the twentieth century but at its beginning he was compared to Poe, Byron, and De Quincey (Pattee, *History* 424, 426, 428). An enigmatic writer, his early stories of Cincinnati are largely conventional realistic accounts, while his later writings became increasingly romantic and mystical (Pattee 423–26). Yet, in spite of the increasing romanticism and mysticism, Hearn continued to write conventionally realistic sketches that would qualify as narrative literary journalism. One example is "Ti Canotie," a sketch about two boys who dive for coins off Martinique, where Hearn lived from 1887 to 1889. Another is "At a Railway Station" (347–50), an account set in Japan in the 1890s about a man apprehended for murdering a child and returned under police guard to the town where the murder occurred. There he confronts the parents of the slain child and in Japanese tradition begs for their forgiveness by offering his own life (285–97).

Among representative examples of Hearn's early and more conventionally realistic literary journalism is "Dolly: An Idyl of the Levee," which appeared in the *Cincinnati Commercial* in 1876. The article recounts how Dolly, an African American, died of a broken heart. Beyond the conventional plot however lies a vigorous use of novelistic technique, such as in the following description:

> Dolly was a brown, broad-shouldered girl of the levee, with the lithe strength of a pantheress in her compactly knit figure, and owning one of those peculiar faces which at once attract and puzzle by their very uniqueness—a face that possessed a strange comeliness when viewed at certain angles, especially half-profile, and that would have seemed very soft and youthful but for the shadow of its heavy black brows, perpetually knitted Medusa-wise, as though by everlasting pain, above a pair of great, dark, keen, steady eyes. It was a face, perhaps rather Egyptian than aught else; fresh with youthful roundness, and sweetened by a sensitive, passionate, pouting mouth. (2)

The vigor lies not only in the concreteness of the description but also in the complexity of a portrait that eschews both journalistic cliché and the sentimentality of the genteel sensibilities of the period that literary realists such as William Dean Howells were challenging (*Criticism and Fiction* 10–12, 27–28). For example, the "heavy black brows, perpetually knitted Medusa-wise, as though by everlasting pain" mediate the redeeming qualities of her face, thus denying the possibility that the face could be exclusively "very soft and youthful." At the same time, the redeeming qualities redeem Medusa—"fresh with youthful roundness, and sweetened by a sensitive, passionate, pouting mouth"—to complete a portrait of paradoxical human complexity, or what more conventionally would be called a realistic portrait. It is in the conflicting suggestiveness of the description that the description's novelistic energy lies. Hearn illustrates Howells's call for a "young writer who attempts to report the phrase and carriage of every-day life, who tries to tell just how he has heard men talk and seen them look" (*Criticism and Fiction* 10). Hearn's literary journalism foreshadows future fictional realists such as Anton Chekhov. Chekhov wrote the following passage in 1886:

> And the dog Wriggles, who had a black coat and a long body like a weasel's, followed him with hanging head. . . . This Wriggles was extraordinarily deferential and demonstrative, looked with equally friendly eyes both at his masters and at strangers, but did not enjoy a good reputation. His deference and meekness concealed the most Jesuitical spite. No one

knew better than he how to creep up behind you and suddenly snap at your leg, how to slip into the icehouse, or how to steal a hen from a peasant. More than once his hind legs had been all but broken, twice he had been hanged, every week he was whipped till he was half dead, but he always managed to revive. (35)

Wriggles, like Dolly, had a disagreeable aspect, even as he was redeemed by his deference and meekness, as was she by her face "fresh with youthful roundness."

As Connery notes of the work of still other practitioners of a narrative literary journalism during the post–Civil War period, "articles containing dialogue, or extended conversation, and scene setting, were characteristic . . . [and] it was common in the 1890s to let a speaker tell his or her own story, so that many articles would consist of paragraphs of quotations" ("Third Way" 11). One example is Hearn's "Why Crabs Are Boiled Alive," which appeared in the *New Orleans Item* in 1879. The brief story is composed entirely of a patois-flavored monologue, without description: "And for why you not have of crab? Because one must dem boil 'live? It is all vat is of most beast to tell so. How you make for dem kill so you not dem boil? You not can cut dem de head off, for dat dey have not of head. You not can break to dem de back, for dat dey not be only all back. You not can dem bleed until dey die, for dat dey not have blood. You not can stick to dem troo de brain, for dat dey be same like you—dey not have of brain" (266).

The degree to which the use of novelistic technique was adapted to journalism has been examined closely by Phyllis Frus in her comparison of Crane's two accounts of surviving the sinking of the ship *Commodore* on New Year's Day 1897 while participating in gunrunning to Cuba. She concludes that there is little difference between the two even though one is traditionally considered fiction and the other journalism. Ultimately, too, she provides an example of how narrative literary journalism has been mislabeled. The two accounts are Crane's well-known short story "The Open Boat," first published in *Scribner's Magazine,* and the news article, "Stephen Crane's Own Story," published in the *New York Press* on 6 January 1897 only five days after the event. As Frus notes: "Both narratives follow the historical sequence of events surrounding the *Commodore* disaster as verified in contemporary newspaper reports, the ship's log and other shipping records, and accounts by witnesses. . . . Neither story invents facts or characters, although both narratives inevitably proceed by invention—in the rhetorical sense of producing the subject matter according to previous literary models while appearing to copy from nature or reality" ("Two Tales" 128). Not only then is "The Open Boat" fundamentally a true story, despite the practice of the English academy to categorize it as a fictional short story, but its alter ego, the acknowledged true story "Stephen Crane's Own Story" engages in the kind of rhetorical invention associated with novel or fiction writing.

Frus, perhaps, needs to fine-tune her argument because both stories by Crane do reflect a difference in tone. Frus acknowledges this in part when she notes that "a tropological inventory of each narrative does show different *patterns* of figures. The number of similes far exceeds that of metaphors in the news feature, for example, whereas these are about evenly divided in 'The Open Boat'" ("Two Tales" 130, Frus's emphasis). Frus claims that deadline pressures would account for the larger number of similes. In contrast, Crane had six weeks to write "The Open Boat." The greater emphasis on metaphor could, however, reinforce critical opinion that "The Open Boat" is a fictional short story, and "Stephen Crane's Own Story" is still only a lowbrow form, that of journalism. But it is how "The Open Boat" was presented in *Scribner's* that helps to level the field. When it appeared in June 1897 it opened with the following preface: "A Tale Intended to be after the Fact: Being the Experience of Four Men from the Sunk Steamer *Commodore*" (277). The article, even though it has been frequently anthologized as a fictional short story, has a claim to being narrative literary journalism, and to represent it as a conventional literary fiction is to engage in an elitist literary strategy that simply elides the narrative's origins by pretending they do not exist.[2]

Still, as Frus has demonstrated, "both narratives inevitably proceed by invention—in the rhetorical sense of producing the subject matter according to previous literary models while appearing to copy from nature or reality" even as both were historically accurate. In rhetorical

---

2. For example, Baym et al. anthologize "The Open Boat" and in a footnote characterize the tale as a "fictional account" (2:722). Crane scholar James B. Colvert takes a similar position in his introduction to *Great Short Works of Stephen Crane* x–xii.

invention, then, there is no reason why both forms cannot partake of the same bag of tropological tricks. The fictional novel and short story could be written solely with the use of simile, eschewing metaphor, and vice versa in narrative literary journalism.

PROFESSIONALIZATION AS a consequence of the means of production is important as a factor in situating modern narrative literary journalism in the American experience for several reasons. One is that the work of journalists has been dismissed as literature not on its merits but because of what journalists do for a living as determined by their means of production. As Frus notes, "The twentieth-century critic comes armed with the attitude that journalism is an inferior form" ("Two Tales" 126). To acknowledge that circumstance is to clear an obstacle to the wider consideration of the form on its own grounds. As a corollary to this, if narrative literary journalism is permitted to be dismissed based on the professional class of the people who engage in it, then it can be conveniently lumped into a broader category of literary nonfiction. In such a critical leveling, the collective work of a professional class can be elided altogether on the basis that it is no different (and rhetorically this can be the case) from such a broader literary nonfiction. The result is that it can continue to be overlooked and ignored. In effect, one can't tell the trees from the forest. The danger of course is that this form would continue to be lost in the critical forest because of the elitist politics of the traditional literature academy.

Another feature that distinguishes narrative literary journalism according to Connery is that "the content of the works come from traditional means of news gathering or reporting" ("Discovering" 15). While certainly to a degree this is true, I suggest refining the argument to identify the practice of professional journalists as a means for further situating the form. The "traditional means of news gathering or reporting" is also available to other writers, such as essayists and anthropologists, or for that matter, scholars. To suggest that information gathering and its analysis and synthesis are the private preserve of journalists is presumptuous. Boswell engages in just this activity in his dedication to *The Journal of a Tour to the Hebrides* when he writes, "In every narrative, whether historical or biographical, authenticity is of the utmost consequence" (155). What is motivating the "traditional means of news gath-

ering or reporting" is also the desire, however problematic as a specular and subjective act, for "authenticity." We might consider Boswell
today an early journalist, but he is also, and so he saw himself, a historian and biographer. One might well add essayist. Instead, the means
of industrial production in the nineteenth century stamped journalists
as a class—in this case a professional class. As Michael Schudson notes,
"It was only in the decades after the Civil War that reporting became a
more highly esteemed and more highly rewarded occupation" (68). By
1898, he notes, all the major newspapers in New York had at least ten
college graduates on their reporting staffs (69). As *New York Tribune*
editor Whitelaw Reid noted in the 1870s, "Our greatest newspapers are
carried on rigorously upon the idea that journalism is a profession"
(qtd. in Mott 405). This was a trend that could be traced back at least
to midcentury, as Frank Luther Mott notes in his seminal history of
American journalism, a trend ultimately made possible by the development of the mass-circulation American newspaper.

Moreover, there is little difference between the professionalized
class of journalists and the way creative writing workshops today profes-
sionalize "creative" writers, some of whom teach in our most esteemed
universities and are considered makers of "literature." They then are
judged by their professionalization. The only difference is that they are
privileged while journalists are marginalized—the latter not according
to what they write but according to their professional class. The professionalization of the narrative literary journalist as such can also be detected in the fact that many, like Hearn, were adept at writing in the
mainstream news styles. The same is true of Lincoln Steffens who has
been described as one of the two best police reporters in New York City
before he took over as city editor of the *Commercial Advertiser* (Hapgood,
Victorian 141). Thus Steffens demonstrated his facility at writing one of
the most common subgenres of mainstream news style, as well as one
of the most challenging, police news. (It should be borne in mind that
he was an advocate of a narrative literary journalism, not necessarily a
practitioner. Nonetheless, his advocacy of the form was as important in
drawing attention to it as the work of practitioners.) Similarly, R. W.
Stallman and E. R. Hagemann characterize Crane as a "star reporter,"
asserting that he was "not the failure as a journalist that almost every
critic has labeled him" (*War Dispatches* 109).

Another factor reflecting the professionalization of narrative literary journalists is that the mainstream press demonstrated considerably more openness to publishing the form than is generally appreciated. One could easily conclude that the example of the *New York Commercial Advertiser* was the exception. But there is sufficient evidence that the practice of a narrative literary journalism by professional journalists was more extensive than has been accounted for. What is true is that the *Commercial Advertiser*'s example is striking, and its commitment to a literary style was reflected in Steffens's attempts to enlist college graduates who aspired to literary writing: "I would take fellows, I said, whose professor of English believed they were going to be able to write and who themselves wanted to be writers. . . . 'We' had use for any one who, openly or secretly, hoped to be a poet, a novelist, or an essayist . . . [and] I promised to give them opportunities to see life as it happened in all the news varieties" (*Autobiography* 314). Steffens particularly favored Harvard graduates, crediting them with an intellectual appetite for examining that "which men do not know and have to discover of 'the True and the Beautiful'" (*Autobiography* 316). The rhetoric may be romantic translated through the eyes of a Victorian sensibility, but it reflects again the literary possibilities in journalism that Steffens detected. He adds: "We talked of such things on our paper. We dared to use such words as 'literature,' 'art,' 'journalism,' not only in the city room itself, but at a fire or in the barrooms where the Press drank. The old hacks hated it and ridiculed us. . . . But we did not care what the old bumbs said" (316–17). Hutchins Hapgood, for one, came from Harvard with a master's degree in English, indeed giving up an instructorship in English at that institution to take a position offered by Steffens (Hapgood, *Victorian* 137). Hapgood notes that Steffens "particularly loved . . . small articles illustrative of city life" (156–57). Among Hapgood's more notable contributions were articles on life in New York's Jewish ghetto to which Abraham Cahan introduced him. The articles would be collected, revised, and published in 1902 as *The Spirit of the Ghetto*. As Hapgood notes in his autobiography, the book was still in print thirty-six years after its appearance (143). In his self-promotion, he reveals the staying power of some of the narrative literary journalism from this era. Indeed the book was republished as late as 1967 by the distinguished Belknap Press of Harvard University Press.

But the *Commercial Advertiser* was not alone. Evidence suggesting that other publications were open to a narrative literary journalism is reflected in a snapshot of Stephen Crane's publishing history. At various times Crane published his true-life sketches of local color in every major New York newspaper, including the *Tribune, Press, Herald, Times, Sun, Journal,* and *World.* Nor was the New York market the only market for the form. Again, Crane's publishing history provides a snapshot of papers from around the country that published the form. These include the *Washington Post,* the *Denver Republican,* the *Philadelphia Press,* and the *Kansas City Star.* Magazines also published his sketches, including such notable publications as *Harper's, Metropolitan Magazine,* and *McClure's Magazine.* Other articles in the form appeared in now largely forgotten publications such as the *Arena,* the *Philistine,* the *Roycroft Quarterly, Town Topics, Pocket Magazine,* and *Truth.*[3]

Nor was Crane the only journalist to benefit from a publishing market willing to print narrative literary journalism. Other practitioners include Norris, who was editor of the *Wave,* a weekly newspaper in San Francisco (O. Lewis 6), and Hearn whose work appeared in Cincinnati and New Orleans newspapers. Others often cited from this period include such notables as Mark Twain, Ambrose Bierce, W. E. B. Du Bois, Richard Harding Davis, and Jacob Riis, as well as writers now largely forgotten such as Julian Ralph, George Ade, Hapgood, and Cahan.[4] Moreover, that other, now-forgotten journalists were practicing the form is reflected in a comment in 1901 in the *Bookman,* one of the leading literary reviews of the time. In an unattributed article, the author takes note of coverage in the *New York Evening Sun* of Carrie Nation's visit to New York, saying that it contained "more humour and insight and clever description than in half a dozen of the typical novels which appear nowadays. It is a pity that really admirable work like this should be so ephemeral, and we take great pleasure in calling attention to it when we can." ("Chronicle and Comment" 111)

But it is Steffens and Hapgood who, by acknowledging the competi-

---

3. All are collected in Crane, *New York City Sketches.*

4. See Nelson on Twain; Fishkin on Du Bois; Bradley on Davis; Good on Riis; Connery on Ralph ("Discovering a Literary Form" 28–29); Connery on Hapgood ("Hutchins Hapgood"); Pauly on Ade ("George Ade"); Rischin on Cahan; and Evensen on Cahan.

tion, provide some of the most compelling evidence that the form had a more widespread practice among journalists at other newspapers in the 1890s than has hitherto been acknowledged. Steffens was to recall: "As for the star men of the other papers, we could see in their printed stuff that they likewise were laboring at the art of telling stories" (317). Similarly, Hapgood recalled: "The newspapers of New York at that time permitted more personal journalism than they do now, not in the way of signed articles, but in individuality of writing, variety of subjects, and a less rigid idea of news. Picturesque interviews, with odd characters, vaudeville actresses, town bums, irrespective of whether the subjects were 'important' or not—many pictures of the character and life of the city—had an opportunity to appear in the newspapers" (138).

Nor was New York necessarily the center for such activity. Chicago had its own homegrown school of narrative literary journalists that included in the 1890s George Ade and to a lesser degree Finley Peter Dunne, who openly engaged in fictionalizing with his "Mr. Dooley" column. (Ade also wrote columns that might or might not contain fictionalized characters and thus his work has to be examined carefully to determine that it is nonfiction.) They would be followed in the first decade of the twentieth century by William Hard, who wrote social reportage, and Ring Lardner, perhaps better known as a short story writer who also wrote sketches of baseball personalities as a sports reporter.[5] Indeed, these Chicago literary journalists would prove to be part of a century-long tradition of narrative journalism practiced there by the likes of Ben Hecht in the 1920s and Mike Royko in the late twentieth century.

But the examples of Ade and Dunne illustrate another point about narrative literary journalism as it has been practiced in the twentieth century. It frequently found an outlet among newspaper columnists who had liberties that conventional hard news reporters often did not. In those liberties can be detected a problem of scholarship. The newspaper columnist has considerable latitude not only in what he or she writes, but in *how* what is written is presented. The vulgarisms of a Ned Ward in late seventeenth-century London may not be permissible, but columnists can write at will in discursive or narrative modes, or like

---

5. See Marmarelli on Hard; and Hettinga on Lardner.

E. B. White they can move between both. Nonetheless, there is no mis-
taking that columnists practiced a narrative literary journalism even if
the result reflected brevity. As scholar Sam G. Riley observes: "My modest protest to the usual definition of 'literary journalism,' which has
often precluded short-form writers such as columnists, was and is that
some of our best remembered and best loved columnists managed to
give their readers good narrative copy, divided as it was by individual
800-word columns" (Riley, email). Moreover, as the examples of Ade
and Dunne illustrate, the adoption of fictional characters to comment
on contemporary life is not uncommon. Indeed, Addison and Steele
did it.

San Francisco was still another center for narrative literary journalism practiced by writers such as Norris, Bierce, and Winifred Black, the
latter better known by her byline as "Annie Laurie" and later a competitor in New York with Elizabeth Cochrane, who wrote under the byline
"Nellie Bly." Ultimately, what all these writers had in common, whether
they worked out of New York, Chicago, or elsewhere, is that they were
practicing professional journalists (and not infrequently columnists)
who engaged in and encouraged a "literary faction," or a journalism
that liberally partook of the techniques associated with the openly fictional novel.

As the *Bookman* article "Chronicle and Comment" suggests, the critical attention the form generated, when coupled with novelistic technique and who practiced it, helps to situate the narrative form as having come of age by the 1890s. That critical consciousness is reflected
in the views of practitioners and critics. One example that appeared in
Steffens's *New York Commercial Advertiser* in 1897 described Crane's
"Men in the Storm" as "one of the most powerful pictures he has ever
drawn of the tragedies of life among the poor of New York" (qtd. in
Stallman and Hagemann, *New York City Sketches* 91). The account of
homeless men in a snowstorm in New York City appeared first in 1894
in the *Arena* and was republished in the *Philistine* in 1897, evidence of
its continuing contemporary appeal. Even though it remains unclear
who the source is of the unidentified comment in the *Commercial Advertiser,* it comes as no surprise that it appeared in Steffens's newspaper.
As Connery notes, Steffens, along with Hapgood and other reporters

at the newspaper, "perceived the possibilities of such a form of writing, envisioned a philosophy or theory of literary journalism, and attempted to enact their philosophy" ("Third Way" 9).

This is reflected in the advice Steffens gave to Cahan on writing a
story about a husband murdering his wife. Steffens added to the advice:
"Our stated ideal for a murder story was that it should be so understood
and told that the murderer would not be hanged, not by our readers.
We never achieved our ideal, but there it was; and it is scientifically and
artistically the true ideal for an artist and for a newspaper: to get the
news so completely and to report it so humanly that the reader will see
himself in the other fellow's place" (317). As a practitioner of the form,
Hapgood offered one of the most extensive attempts at theorizing it in
a 1905 *Bookman* article. He echoes Steffens by observing that when he
writes of his subjects, "I should become identified for the time being
with their lives." He added, "All that is wanting, is for our authors to
pick up the material that abounds, forget their romantic and historical
conventions, and impersonally reflect, with understanding, the drama
of real life. By so doing, they would help vitalise our present anaemic
literature" ("New Form of Literature" 425).

As literary realists and naturalists at the time theorized their own
writings, narrative literary journalists did the same. Indeed Howells was
also calling for the abandonment of romantic and historical conventions in his 1891 volume *Criticism and Fiction:* "It was still held that in
order to interest the reader the characters must be moved by the old
romantic ideals. . . . How false that notion was few but the critics, who
are apt to be rather belated, need now be told" (27). Narrative literary
journalists similarly were stepping back from a creative to a critical
stance and in that perspective on their own work helped to situate it.

But critical recognition of the form extended beyond the presumably self-serving purposes of its practitioners. In 1894 Hamlin Garland
would remark in *Crumbling Idols* that even though American newspapers were generally "conservative" in how they attempted to portray the
phenomenal world—a remark reflecting the emergence of disengaged
journalisms that objectified the world as something different from the
viewing subject—nonetheless many contained "sketches of life so vivid
one wonders why writers so true and imaginative are not recognized
and encouraged" (14). The accolade from Garland is significant be-

cause he was one of the leading theorists of the movement in literary naturalism and *Crumbling Idols* one of the major treatises of that movement (Pizer, *Realism and Naturalism* 55). Moreover, the year before, in 1893, a trans-Atlantic quarrel erupted between the *New York Herald* and the *Pall Mall Gazette* about whether journalism could be literature. The *Spectator,* one of the leading British journals of opinion at the time, attempted to provide moral support for its countryman in insisting that journalism could not, notwithstanding the *Herald*'s point of view that American newspapers had published Longfellow ("Borderland of Literature" 513–514). To be sure, the discussion goes beyond the more limited focus of a narrative literary journalism. But it reveals cultural battles that apply to the modern emergence of that form. And the *Spectator* betrays its own argument when it cites examples of journalism that could also be characterized as literature: "Some of Richard Jefferies' work, for instance, made its first appearance in the columns of an evening paper, and was as undoubtedly literature in its fragmentary shape as it was when collected into the form of a book." Jefferies, who wrote essays and poems on nature, began his publishing career with the *Pall Mall Gazette.* Elsewhere, the *Spectator* article comes closer to acknowledging the form of narrative journalism when it cites the example of Boswell's *Life of Johnson* as both literature and journalism (513). Critics in the United States similarly took note of a narrative literary journalism, reportedly including Howells. As Steffens recalled, Howells, the arbiter of literary taste in American letters at the time, "said that no writer or artist could afford not to read the *Commercial Advertiser*" (*Autobiography* 321).

By the turn of the century, the debate had intensified, surfacing regularly in journals of opinion and letters. In a 1900 article in the *Atlantic* Gerald Stanley Lee said, "It is the business of the average reporter to put a day down, to make a day last until the night. It is the business of the poet reporter to report a day forever, to make a day last so that no procession of flaming sunsets shall put that day out" (232). Citing the British journalist and writer J. M. Barrie, he noted that "it is not in spite of being a reporter that J. M. Barrie is an artist, but it is. . . because he is so much more a reporter that he can report an out-of-the-way town like Thruhms, and make it as famous as London" (233). Lee was referring to the now largely forgotten *Window in Thrums* (the article misspelled the name of the community), one of a collection of sketches of parochial Scottish life appearing in 1889 by the future author of *Peter Pan*. Lee called for "transfigured" journalists to create future literary art: "To be a transfigured reporter, a journalist who is more of an artist than the artist, an artist who is more of a journalist than the journalists,—this is the inevitable destiny of the next great writer who shall succeed in making headway in the public mind" (237).

Lee's statements reflect a critical view that granted literary possibilities to journalism beyond the aspirations of self-serving practitioners such as Hapgood. In another *Atlantic* article in 1904, Henry W. Boynton, a noted critic, observed: "More to our purpose are the many writers of power whose permanent and absorbing task is journalism, but whose work is so unmistakably informed with personality, so pure in method and in contour, as to outrank in literary quality the product of many a literary workshop" (847). Calling such reportage a "higher journalism," he assaults the elitism of conventional literary wisdom that dismisses journalism by noting that "between literature and 'the higher journalism' the partition is extremely thin" (850). A 1906 article in the *Critic*, a book review by Langdon Warner, attempts to eliminate that partition altogether by grandiloquently proclaiming: "What we need . . . is to re-wed literature with journalism, for surely God hath joined them together, and it was man who put them asunder" (469).

To be sure, there were those who assaulted the thesis behind a narrative literary journalism, namely that it could be literature at all. This can be detected in the trans-Atlantic quarrel of 1893 between the *New York Herald* on the one hand, and the *Pall Mall Gazette* and the *Spectator* on the other. Similarly, Warner's article in the *Critic* was in response to an earlier one in that publication, "Journalism the Destroyer of Literature," in which critic and novelist Julian Hawthorne, the only son of literary giant Nathaniel, took an elitist view of literature, describing journalism's concerns as fundamentally "material" while those of literature were "spiritual" (166). His judgment would prove ironic, because he later turned away from the pursuit of literature and engaged in yellow journalism (Pattee, *History* 408).

Others attempted to steer a more sober and critical middle course but one that nonetheless reveals the influence the form was having on literary discourse. An unsigned 1906 article in *Scribner's Magazine*, "The Point of View," notes "a subtle interplay of relation between journalism and fiction of which little account is currently taken" and adds, with a McLuhanesque prescience that anticipates later acknowledgment of the influence of the media on society, "story quality that passes for news modifies the reading habits of a constituency including almost all the reading public" (122).

Thus the form had achieved an identity among critics *outside* that of its practitioners, even if some of those critics attempted to dismiss it. Even a dismissal is testimony to the site of a presence reflected in the give and take of the debate. There is evidence, then, that a modern narrative literary journalism had emerged in the United States after the Civil War, one designed not to report objectified "facts" but to provide a "story" as Steffens called it in his advice to Cahan, one that fundamentally engages the subjectivities of author and reader. Although little recognized as such today, the form has a historical locus, one situated at the intersection of true-life stories—or at least those stories making truth claims to phenomenal experience—that utilized novelistic techniques, were practiced by professional journalists, and of which literary critics took considerable note. To be sure, critical problems remain. One is that the terminology of literary journalism as such was not well understood at the turn of the century in terms of its boundaries. For example, in 1902 Edith Baker Brown made "a plea for literary journalism" in *Harper's Weekly*. In it, literary journalism applies clearly to literary criticism and the discursive literary essay ("A Plea" 1558). This is a usage still very much current in England if references in the *Times Literary Supplement* are any indication (Easthope).

But if this chapter presents evidence of the emergence of the modern form of narrative literary journalism, it does not account for *why* it appeared when it did. That question is examined in the next chapter.

2 Narrative Literary Journalism's Resistance to Objectified News

IN 1898 Stephen Crane, writing as a correspondent covering the Spanish-American War, filed a dispatch to the *New York World* in which he observed that career soldiers often failed to receive the kind of media notoriety that prominent members of society had who volunteered for service in the conflict: "The name of the regular soldier is probably Michael Nolan and his life-sized portrait was not in the papers in celebration of his enlistment. . . . If some good Spaniard shoots him through he will achieve a temporary notoriety, figuring in the lists for one brief moment in which he will appear to the casual reader mainly as part of a total, a unit in the interesting sum of men slain" ("Regulars Get No Glory" 171). Crane thus intuited one of the epistemological consequences, and ultimately liabilities, of mainstream journalistic practice in the second half of the nineteenth century, namely that an account of the phenomenal world committed to the "facts," in this case "a unit in the interesting sum of men slain," failed to do justice to the "subject" of Michael Nolan. I suggest that, at least in part, it would be because of the reaction by Crane and other U.S. writers to this rhetorical objectification of "Michael Nolan" that narrative literary journalism would emerge by the 1890s, providing a challenge to or resistance against mainstream "factual" or "objective" news, much as the form still does today.

The drafting of novelistic technique by working journalists of which critics took considerable note at the turn of the century helps to situate the modern origins of the form to this period, but such factors fail to explain *why* the form should be taken up with such fervor by a group of journalists who so openly advocated a practice outside both the literary and journalistic mainstreams. In other words, why did the form's practitioners engage in the practice, and why did critics outside its practice take more than passing notice of it? There are compelling reasons, I propose, that stem from what was a fundamental epistemological crisis identified by Crane and other critics, a crisis wrought by the development of modern journalism precisely at a time of social and cultural transformation and crisis. One feature of that crisis was that narrative literary journalists recognized at some level the impossibility of ever adequately rendering a contingent world and thus confronted phenomenological fluidity or what the critic Mikhail Bakhtin calls the "inconclusive present" (39). Their efforts could be characterized as one variation on the Bakhtian "novel" and have been part of an attempt to resist unsustainable critical totalizations or closure because of that phenomenological fluidity. As uncomfortable as such a confrontation might prove, narrative literary journalists sought more honest interpretations of the phenomenal world that challenged safe critical assumptions.

A second feature had to do with the rhetorical intention of modern journalistic styles, styles fundamentally alienating of subjectivity, a condition only exacerbated by the considerable social and cultural transformation and crisis of the time. It is in the space created by that transformation, by a critical consciousness of phenomenological fluidity, and by the alienation of subjectivity—including that of the journalist's, the subject of the report, and the reader's—that offered an opening for narrative literary journalism to appear in its modern form, still-prevalent conditions likely to assure its survival as it enters into its second century as a compelling discourse. Viewed in this way narrative literary journalism has been working across a spectrum designed to narrow the distance between the alienated subjectivity and the indeterminate object in a narrative strategy opposite that of objectified versions of journalism. In effect, narrative literary journalism's ambition is to engage the objectified Other. Such a form proves dynamic rather than static, spilling over into conventional objectified journalisms at one end and solipsistic memoir or fiction at the other.

Such an interpretation provides a historical modus for the form, one that can be detected as emerging during the post–Civil War period generally, and the 1890s more particularly, in what Thomas B. Connery has described as the form's first major period (preface xii–xiii). But the modus, it should be emphasized, also can be traced up through the form's second major period in the 1930s and 1940s and eventually to the new journalism of the 1960s. One consequence to viewing the form by means of such a modus is to provide insight into why, not infrequently, narrative literary journalists associated with Populist and Progressive political causes, or at the least found themselves politicized by the subjectivities they examined.

I explore, first, the intellectual and critical context against which narrative literary journalism was emerging by the 1890s. That emergence was taking place against some of the main intellectual currents of the period that include the attempt to graft scientific method to journalistic practice, the emergence of literary realism and naturalism, and ultimately the pervasive influence of positivism in the late nineteenth century. Next, I examine the theoretical foundation for characterizing the discourse as a form of the Bakhtian "novel" that resists comfortable critical closure. Following that, I examine the growing awareness of the epistemological gulf created by factual or objective journalism and how that was reflected in the mainstream journalism profession. Then I examine how such an epistemological gulf occurred precisely at a moment of social and cultural transformation and crisis. Finally, I examine the reaction against the alienation as reflected in texts of narrative literary journalism.

LOOKING BACK on his career as a newspaper reporter, Theodore Dreiser recalled walking into the city room of the *New York World* on his first day of work: "I looked about the great room, as I waited patiently and delightedly, and saw pasted on the walls at intervals printed cards which read: Accuracy, Accuracy, Accuracy! Who? What? Where? When? How? The Facts—The Color—The Facts!" So thoroughly then had the concept of writing "factually" become a part of journalistic culture in the 1890s. But it left Dreiser, the future novelist and a sometime literary journalist, uneasy: "Most excellent traits, I thought, but not as easy to put into execution as comfortable publishers and managing editors might suppose" (*Newspaper Days* 624–25).

In that unease can be detected a simmering revolt against the positivist spirit that had influenced American journalistic practice and against what may seem now to our postmodern world as the naive belief that scientific materialism was the panacea for our earthly pains. The rise in newspaper practice of a factual or objective news style had been driven by that spirit. As Michael Schudson notes: "Reporters in the 1890s saw themselves, in part, as scientists uncovering the economic and political facts of industrial life more boldly, more clearly, and more 'realistically' than anyone had done before. This was part of the broader Progressive drive to found political reform on 'facts'" (71). As an example of such efforts at reform, by 1900 state and federal agencies were routinely gathering data on economic and social issues. "In the first decade of the twentieth century, systematic social investigation practically became a craze" (72). Schudson adds that such "realists," in which he lumps journalists, sociological data collectors, and William Dean Howells and his literary circle, conflated reality with external phenomena, "which, they believed, were subject to laws of physical causality as natural science revealed them and as social science might reveal them" (74).

Thus journalists, litterateurs, and budding social scientists inscribed their beliefs in a determinable knowledge, one that was grounded in a cryptotheological faith in positivism. However, at some point a shift began to occur as doubts arose over what the positivist influence could accomplish. In this shift can be detected one reason for the emergence of a narrative literary journalism during the post–Civil War period. The shift can be found in the changing attitudes in the movement advocating literary realism and its offspring, literary naturalism, the latter especially influencing many of the major narrative literary journalists and proponents of narrative literary journalism. Naturalism always had a close association with journalism broadly conceived. As June Howard notes, "Naturalism combines a particularly complex group of generic messages, including . . . the important emergent form of documentary. . . . Almost all the American naturalists, in fact, worked as journalists at some point in their careers. That biographical connection indicates the deeper structural connection between the specular world of naturalism and the specular world of the newspaper" (155).

In the case of Lincoln Steffens, editor of the *Commercial Advertiser* and one of the major proponents of a narrative literary journalism dur-

ing the 1890s, one important "biographical connection" was his reporter Abraham Cahan, later editor of the Jewish newspaper *Daily Forward* and author of the novels *Shtetl* and *The Rise of David Levinsky*.
Cahan introduced Steffens and Hapgood to the now all but forgotten
but at that time vigorous debates about realism in the active Yiddish
theater in New York:

> The Ghetto and the Russian Jews . . . were splitting just then into two
> parties over the question of realism in the arts. Cahan took us, as he
> could get us, one by one or in groups, to the cafés where the debate was
> on at every table and to the theaters where the audience divided: the
> realist party hissing a romantic play, the romanticists fighting for it with
> clapping hands and sometimes with fists or nails. A remarkable phenom-
> enon it was, a community of thousands of people fighting over an art
> question as savagely as other people had fought over political or religious
> questions, dividing families, setting brother against brother, breaking up
> business firms, and finally, actually forcing the organization of a rival
> theater with a company pledged to realism against the old theater, which
> would play any good piece.
>   I rejoiced when this East Side controversy flowed over into my newspa-
> per. (Steffens, *Autobiography* 317–18)

As Steffens further recalled in his autobiography, Cahan "made inces-
sant propaganda among us for the Marxian program and for Russian
realism" (314).

Moreover, in a prescience that anticipates those biographical con-
nections—in this instance not only from an early realist to later narrative literary journalist but also from mother to son—the writer Rebecca
Harding Davis, whose only son, Richard, became a war correspondent,
narrative literary journalist, and writer of historical romances, issued
one of the early American manifestoes of realism and its offshoot naturalism before the literary movement was enunciated by Howells in the
1870s. It is a manifesto that anticipates not only realism/naturalism
but also, remarkably, muckraking and narrative literary journalism before the emergence of those forms in a fuller if somewhat more rancid
flower. As the unmarried Rebecca Harding she was the author of "Life
in the Iron-Mills," which appeared in the *Atlantic* in 1861. The account
of that "life" in Wheeling, in what was at the time the state of Virginia,
is largely forgotten today not only because she was a woman but also

because what she was attempting to do—understand the subjectivities of iron workers—was undoubtedly overshadowed by civil war which broke out the month her article appeared. Harding's manifesto of realism appeared in still another article in the *Atlantic* that same first year of the Civil War when the narrator reproaches the reader: "You want something, in fact, to lift you out of this crowded, tobacco-stained commonplace, to kindle and chafe and glow in you. I want you to dig into this commonplace, this vulgar American life, and see what is in it. Sometimes I think it has a raw and awful significance that we do not see" ("A Story of To-Day" 472). Narrative literary journalism, among other literary and journalistic forms, would go in search of that raw and awful significance, and in that lies the germination of a form of social or cultural portraiture. So, too, would Rebecca Harding Davis's son, Richard, go in search of that awful significance when in his narrative literary journalism he explored the horrific experience of the German invasion of Belgium in 1914.

It is William Dean Howells, however, who as editor of the *Atlantic* is generally credited as the principal advocate of American literary realism. For Howells, realism would "assert that fidelity to experience and probability of motive are the essential conditions of a great imaginative literature" (*Criticism and Fiction* 15). It is worth noting that the influence of literary realism (and naturalism) on narrative literary journalism was more on the order of the discovery of a critical *articulation*. The techniques of literary realism and naturalism were long practiced in nonfiction narrative forms—including premodern narrative literary journalism. They even predate the modern novel, which borrowed techniques attributed to realism from earlier nonfiction narratives. Nonetheless, the articulation of literary realism and, later, naturalism was important in terms of providing critical models. Naturalism, especially, would call for an examination in which the material world would dictate its "transcription." Perhaps not surprisingly the naturalists concluded that in scrutinizing a material world without looking for a moral conclusion, the result was that a material world was merely an indifferent material world whose indifference made an irony of human aspiration, no matter how noble or moral that aspiration might prove. Moreover in the close examination of the material world, what became evident was that it was by no means a rational and orderly one—no matter how rigidly enforced by convention, whether social, scientific, intellectual, religious, or aesthetic (historical romance is an example in this latter category), or some combination of these. It is in the randomness that literary naturalists detected the phenomenal world became "subject" to the whims of subjectivity. Hamlin Garland, for one, attempted in his literary theorizing in *Crumbling Idols* to strike a balance between an acknowledgment of the existence of a phenomenal world, however contingent, and the existence of a phenomenal world only perceivable through the fallibilities of consciousness, a critical stance that reflects remarkably the modus I suggest is at work in narrative literary journalism.

Garland provides a useful point of examination for outlining those critical positions not only because he was a critic and novelist but also because he was a nonfictionist whose memoirs frequently straddle the boundary with narrative literary journalism. His nonfiction is as much outward-directed in its social or cultural portraiture, like much of narrative literary journalism, as it is inward-directed toward the writing self. Because he provides then a "biographical connection" between his work as a nonfictionist and critic when examining the "important emergent form of documentary," to borrow from Howard, his critical positions reflect an important reflexivity about his creative nonfiction. Equally important, those positions are reflective of a larger philosophical resistance at the time against the totalizing inclination of an emerging modernism.

For Garland, the indeterminacy of the phenomenal world is reflected in two observations he makes in *Crumbling Idols,* the title itself suggestive of the resistance to critical totalization: "Life is always changing and literature changes with it. It never decays; it changes" (77). Also: "The sun of truth strikes each part of the earth at a little different angle" (22). In unending change and the atomization of "each part of the earth" Garland strikes a pose worthy of Heraclitus.

What we see increasingly then at the turn of the century is a growing unease with positivist assumptions. A similar position to Garland's is sounded in a 1906 *Scribner's* article in which the unidentified author, in noting the emergence of journalistic texts of potential literary merit, observes: "This encroachment of the newspaper on the province of ordinary story-telling, vitiating the popular taste and to some extent that of the more thoughtful, has also had its part in delimiting the sphere of fiction as art. . . . [The result is an] endeavor to reproduce, sometimes dramatically, sometimes incidentally, the incompleteness of life. Then, too, the newspaper usually depicts life as it is embodied in a constantly shifting series of individuals, selected haphazardly" ("Point of View" 122). The statement is revealing for two reasons. First, "delimiting the sphere of fiction as art" suggests just how fine is the line between the traditional fictional novel and narrative literary journalism. Second, the "incompleteness of life" "constantly shifting" in a "haphazard" world reflects Garland's changing and indeterminate world.

Comments from both Garland and the *Scribner's* article are particularly remarkable, however, in that they anticipate postmodern positions on narrative in general and narrative literary journalism in particular, this before the ascendancy of the literary modernists and their aesthetic essentializing. But that should come as no surprise considering the critical ferment of the last half of the nineteenth century. In that ferment, Nietzsche composed in 1873 his essay "Truth and Falsity in Their Ultramoral Sense." The essay provided one of the foundations for the later deconstructive position and subsequent poststructural and postmodern challenges to critical totalizations (Childers and Hentzi 74). In the essay, Nietzsche takes note of the tendency to essentialize or totalize distinctive phenomenal experiences into comprehensive abstract generalities by the exclusion of differences between those experiences (179). He characterizes such a cognitive process, reflected of course in language or given its measure by language, as "volatilization" (181). Clearly, the abstracting nature of factual or objective journalism is likewise the result of a cognitive volatilization. But narrative literary journalism engages in a kind of reverse volatilization, or perhaps more appropriately a critical precipitation because of its focus on the concrete particular—scene construction and dialogue, for example—as applied to a certain time and place. Because such particulars are distinctive, they can make no claim to critical closure or totalized volatilization and thus must continue to exist in resistance to such volatilization. While such narratives can *aspire* to closure, say a structural closure with climax and denouement according to a cultural construction of Western narrative, distinctive phenomena must always exist in resistance to that closure because of their one-of-a-kind, or "antivolatil-ized," nature.

Such early critical positions by Nietzsche, Garland, and the author of the *Scribner's* article provide critical evidence that a narrative de-signed to reflect distinctive phenomena served a very different func-tion from a factual or objective news style. It is this "antivolatilized" nature of narrative literary journalism that anticipates Mikhail Bakhtin, who offers an interpretation of the novel that places narrative literary journalism in a larger context as part of a narrative evolution. That evolution could be called the "Bakhtian" novel as opposed to the tradi-tional canonical novel. As Bakhtin notes:

> The novel took shape precisely . . . when the object of artistic representa-tion was being degraded to the level of a contemporary reality that was inconclusive and fluid. From the very beginning the novel was structured not in the distanced image of the absolute past but in the zone of direct contact with inconclusive present-day reality. At its core lay personal ex-perience and free creative imagination. Thus a new, sober artistic-prose novelistic image and a new critical scientific perception came into being simultaneously. . . . A lengthy battle for the novelization of the other genres began, a battle to drag them into a zone of contact with reality. (39)

The novel by Bakhtin's definition is "ever questing" as a result of com-ing into contact "with inconclusive present-day reality." Bakhtin's "con-temporary reality that was inconclusive and fluid" because of its em-phasis on the present reflects the indeterminacy of Garland's and Nietzsche's phenomenal worlds. Also remarkable is how the *Scribner's* article, when it notes that narratives were "delimiting the sphere of fiction as art," similarly anticipates Bakhtin's position.

One version of the Bakhtian novel that has developed, one that is in opposition to the canonical novel, is the "novel" or "narrative" of narra-tive literary journalism, or to cite some of the other terminologies that have been applied to such texts, literary nonfiction, or documentary reportage, or new journalism, ad infinitum, indeterminate and fluid, like the shifting form's attempt to mirror reality. As Bakhtin intuited: "A lengthy battle for the novelization of the other genres began, a battle to drag them into a zone of contact with reality."

To characterize narrative literary journalism as part of a "novel" form is fraught with danger since to do so only increases the invitation to dismiss it as just another fiction.[1] But then any textual mediation can be dismissed as a fiction given the specular nature of language. One consequence is that we have the Holocaust deniers. As John J. Pauly notes, "Literary critics enjoy debunking the realism of nonfiction stories, for they hope to affirm the fictiveness of all narratives. Having settled journalism's hash, philosophically speaking, critics can deny all claims to representation, and hence free the literary imagination from its earthly entrapments" ("Politics" 122). What remains to be acknowledged, as Pauly implies, is that not all fictions are equal, or rather not all are of the same degree of fictiveness. This acknowledged, Bakhtin's analysis describes a "novel" that is more like narrative literary journalism than a text timelessly frozen in an essentialized literary heaven, or in "the distanced image of the absolute past," as he has characterized it. Moreover, such an interpretation is not without historical legitimacy, a legitimacy that has been largely overlooked in the marginalizing politics of the literary academy and in the origins of the meaning of the word "novel": "Our word, stemming from the Italian *novella* and roughly equivalent to 'news,' suggests a new kind of anecdotal narrative that claims to be both recent and true. Thus the development of the novel touches heroic legend at one extreme and modern journalism at the other" (Levin 283). Bakhtin might well quibble with the novel touching "heroic legend" because to do so is to run the risk of freezing the novel once again in "the distanced image of the absolute past" and to deny what about it makes it a distinctive form of discourse, namely, that it is fluid in its coming into contact with indeterminacy, or the "inconclusive present." Nonetheless, it is no accident that early examples of newspapers in English were in fact called "novels." In 1640 one English editor and printer of newspapers wrote in his paper: "It is well known that these novels are well esteemed in all parts of the world" (qtd. in Andrews 30). It has only been with the rise of the elitist literary academy that the "novel" has been press-ganged into a kind of essentialized literary servitude, denying it its earlier robust and freewheeling epistemological intention. Bakhtin comes closer to the truth in acknowledging the novel's fluid and indeterminate nature.

---

1. See Hellmann, *Fables of Fact.*

While Bakhtin does not specifically acknowledge a narrative literary journalism, other critics do, while at the same time taking positions that bear a strong resemblance to Bakhtin's before his work was widely available to the West. Mas'ud Zavarzadeh, in an analysis of the "nonfiction novel," suggests that his variation on narrative literary journalism, such as Truman Capote's *In Cold Blood,* derived from the pressures of an increasingly "technetronic" society that resulted in a "discontinuous present" that is fundamentally absurd (9). Similarly, James Boylan has observed of narrative literary journalism in the 1930s, or what he calls "documentary," that it "was designed to upset the status quo" (169). In both Zavarzadeh and Boylan, reality, or the unreality of reality, defies the status quo dictated by closed critical systems, or what Bakhtin characterizes as "the distanced image of the absolute past." In its documentary concern then, narrative literary journalism has the courage to acknowledge a phenomenal world that is fundamentally indeterminate and in doing so not to reinscribe it in a cryptotheological faith.

Such a narrative ambition is daunting, even terrifying, which has made the historical enterprise in narrative literary journalism all the more existentially courageous in the face of essentializing critical cryptotheologies. For narrative literary journalism, with its emphasis on representing the phenomenal particular such as character, inanimate spatiality, and a moment in time, "the object of artistic representation was being degraded to the level of a contemporary reality that was inconclusive and fluid."

BAKHTIN AND ZAVARZADEH, along with Garland and the anonymous author in *Scribner's,* also take positions that acknowledge, whether implicitly or explicitly, the important role of subjectivity for perceiving and conceiving of that indeterminate world. If journalism is to be "truthful" in its "transcribing" interpretation of the world, it must also be truthful in its means. The rise of a factual or objective journalism style provoked an epistemological crisis for subjectivity, whether the journalist's, the reader's, or that of the object of the report. Narrative literary journalism was a response to that crisis in an attempt to reestablish what critic John Berger ably calls the "relation between teller, listener (spectator) and protagonist(s)" ("Stories" 286). This then is another reason I detect for the rise of a narrative literary journalism by the 1890s. Nor should one reason be privileged over the other. Rather, I see both reasons in an ongoing negotiation, a negotiation that ultimately results in a space across which narrative literary journalism operates between an open subjectivity that in the extreme runs the risk of slipping into solipsism and a covert subjectivity outward-directed in its aspiration to render a narrative about fluid phenomenal experience.

For Garland, the role of subjectivity is reflected in the following passage: "Art, I must insist, is an individual thing,—the question of one man facing certain facts and telling his individual relations to them. His first care must be to present his own concept. This is, I believe, the essence of veritism: 'Write of those things of which you know most, and for which you care most. By so doing you will be true to yourself, true to your locality, and true to your time'" (35). In emphasizing that the artist should tell of his or her individual relations to "facts," Garland not only foregrounds the writer's subjectivity but also reverses the emphasis of an ascendant mainstream factual or objective journalism that in its objectification was attempting to deny or neutralize subjectivity. Garland's comments reveal a naturalism that has established for itself what ultimately must be an impossible goal because not only is the world indeterminate but also the subjective or impressionistic rendering of the world must in the subjective choices be indeterminate. As Donald Pizer notes, "Throughout *Crumbling Idols* Garland used *impressionism* and *veritism* interchangeably" (*Realism and Naturalism* 93). Thus the *truth* of "veritism" lies in the *subjective* "impression." In the *Scribner's* article, the role of subjectivity is reflected in the "haphazard selection." As the physicist Werner Heisenberg observed, "what we observe is not nature in itself but nature exposed to *our* method of questioning" (55, emphasis added). That exposure determines how nature will appear in accordance to the whims of the questioning we choose to apply. What we choose then is "telling our individual relations" to the world, and Heisenberg, who articulated the "Uncertainty Principle" in physics, well understood how our subjectivity provides only one limited vantage point on phenomenal experience.

Indeed, chroniclers of the phenomenal world have long acknowledged that this is the case. Samuel Johnson did so in the eighteenth century when he observed in his *Journey to the Western Islands of Scotland,* an early variety of narrative literary journalism: "He who has not made the experiment, or who is not accustomed to require rigorous accuracy from himself, will scarcely believe how much a few hours take from certainty of knowledge, and the distinctness of imagery; how the succession of objects will be broken, how separate parts will be confused, and how many particular features and discriminations will be compressed and conglobated" (139). Johnson provides a portrait of indeterminacy and the limitations of one's cognition.

Similarly, at the center of Bakhtin's position "lay personal experience and free creative imagination." In a circumlocution, one that may explain why Bakhtin fell afoul of the Soviets and was banished to Kazakhstan, he notes that "in the novel [or at least the Bakhtian novel of the inconclusive present] the individual acquires the ideological and linguistic initiative necessary to change the nature of his own image (there is a new and higher type of individualization of the image)" (38). The text suffers from abstraction, perhaps in part because it suffers from Soviet critical language. But as Cathy N. Davidson translates the passage: "Bakhtin also notes [that] the complex intellectual and emotional activity of reading fiction empowers the hitherto powerless individual, at least imaginatively, by authorizing necessarily private responses to texts" (303). Bakhtin's position that an individual acquires "initiative" reflects the subjectivity implicit in the "complex intellectual and emotional activity" and the authorization "imaginatively" of "necessarily private responses." Again, Davidson's interpretation corresponds with remarkable likeness to Garland's "one man facing certain facts and telling his individual relations to them."

Narrative literary journalism, then, has attempted to drag the journalistic concept of a verifiable reality reflected in a truth claim "into a zone of contact with reality" that can only be shaped by subjectivity. Bakhtin hints at this, as well as the continuing evolution of his version of the novel, when he notes: "The process of the novel's development has not yet come to an end. It is currently entering a new phase. For our era is characterized by an extraordinary complexity and a deepening in our perception of the world; there is an unusual growth in the demands of human discernment, on mature objectivity and the critical faculty. These are features that will shape the further development of the novel as well" (40). While "mature objectivity" may be open to debate, the "deepening" of "perception" and the "unusual growth in the demands of human discernment" speak to the important role accorded to subjectivity in the discernment, which by definition is not capable of omniscience or an objectivity free of the limitations of subjectivity.

Zavarzadeh's similar position on subjectivity is reflected in a statement that also helps to distinguish the difference between the more traditional canonical and overtly fictional novel, and narrative literary journalism as a kind of novel, admittedly covertly fictional because of the specular nature of language. Zavarzadeh notes that the events and actions of narrative literary journalism "are actual phenomena in the world accessible to ordinary human senses and, unlike the contents of fictive novels, exist outside the cover of books. The subjectivity involved in all acts of human perception of the external world does not deny the phenomenalistic status of the experiences transcribed" (226). His observation does justice, for example, to the "facts" that lie in a cemetery in Garden City, Kansas, graves containing the remains of the Clutter family who were portrayed in *In Cold Blood* because they give testimony to "the phenomenalistic status of the experiences transcribed." The choice is whether to acknowledge that there can be a phenomenalistic status, or slip wholly into the safety zone of a consciousness' solipsism. At the same time, as Zavarzadeh implies, the phenomenalistic status of transcribed experience does not deny the subjectivity involved in all acts of human perception. Once again, it is this conundrum that informs narrative literary journalism.

Connery takes note of a literature of fact of the 1890s that acknowledges the role of subjectivity in its practice. A "literary journalistic account did not just record and report, it interpreted as well. It did so by subjectively placing details and impressions no longer considered appropriate for the standard newspaper article into a storytelling form that was also being cast aside by the institutionalized press" ("Third Way" 6). Indeed, one of the distinctive features of narrative literary journalism, as Ronald Weber ("Some Sort" 18, 20–21), Dan Wakefield ("Personal Voice" 41–44, 46), Norman Mailer (*Armies of the Night* 65–66, 243–44), and others have noted, is the heightened and at times foregrounded subjectivity of the author. This is true even in accounts that posture novelistic omniscience, because as Weber observes, "in the obvious . . . novelistic artistry of scene and characterization the writer makes his presence and his shaping consciousness known" ("Some Sort" 20).

BUT WHILE writers and scholars have long noted the evidence of a more openly acknowledged subjectivity in narrative literary journalism, it remains unclear why journalists chose to indulge their subjectivities so flagrantly. To understand this, it is necessary to understand the contrasting epistemological nature between narrative literary journalism style on the one hand, and the news style of objective or factual journalism, along with sensational journalism, on the other. Narrative literary journalism could also be placed under what has been characterized by Michael Schudson as the "story" model of journalism and objectified factual journalism under what he characterizes as the "information" model of journalism (89), or what is analogous in more traditional rhetorical theory to "narrative" and "discursive" modes, respectively. The exception is sensational journalism, which can fall under both, an issue I explore in chapter 4. In any event, the period after the Civil War is considered the period when both objectified factual reporting—what today we call objective reporting—and sensational yellow journalism were ascendant at the expense of the older partisan journalism. A consequence of the development of factual or objective news reporting was a paradox in human perception, Alan Trachtenberg suggests, in which American newspapers appeared to bring the world closer to their readers when in reality they were alienating them from the *experience* of the world. While much of what he says focuses on the information model, similarities exist with sensational yellow journalism. Trachtenberg notes:

> Monopolized by telegraphic press services, the older kind of news, a record of a significant event, now arrived at the offices of the dailies in packaged form. The telegraphic system, observed a writer in 1870, has "made all the leading papers so nearly alike as to their news that one does not differ in that respect materially from the others." The conditions themselves of gathering what had been thought of as news, then, made the world seem the same regardless of the name of the newspaper. . . . Thus the dailies dramatized a paradox of metropolitan life itself:

the more knowable the world came to seem as *information,* the more remote and opaque it came to seem as *experience.* . . .

Yet in providing surrogate experience, the newspaper only deepened
the separation it seemed to overcome—deepened them by giving them
a precise form: the form of reading and looking. Each individual paper,
a replica of hundreds of thousands of others, served as a private opening
to a world identical to that of one's companion on a streetcar, a companion likely to remain as distant, remote, and strange as the day's "news"
comes to seem familiar, personal, and real. (*Incorporation* 124–25, Trachtenberg's emphasis)

Elsewhere, Trachtenberg notes, "In technologies of communication,
vicarious experience began to erode direct physical experience of the
world. Viewing and looking at representations, words and images, city
people found themselves addressed more often as passive spectators
than as active participants" (*Incorporation* 122). The observation, of
course, is resonant with meaning in the current television age, when
television is often cited as turning viewers into passive spectators.

Trachtenberg's analysis draws on critic Walter Benjamin who observed that the intention of the modern newspaper is "to isolate what
happens from the realm in which it could affect the experience of the
reader. The principles of journalistic information (freshness of news,
brevity, comprehensibility, and, above all, lack of connection between
the individual news items) contribute as much to this as does the make-
up of the pages and the paper's style. (Karl Kraus never tired of demonstrating the great extent to which the linguistic usage of newspapers
paralyzed the imagination of their readers.)" ("On Some Motifs" 159).
A factual or informational news style separated individual subjectivity
from what has now become a distanced object. This is still reflected in
the advice of contemporary journalism textbooks. In what one author
calls the "most important part" of the "objective" news story, the story
lead, he prescribes that "the lead immediately reveals every major detail" (Fedler 139, 214). The *aspiration* then of what is also called the
"summary lead" is to attempt to leave no questions—meaning contin-
gencies—unanswered.

Aside from the epistemological problems of such an ambition, the
result is that the tendency of mainstream news style is to *deny* questioning by the reader, thus opening an epistemological gulf between
the reader's imaginative participation and what has become an objec-

tified world. In a manner of speaking, an "objective" news style is aspiring to the Platonic ideal, as demonstrated in an early example of factual news. The bulletin, written by Associated Press reporter Lawrence A. Gobright on the assassination of Abraham Lincoln, was printed in Horace Greeley's *New York Tribune:* "The President was shot in a theater tonight, and perhaps mortally wounded" (151). While the language is perhaps archaic from our contemporary perspective, nonetheless it is an early version of factual objectified news style for several reasons. First, Lincoln the man has been reified to president thus eliding his identity and symbolically his human subjectivities. Second, he has been shot in a generic and thus abstracted theater. Third, the issue of Lincoln's mortality has been foregrounded precisely to foreclose asking the question, Is he alive or dead? The reader is told that this must still be determined. However, since the reader has already been excluded from asking the question, the implication is that the answer must come from somewhere else. The news of Lincoln's assassination then has been distilled or abstracted of its subjectivity and impersonally objectified to be presented as an unarguable given in which there is little opportunity for dispute, other than to answer the question the reader has already been directed to ask, Is Lincoln dead or alive? Ultimately, the reader's subjectivity is excluded from imaginative participation. Imaginations indeed have been paralyzed.

A not-dissimilar conclusion can be made about the emergence of sensational yellow journalism during this era. Sensational journalism attempts to cause repugnance, horror, or terror by emphasizing differences between subjectivities, not by attempting to narrow the gulf between them. In emphasizing difference, or what makes us different from the Other, sensational yellow journalism reenacts the epistemological problem inherent in objectified, "factual" journalism.

BUT SUCH an alienation alone might not have been enough if the rise of "objective" news and yellow sensational journalism had not come at a time of extraordinary social and cultural transformation and crisis. They came to dominate journalistic discourse precisely at a time when if anything people needed to understand *more intimately* the consequences of what was happening in American life—and to their own lives. It was a time of major shifts in population from the country to the burgeoning cities; it was a time of mass immigration; and it was a time of economic upheaval and labor strife. While such problems are generally common knowledge, it is easy to forget just how momentous were the transformations and crises.

From 1860 to 1890 the population of the United States had doubled; wealth per capita had doubled; and the national wealth had quadrupled (Schlesinger, *Political and Social Growth* 132). Towns with a population of 8,000 or more had gone from accounting for only 16.1 percent of the population in what was largely an agrarian society in 1860, to accounting for nearly 30 percent in 1890. It is worth emphasizing that if the national wealth had quadrupled, clearly that wealth was not shared proportionally by the average worker who only saw income double. In that, one can detect various economic disparities. For example, before the Civil War there were only a handful of millionaires; by the time of the 1893 Columbian Exposition in Chicago there were more than 4,000 (Martin 3). The robber baron had become a staple of American society and culture. But such disparities were more than just a matter of the emergence of a new upper class and a new proletarian class: by 1893 the average family wealth of city dwellers was $9,000 compared to $3,250 for those living in rural areas (Ziff 21).

Meanwhile, in the thirty-five-year period between 1865 and 1900, 13.26 million foreigners entered the United States (Schlesinger, *Political and Social Growth* 281). In less than half that time, between 1900 and 1914, immigration accounted for an additional population of 13.3 million, mostly from Central and Eastern Europe (353). When World War I broke out, fully one-third of the 100 million U.S. residents were foreign born or of foreign-born parents (396). The consequences, particularly for urban centers, were dramatic. In 1890 Greater New York had twice as many Irish as Dublin, as many Germans as Hamburg, two-and-a-half times as many Jews as Warsaw, and half as many Italians as Naples. In Massachusetts, Brahmin dominance of politics had declined, and in 1889 sixty-eight towns and cities in that state were governed by those with Irish surnames (281–82). In the Midwest at least every sixth person was of foreign birth in 1890 (Schlesinger, *Rise of the American City* 64). And in that same year the foreign-born population of Chicago, numbering about 450,000, almost equaled that city's population ten years earlier (65).

Such changes alone would assure social transformation and cultural crisis for all citizens. But such transformations were exacerbated by severe cycles of boom and bust. First came the financial panic of 1873, then that of 1884–85—sometimes characterized as the Great Upheaval—and then the financial panic of 1893. Nor were these short-lived, often stalling the American economy, and unemployment and wages, for years at a time. In the panic of 1873, more than 5,000 businesses failed and more than 3 million wage earners lost their jobs. The U.S. economy took five years to recover (Schlesinger, *Political and Social Growth* 159–60). The panic of 1893 resulted in 8,000 businesses failing between 1 April and 1 October of that year; 156 railroads went into receivership (264). Under such circumstances, it is little wonder that this was the era in which labor unions first began to form with some real success, accompanied by labor strife as workers called for higher wages, job security, an eight-hour workday, and abolishment of child labor—all these demands aggravated by cheap immigrant labor vying for the same jobs as the native born (203). The membership of the American Federation of Labor grew from 150,000 in 1886 to 550,000 by 1900. Nearly 24,000 strikes and lockouts occurred between 1881 and 1900, involving some 128,000 businesses and more than 6.6 million workers. The total loss for both employees and employers has been estimated at $450 million (205).

Given such a social context, it is no wonder that the alienating nature of the information and sensational models of objectified journalisms would fail to account for what was happening in people's lives. The social psyche was being fed what could not sustain it.

To be sure, narrative literary journalism is as mediated as objectified journalisms because of its fundamentally specular nature. But its ambition is to narrow the gulf between subject and object, not to widen it. This is not to suggest that such attempts were or are ultimately entirely successful. The problem is an epistemological one, one that must place the critical emphasis first on *how* we attempt to know the phenomenal world before we can know the *what* that matters. Trachtenberg comes to a not-dissimilar conclusion in an examination of two of Crane's New York City sketches, "An Experiment in Misery" and "The Men in the Storm": "In their daily recurrence newspapers express concretely the

estrangement of an urban consciousness no longer capable of free intimacy with its own material life." While Trachtenberg does not acknowledge the existence of an extant narrative literary journalism during the
period, he does acknowledge that Crane "wrote as a 'literary' observer." Similarly, he notes that Crane's "sketches present themselves
as personal reports from and on *experience,* frankly colored by personal
style." More broadly, Trachtenberg observes that a story model of journalism was pervasive, but that as conceived in the mainstream press it
served as "an expression of the newspapers' need to transform random
street experience into *someone's* experience." One consequence was
that newspapers turned to publishing human-interest stories. Trachtenberg adds: "The tactic of searching out 'human interest,' of making
the commonplace seem picturesque or dramatic, is an attempt to fill
the distances inherent in mystified space with formulaic emotion fos-
tering the illusion of distance transcended" ("Experiments" 269). Such
was the nature of the conventional human-interest feature story, and
narrative literary journalism would attempt to move beyond that formulaic emotion, as reflected in Crane's sketches. As Connery notes of
the relationship between the feature story and narrative literary journalism, "Although some literary journalism bore a striking resemblance to what was coming to be known as newspaper feature writing,
it eschewed the evolving formula of that article type, with its predictability and clichés" ("Third Way" 6).

It is important to understand that amid the cultural and social transformation and crisis of the period, and amid the rise of objectified and
yellow journalisms, the result could only be epistemological crisis. It
is to this that narrative literary journalists such as Crane responded.
Indeed, they and the literati of the day such as Howells and Dreiser
critically detected this alienating gulf between subject and object in
mainstream journalistic practice. For example, journalist Jacob Riis expressed his antipathy toward the concept of objectified transcription
(although in this instance he is discussing his photojournalism): "I do
not want my butterfly stuck on a pin and put in a glass case. I want to
see the sunlight on its wings as it flits from flower to flower, and I don't
care a rap what its Latin name may be. Anyway, it is not its name. The
sun and flower and the butterfly know that. The man who sticks a pin
in it does not, and never will, for he knows not its language" (266).

Sticking the butterfly on a pin and placing it behind glass makes a dead and distanced object of it, denying the experience of watching its motion and acknowledging one's impressionistic experience of observing its vital flight.

Howells also took note of the depersonalizing nature of objectified journalistic practice in two of his major novels, *A Hazard of New Fortunes* and *A Modern Instance*. Howells's own feelings about journalism broadly conceived were ambivalent. On the one hand he recalled fondly his years as a printer's devil on his father's newspaper in Ohio (*Years of My Youth* 131). Moreover, there is evidence that he was favorably inclined toward the narrative literary journalism of the fin de siècle; as Steffens observed: "William Dean Howells, the novelist, once said that no writer or artist could afford not to read the *Commercial Advertiser*" (*Autobiography* 321). But Howells was ill at ease with the rise of objectified journalism: "Howells . . . saw the new journalism as the vulgar and pernicious violator of private experience" (Ziff 148). Here, the "new journalism" is not that of the 1960s variety but a factual, or what would eventually be characterized as an objective, journalism.[2]

Howells's acknowledgment of the growing gulf between subjectivity and objectification found expression in 1890 in the publication of *A Hazard of New Fortunes*, which still serves as an insightful cultural critique of mainstream journalistic practice. In the novel Howells explores both the potential for a narrative literary journalism and the alienation wrought by mainstream factual journalism that had emerged after the Civil War. In one passage the character Fulkerson suggests that the journalist Basil March write an account of a labor strike in "Defoe's Plague-of-London style" (*Hazard* 357). The observation is telling because Daniel Defoe attempted to pass off his *Robinson Crusoe* and *A Journal of the Plague Year* as true-life accounts, when instead they are fictions based on true-life accounts. Nonetheless, Defoe clearly understood the potential of a narrative literary journalism, and Fulkerson detects that potential in the emerging modern era when he adds that he would like March to join with an illustrator to "take down [the

---

2. The new journalism of the era was the new style of objectified news, as George A. Hough has noted in his discussion of the different "new journalisms" in journalism history.

strike's] aesthetic aspects. . . . I tell you it's imposing to have a private war, as you say fought out this way, in the heart of New York, and New York not minding it a bit" (357). March, however, does not act on Fulkerson's advice. Presumably readers continue not to mind the strike "a bit" because their subjectivities are alienated from it by the epistemological nature of objectified journalism practiced by the mainstream press.

Nor is this the first time March is advised to engage his subjectivity in the experience of the phenomenal world. The character Conrad Dryfoos counsels March that the "city itself is preaching the best sermon all the time" (Howells, *Hazard* 138). March's response is not hopeful. He reveals the alienation of his subjectivity from an objectified world when he responds, "I don't know that I understand you." As Daniel H. Borus observes, when March rejects Conrad Dryfoos's advice it is because the journalist "'philosophizes'—devises concepts to remove himself from the immediacy of life. . . . This pose prevents March from finishing the sketches for which his trip around the city has provided material" (180). In denying then the imaginative participation of his subjectivity in experience, March ultimately is denying his own subjectivity; he has reenacted in his own life the gulf reflected in the alienation of reader from the object. In the philosophizing, he has engaged in Nietzsche's volatilization. Indeed, Ziff is accurate: the pernicious violation of personal experience lies in the evidence that mainstream factual or objective journalism does not personalize, or attempt to engage in an exchange of subjectivities, in its reports. The cryptotheological hold that factual or objective journalism had begun to have in the minds of journalists of the era, as Michael Schudson suggests, is reflected in March's conscious detachment from the phenomenal world when he finds himself being drawn into the experience of the strike: "he began to feel like the populace, but struggled with himself and regained his character of philosophical observer" (Howells, *Hazard* 360). The cryptotheological hold of factual or objective journalism according to which the world must be interpreted is reflected when, after March is told that "the city itself is preaching the best sermon all the time," the character Mela observes of March that "he dresses just like a priest, and he says he *is* a priest" (138, Howells's emphasis).

Similarly, in Howells's *Modern Instance,* published in 1882, the protagonist and newspaper editor Bartley Hubbard outlines his ideal of a newspaper that "must cease to have any influence in public affairs" (22). As Amy Kaplan observes of the passage, Hubbard advocates an independent journalism that "involves the separation of journalism from party allegiances." In effect, Hubbard "divorces the public from an active political body." Aside from the irony that one of the book's major themes is the divorce of husband and wife and the consequent breakdown of moral order in both private and public life, Hubbard's idea of journalism "transforms readers from political participants into passive spectators" (29–30).

This perception at the turn of the century in literary circles that conventional mainstream journalistic practice divorced readers from experience and alienated their subjectivities is examined perhaps most forcefully in Theodore Dreiser's *Sister Carrie*. Here, however, the author examines the alienation of the reader. In the novel, the unemployed Hurstwood "substitutes," as Kaplan calls it, reading a newspaper in place of looking for a job (153). Thus the newspaper serves as a surrogate for life. But after reading about a streetcar strike Hurstwood is prompted to answer an advertisement to be a strikebreaker. His experience so far with the strike has been in its objectified version distanced from his subjectivity in the form of a newspaper report. On the job, however, he finds that "the real thing was slightly worse than the thoughts of it had been," thoughts formed of course by the objectification of experience by newspapers (Dreiser, *Sister Carrie* 308). Finally, when his streetcar is attacked and he is shot at, he deserts his job, concluding that "it was an astonishing experience for him. He had read of these things, but the reality seemed something altogether new" (310). Clearly, the "reality" of what one reads, objectified and placed at an emotional distance from one's own subjectivity, is not the same as the "reality" of that subjectivity engaged in an imaginative intimacy with the experience. As Kaplan notes, "When [Hurstwood] ventures out of his apartment as a scab, he is not prepared for the intensity of the social conflict, and is forced to take sides. He must either be seen and attacked as a scab, join the strikers, or leave. There is no neutral position" (154). He chose to leave, his subjectivity defeated, and afterward he again takes refuge in the newspaper with the illusion of living an engaged life.

What remains remarkable is how much literary realists such as Howells and Dreiser, both former journalists (and sometime literary journalists), discerned and intuited the divorce of subjectivity from the experience of the world in factual or objective journalism. It was this that
Steffens detected when, looking back on his newspaper career, he
observed that during the financial panic of 1893, while working as a
Wall Street reporter, style restrictions prohibited him from reporting a
ruined financier weeping. "I picked up not the hysterical man but the
confession, and that I wrote without tears, statistically" (*Autobiography*
186). This was when he was a reporter at the *New York Evening Post,*
before he took over as city editor of the *Commercial Advertiser* where he
could advocate his version of narrative literary journalism. "Reporters
were to report the news as it happened, like machines, without preju-
dice, color, and without style; all alike. . . . As a writer, I was perma-
nently hurt by my years on the *Post*" (179).

NOR WAS he the only one. This is important to understand if we are
to comprehend just how wide was the gulf between what a factual objectified journalism was attempting to do and what a narrative literary
journalism was attempting to do. The epistemological consequences of
journalistic objectification found revealing ontological expression at
the turn of the century in the life of a man who has been characterized
as the model of the desk-pounding, irascible city editor, Charles E.
Chapin of the *New York Evening World.* Ultimately, too, his example reveals why narrative literary journalism has continued to have its advocates: Chapin's story provides a cautionary story about the dangers of
divorcing one's subjectivity from phenomenal experience. Characterized by journalism historian John Tebbel as "a sadistic psychopath who
gloried in his reputation as the toughest man who ever sat at the city
editor's desk" (324), Chapin's position as an editor recalls journalist
Dreiser's response several years earlier to the demand for "the Facts—
The Color—The Facts!" "Most excellent traits, I thought, but not as
easy to put into execution as comfortable publishers and managing
editors might suppose" (*Newspaper Days* 624–25). Dreiser detects that
behind a desk in the city room, in an enterprise dedicated to objectifying the world, the gulf can only widen between an alienated subjectivity and that world. Thus Chapin could sit back in the safety of his city

room without engaging his subjectivity in the stories his reporters covered.

In that sense Chapin is reminiscent of the protagonist Hurstwood in *Sister Carrie*. However, compared to Chapin, Hurstwood is benign in his unwillingness to engage his subjectivity. In a dark and disturbing real-life parody of the sensationalism practiced at Joseph Pulitzer's *Evening World*, an eyewitness recalls how Chapin, on hearing of the sinking of an excursion steamer on the Hudson River, "capered about the city room with every trace of enjoyment, to make him seem a figure of jerking, hysterical life in a ballet with a background of morbid death. He would run up and down, peering over shoulders to read the nauseating details of the tragedy as they were typed out. Then, standing erect, he would shout, 'Women and children jumping overboard with clothing afire! Water full of charred bodies!' And between these jackal outcries he would strut exultantly up and down, humming a simpering, happy, tuneless tune" (Churchill 249). Given that his only experience with the sinking ship was from the vicarious distance of the city room, Chapin had the luxury, like Hurstwood, of not having to engage his subjectivity. His mission was the opposite of Steffens's, who had announced at the *Commercial Advertiser* that he wanted "to get the news so completely and to report it so humanly that the reader will see himself in the other fellow's place" (*Autobiography* 317).

In a revealing autobiographical note, Chapin later said of himself: "And in all those twenty years I never saw or spoke to a member of the staff outside the office or talked to them in the office about anything except the business of the minute. I gave no confidences, I invited none. I was myself a machine, and the men I worked with were cogs. The human element never entered into the scheme of getting out the paper. It was my way of doing things. That it was not a bad way is proven by the fact that I stayed in my job for twenty years and was the highest salaried city editor on earth" (qtd. in Walker 5). The passage and Chapin's behavior during the sinking of the excursion steamer recall William Barrett's observation of Fyodor Dostoyevsky's "underground man" in the novella of the same name. As Barrett notes of the protagonist Underground Man, "If science could comprehend all phenomena so that eventually in a thoroughly rational society human beings became as predictable as cogs in a machine, then man, driven by [his] need to

know and assert his freedom, would rise up and smash the machine"
(139). Chapin had committed himself to the objectifying ideal that was
the result of the scientific spirit of the nineteenth century, one that in
turn alienated Chapin in his view of the world and in his relations with
his colleagues. The narrative literary journalists would attempt to rise
up and smash the machine of objectivity in order to escape the totalizing formulas and to acknowledge the world for what it is: indeterminate, subjectively perceived, but also free of totalizing prescriptions
that demand alienated uniformity as cogs in a machine. Trachtenberg
has suggested this when he notes the uniformity of the newspaper read
by readers on a street car who as a result are "likely to remain as distant,
remote, and strange" (*Incorporation* 125). In other words, alienated.

The capering and exultant strutting of Chapin's alienated subjectivity, its sham challenge to the Other that remains safely constrained beyond the margin of the city room also recalls Barrett's other observation about the alienated subjectivity of Rodion Raskolnikov in *Crime
and Punishment,* that "the more it is cut off and isolated from the rest
of the human personality, the more desperate, in its weakness, it can
become" (137). The result of the desperation of a negative, defeated
consciousness incapable of engaging with other subjectivities was Raskolnikov's murder of the pawnbroker. The same would prove true of
Chapin: "In the end, Chapin's megalomania led him to frantic speculation in the stock market and ultimate financial ruin. In a suicide pact
with his wife, Nellie, he shot and killed her but failed to turn the gun
on himself" (Tebbel 324–25).

Chapin was sentenced to twenty years to life in Sing Sing for killing
his wife. And proving the maxim that life can indeed be stranger than
fiction, in prison he carried on a love affair by correspondence with a
young woman from Cleveland. According to Tebbel, Chapin's "personality changed completely as a result." He successfully edited a prison
newspaper and built a prison garden, where he raised roses. "When he
died in 1930 it was, in effect, from a broken heart over the destruction
of his garden to make room for prison expansion" (324–25). Whether
Chapin died because his subjectivity was confronted with being alienated from his roses by more prison walls is of course conjectural. But
there is ample evidence that his was indeed an alienated personality,
one that engaged in a desperate attempt to recover its humanity

through love and a rose garden. Moreover, evidence exists that Chapin's alienation was fed by the expectations of his profession, as reflected
in a comment he made to one of his reporters who had been beaten up
and kicked out during a news interview. In the safety of his objectifying
newsroom, he told the reporter, so the story goes, "You go back and tell
that sonofabitch he can't intimidate *me*" (qtd. in Tebbel 324). Chapin is
a true-life grotesque of the fictional Hurstwood, and Chapin's is the
true-life story of an American *Crime and Punishment*.

As part of a scholarly consideration, perhaps Chapin's story can only
appear sensational. But in its larger critical ramifications it illustrates
the problem of objectification. It also recalls what Steffens says about
his refusal to hire burned-out hacks who had turned to drink (*Autobiography* 312–13), as well as what the anonymous writer said in "The Confessions of 'a Literary Journalist,'" that so many turned to drink (373).
What the burned-out and alcoholic hacks were doing as objectifying
journalists had nothing, epistemologically or ontologically, to do with
their own lives, or rather their own subjectivities. Moreover, they engaged in what did not engage them day in and day out, thus reinforcing
their fundamental alienation. To address that subjectivity—to whatever
degree—was what narrative literary journalism would attempt to do.

INTO THIS epistemological crisis narrative literary journalism entered,
directly influenced by the movements in literary realism and naturalism, the rise of objectified journalism, a critical reaction against positivism, and significant social and cultural transformation and crisis. In
his examination of Crane's "An Experiment in Misery" and "The Men
in the Storm," Trachtenberg outlines the implicit doctrine to the narrative literary journalist's ambition: "Crane had discarded the moral
posture of the tourist and had tried to convey physical landscapes
equivalent to his perception of the subjective lives of his characters"
("Experiments" 273). The observation deserves further examination.
First, the moral posture of the tourist is fundamentally an objectifying
one, disengaged from what is being viewed. Second, in landscape—
and by extension in scene setting, concrete detail, dialogue and the
other techniques associated, however erroneously, with novel-writing—
an attempt was made to establish a common epistemological ground
for what Trachtenberg calls an "exchange of subjectivities" (273). What

the abstracting nature of factual or objective mainstream journalism failed to provide then was the rhetorical common sense–appeal of the shared common senses, or what Trachtenberg elsewhere describes as "felt detail" (278).

Crane unequivocally announces his intention to close the gulf between subjectivity and an objectified world in "An Experiment in Misery" when, after observing a homeless person on the streets of New York, he decides to spend a day and a night living like him. He does so, he says, because "perhaps I could discover his point of view or something near it" (34). Thus he attempts to engage his subjectivity with what until now has been an object. According to Trachtenberg, Crane deftly reverses spatial and with it social perspective in "An Experiment in Misery" and "The Men in the Storm" so that the reader imaginatively feels he or she is in the position of a homeless person ("Experiments" 273, 282–83). For example, in "The Men in the Storm" the reader follows what becomes the psychological progress of homeless men in a February blizzard as they wait outside for entrance to a homeless shelter. In one passage, Crane describes a "stout," "well-clothed" merchant in his warmly lit display window who looks out at the cluster of homeless men, stroking his beard, with "supreme complacence." "It seemed that the sight operated inversely, and enabled him to more clearly regard his own environment, delightful relatively," Crane writes (95). But when the homeless men begin shouting at the merchant with "familiar and cordial greetings" in a good-natured outburst of the envy of the disenfranchised for the economically and socially enfranchised, the merchant flees the showcase window. For readers who have until now followed the narrative progress of the homeless men in the spatial setting of the blizzard and whose subjectivities are then placed among the homeless, they have discovered themselves rebuffed in a spatial reversal by one whose material comfort in life may well be their own, or at least a comfort to which presumably they could aspire. They are on the outside looking in, and as Trachtenberg notes, "Crane forces the reader to free his own point of view from any limiting perspective" (276). Moreover, the irony of the merchant's being placed on display in his own display window, described as looking like the "Prince of Wales," reenacts allegorically the epistemological problem Crane confronted and attempted to overcome, in this instance by spatially reversing the reader's perspective. Cast out because of what Bakhtin characterizes as "direct contact with inconclusive present-day reality," the reader has resisted social critical closure by means of the evidence of the concrete particular and ultimately has resisted the implicit ideological closure that consigns the homeless as Other.

Such is also the case in "An Experiment in Misery." In the sketch, Crane, after having lived for a day as a homeless person and having been rebuffed by the ideological prescriptions that make of the homeless outcasts, acknowledges the reversal of his fortunes to himself (in the third person): "He confessed himself an outcast, and his eyes from under the lowered rim of his hat began to glance guiltily, wearing the criminal expression that comes with certain convictions" (43). Outcast, Crane too has resisted the implicit closure that consigns the homeless person as Other. To attempt to engage with the Other is an attempt to move beyond ideological prescription and ultimately beyond the critical closure or totalization drafted to contain such prescriptions. Doing so embraces the uncontrolled and inconclusive present of the Bakhtian novel.

The attempt to "exchange subjectivities" in a narrative literary journalism—or perhaps more precisely to narrow the gulf between subjectivity and an objectified world given the mediated nature of any text that can never result in a complete exchange of presence for the linguistic figure—can be detected in the work of other narrative literary journalists of the period as well. One now largely forgotten practitioner of the form who illustrates the point is Lafcadio Hearn. A transitional figure in the form, he began writing sketches in 1872 for Cincinnati newspapers. Most of them examined life among African Americans who lived and worked on the docks of that city (Ball 7). Hearn would later live in New Orleans, then the West Indies, and finally Japan.

Hearn's resistance to an alienating objectification of the phenomenal world was dramatically expressed in 1890 when he arrived in Japan on assignment for *Harper's*, "where, in the rush and tumult of new sensation, he forgets his commission and loses himself completely in the new delicious world of impression" (Pattee, *History* 425). Moreover, Hearn's reportage illustrates the near-solipsistic extreme to which the effort to narrow the distance between subjectivity and objectification can conceivably lead. In essence his example illustrates the journey that was traveled to varying lengths by different narrative literary journalists on a spectrum or continuum between objectification at the one end and their own subjectivities at the other. Fred Lewis Pattee says of an account Hearn wrote while living on Martinique in the late 1880s that it is "a chaotic book, flashlights, impressions, but no single completed impression, no totality, but the soul of the West Indies none the less, revealed with a rare, queer art that was individual" (*History* 425). In noting that Hearn provided no aesthetic "totality," Pattee perhaps unwittingly touches on one of the distinctive features of narrative literary journalism, articulated so well by Garland: the form resists critical totalization or closure. As part of that narrative dynamic however, Pattee also acknowledges a subjectivity to Hearn's writing that attempted to narrow the distance between it and an objectified world when he notes Hearn's "impressionism" in the "queer art that was individual." Pattee's comments, written in 1915, suggest the degree of awareness in the English academy of what Hearn had attempted to do.

Hearn's romanticism is reflected in his affirmation of his subjectivity, when he observed of Japan, "this is a land where one can really enjoy the Inner Life. Every one has an inner life of his own,—which no other eye can see, and the great secrets of which are never revealed, though occasionally when we create something beautiful, we betray a faint glimpse of it" ("To H. E. Krehbiel [1878]" 196). Hearn acknowledges his inability to come to closure: only a faint glimpse of an "inner life" is available and not the full view. Moreover, the purpose of the phenomenal world is to provide passage to the inner subjective life that no other life can know. Hearn is approaching the end of the journey on the spectrum between objectification and a gorgeously affirmed subjectivity. It is an end that must of course keep receding from realization lest solipsism be fully realized in silence. In that, Hearn is anticipating stream of consciousness.

Hearn's earlier literary journalism is generally more accessible as conventional realism than the later mystical writings. One example is "A Child of the Levee," published in the *Cincinnati Commercial* in 1876, which is a story about Albert Jones, an African American resident of Cincinnati's Ohio River levee. In a strategy that evokes the social distance between white and black Americans in the 1870s, Hearn begins the story as if it were a conventional news story: "Shortly before day-break on Saturday morning a drunken 'negro' was pulled out of the river at the foot of Broadway by two watchful patrolmen" (4). The lead reads just as any number of "objective" police beat reports would read with a summarization of the main points. Moreover, the story could easily deteriorate into racist stereotyping on the order of a portrait of a drunken, irresponsible "negro" inadmissible to the Victorian parlors of polite, genteel Cincinnati society. The story seems poised to do that with its laudatory appraisal of the behavior of the policemen who represent and guard the class authority of that society: they were "watchful" and thus doing their duty in behalf of class authoritarianism. The story would seem to reinforce the perspective that Jones represents the social and racial Other.

But when, under questioning, Jones gives his name at the station house, standing "before the desk with an air of frightened bewilderment, like a sleepwalker suddenly aroused from his dangerous dreams," the desk sergeant responds, "Albert Jones! . . . that man can imitate the whistle of any boat on the Ohio or Mississippi River" (9–10). Thus encouraged, Jones does so. Once again, Hearn's portrait could easily deteriorate into one of a freak or "brute" who can imitate the *Robert E. Lee* and thus reinscribe Jones's racial status as Other. However, Hearn is judicious in his selection of detail and value-laden adjectives when describing Jones's efforts, or rather in making a rhetorical common sense–appeal to the common senses and thus inviting the reader to share in the experience: "He suddenly threw up both hands, concave-fashion, to his mouth, expanded his deep chest, and poured out a long, profound, sonorous cry that vibrated through the room like the music of a steam-whistle. He started off with a deep nasal tone, but gradually modulated its depth and volume to an imitation of the steam-whistle, so astonishingly perfect that at its close every listener uttered an involuntary exclamation of surprise" (10). So the allegorical "savage other" begins to conquer the senses and sensibilities of the reading, civilized gentility and to resist by means of the distinctive phenomenal particular a culturally determined closure in order to gain social admittance. Hearn's value judgments, those injections of his overt subjectivity, are respectful: the cry is "sonorous and profound," like the "music" of a steam whistle (instead of, for example, the dissonant shriek of a steam whistle), a music that is "astonishingly perfect" and that leaves his listeners expressing "an involuntary exclamation of surprise."

Hearn also draws on the cultural sensibility of American genteel society to persuade it that Albert Jones, and by implication Albert Jones as representative of the social Other, should be viewed seriously and respectfully, when he notes that "the steamboats seem to his rudely poetic fancy vast sentient beings, as the bells of Notre Dame to the imagination of Quasimodo, and their voices come to his ear as mighty living cries, when they call to each other across the purple gloom of the summer night—shouting cheery welcomes in sweetly-deep thundertones" (11). The reference to *Notre Dame de Paris* invokes, of course, one of the world's most widely recognized novels and one of the most recognized writers of the time, Victor Hugo. Hearn is attempting to bring into the parlor the portrait of Jones as an American version of the redeemed figure Quasimodo. It is at that moment, when Jones is poised to enter the parlor, that Hearn attempts to account for why Jones has taken up the peculiar habit of imitating steamboat whistles: "Other melody he seems to have little conception of—neither the songs of the stevedores nor the vibrant music of banjo-thrumming. The long echoes of the steam calls and the signal whistles of the night patrolmen—sounds most familiar of all others, indeed, to those who live on the levee-slope—form the only chords of melody in his little musical world" (11). At issue then is denied opportunity and not racial difference. But Hearn does not end with a pitying portrait of denied opportunity. Instead, he takes the occasion of the human steamboat whistle to suggest, as social allegory, that it provides for Jones visions and insights into "other" worlds not otherwise available to genteel society:

> Possibly to him the Song of Steam is the sweetest of all musical sounds, only as a great tone-record of roustabout memories—each boat whistle, deep or shrill or mellow, recalling some past pleasure or pain in the history of a life spent along the broad highway of brown water flowing to the Crescent City of the South. Each prolonged tone awakes to fresh life some little half-forgotten chapter in the simple history of this Child of the Levee—some noisy but harmless night revel, some broil, some old love story, some dark story of steamboat disaster, a vessel in flames, a

swim for life. Probably the first sound which startled his ears in babyhood was the voice of a steamboat passing by his birth place; and possibly the same voice may serve for his requiem some night when patrolmen do not happen to hear a sudden splash in the dark river. (11–12)

To be sure, the reference to "this Child of the Levee" will not entirely escape the charge of paternalism from our contemporary perspective. But that Hearn undertook a sympathetic portrait of a member of a marginalized race at that time is remarkable, and in the case of Hearn not unusual. He frequently wrote about African American life on the levee. Moreover, he lived openly with a mulatto woman, which eventually cost him one of his newspaper jobs. But what is perhaps most remarkable about the passage is that in the open speculation Hearn has flagrantly acknowledged his own subjectivity in the attempt to understand Jones's. It is a theme Hearn addresses further in trying to close the gulf between subjectivity and the object in the last sentence of the story, which follows with ominous suggestion from the previous quote. It is also a passage that clearly portends Hearn's later and more open romanticism: "We left him slumbering in his wet and muddy rags, dreaming, perchance, fantastic dreams of a strange craft that never whistles, and is without name—a vessel gliding noiselessly by unfamiliar banks to a weird port where objects cast no shadows, and even dreams are dead" (12). The symbolic "transmigration" has been rhetorically completed because there are no more dreams of that "other" world. Furthermore, objects that cast no shadows are no longer phenomenal objects. Hearn, in a sense, has escaped critical closure, initially via the distinctive phenomenal particular, to eventually embrace an imaginative indeterminacy.

Still another writer from this period is Abraham Cahan, who, when he joined the staff of the *Commercial Advertiser* in 1898, introduced his colleagues to Russian realism (and the "Marxian program"), as Steffens recalled. As a Russian Jew who immigrated to the United States in 1882, he brought a unique perspective to the immigrant experience in the new country. According to Moses Rischin, a Cahan scholar largely responsible for identifying and salvaging Cahan's stories in the *Commercial Advertiser* and other publications, Cahan "labored to bridge the chasm between newer immigrants and older Americans, between Old World and New" (xxvi). A favorite approach of his was to visit immigrants at the immigration receiving center at the Battery in New York City. (The Ellis Island facility was being rebuilt after a fire.) In doing so, Cahan wrote not only about the Jewish experience in the U.S. but also about the experiences of other ethnic groups. In "Can't Get Their Minds Ashore," Cahan captures the polyglot nature of immigration at the time. He takes what on the surface hardly seems a sophisticated approach by simply describing sequentially the fear of different immigrants and their families that they will not receive approval to enter the country. The seeming lack of sophistication lies in the unremitting despair born of what seems like endless waiting on the part of the immigrants. As an approach it can get old very quickly: first he interviews Italian immigrant families, then a Lithuanian woman, then Ruthenians (Ukrainians from the historic lands of the old Polish kingdom), then Russian Germans, and finally a Russian Jewish family (the tsar's citizens seemed to be deserting all the Russias en masse). As if to compound the despair, the Russian Jews refuse to eat when dinner is announced because the food is not kosher (113–16).

But the cultural mosaic does not conclude with a one-dimensional portrait of immigrant despair. Cahan adds a subtle complexity by showing those who in counterpoint unwittingly resist despair by finding something else to focus their energies on. Thus they engage in denial. For example, an Italian woman calls an Italian man an "idiot" behind his back because he stutters badly but must serve as the interpreter for other Italians. Later another Italian woman calls her "the idiot," revealing a community politics that distracts them from their waiting for approval—or disapproval—to immigrate. There is the young Lithuanian woman who believes that once her betrothed, who preceded her to America, comes for her, "we shall live like noble folk in America." The true nature of the American experience for many immigrants in the late 1890s—that of ghetto slums and sweat shops, especially if they were from Eastern or Southern Europe—has yet to be seen.

Cahan's portrait adds still further dimensions at the conclusion when a young German American woman, who is wearing a hat "with a forest of ostrich feathers" and works as a serving girl in America, comes to the immigration center to pick up her brother newly arrived from Germany: "'Here he comes! Here he comes! Hugo!' the servant girl said, with a ringing chuckle, and flinging herself upon her brother's shoulder, she burst out crying" (116). There is much here in this scene of the inconclusive present that resonates with different possibilities of meaning. To begin with, the brother's good fortune is in sharp contrast to that of the earlier mosaic of immigrants. Someone has come for him. He has realized what the others can only dream of: rescue. Second, his sister's dress, which included not only the ostrich feather hat but "a brand-new jacket of blue cloth overladen with trimmings of every color in the rainbow" provides a measure of her American assimilation and success, again in contrast to the immigrants and their families described earlier (116). What makes her dress in its rainbow colors and the forest of ostrich feathers all the more remarkable is that her realization of the American dream is that of a serving girl. She has clearly dressed up to show off even though she occupies a low social echelon. To the immigrant families awaiting their rescuer, fearful at any moment they may be sent back to Europe and what they fled—pogroms, poverty, rigid class structure—the German American serving girl must seem as far away from them as she well could have felt when she first arrived and was equally awaiting an unknown and alien country. Finally, if she had only flung "herself upon her brother's shoulder" and not burst out crying, the story might have ended as a homily on the promise that awaits immigrants in America. But when Cahan concludes that "she burst out crying," he injects a dissonant note of ambiguous meaning, and therein lies his art. Because we can only puzzle over his meaning. Does she burst out crying from happiness because she sees her brother? Cahan does not tell us. Does she do so because she has realized the American dream and is grateful? Again, we are not told. Or does she burst out crying because of her own personal memory of what she and every immigrant to the United States has had to confront, what Rischin characterizes as the "chasm" between cultures and whether one would be able to bridge it? Cahan does not tell us. Does she burst out crying because despite her forest of ostrich feathers and the bright rainbow colors of her dress, they are only a temporary (and unconscious?) disguise and ultimately denial of the reality of her American dream? After all, she is only a serving girl. Cahan does not tell us. And so the speculation could continue. Cahan, indeed, teases us out of thought with the inconclusive present in sketching this mosaic of immigrant pathos.

One of Cahan's other strengths was capturing colloquial dialogue. In the following passage a fortune teller is peddling his fortunes on Passover in the Jewish ghetto on the lower East Side of New York City. Unfortunately, his captive mouse, who chooses the fortunes, selects one more appropriate for a Roman Catholic audience than a Jewish one:

> "What does it mean?" several girls asked, in consternation.
> The wizard would not say. "Mousie ought to know what she is talking about," he answered.
> "Who writes your tickets?" asked the snooper.
> "They are not written, they are printed. *Pleellii — pleellii — li.*"
> "Maybe you bought them of a Catholic or you got them mixed up with Catholic fortunes?"
> "Mousie never mayx up nayting," the wizard answered, in haughty English. "*Trulitu-lu, trulilu-lu-lulu!*"
> "Never mind your *trulilulu!*" screamed one of the girls. "What do you mean by working off ungodly fortunes on daughters of Israel?"
> "I want my two cents!" stormed another.
> "And I want mine!"
> The wizard shouldered his burden, organ, mice, parrots, "Fortunes" and all, and fled.
> "That's it! Let him fly to all the black years!" the market women shouted after him. "Now we will do some business in honor of the holiday."
> "Carrots, carrots. Fish, living fish." ("Pillelu" 58–59)

So the sketch of city street life in the immigrant's new world concludes. Cahan's strengths as a literary journalist were that "he developed a style of compassionate interviewing, and of reporting through extended dialogue. Without recourse to dialect spelling, Cahan captured the idiom and imagery, and the elation and bewilderment, of people from every corner of the world" (Kerrane and Yagoda 76). In the compassion, in the direct words of others speaking for themselves, in the common sense–appeal of the imagery and idiom, Cahan was attempting to narrow the rhetorical and cultural distances—to cross over the "chasm" as Rischin describes it—between alienated subjectivities confronting each Other. In this lies a cultural allegory.

It is perhaps fitting, then, to discover that narrative literary journalism from this period proved subversive not only in challenging the objectification of mainstream journalism but also in subverting the literature academy as well: Theodore Dreiser included in *Sister Carrie* earlier published material that qualifies as narrative literary journalism. In 1897, after he left his position as editor of the publication *Ev'ry Month*, Dreiser took up magazine freelancing and between that time and the appearance of *Sister Carrie* published more than 120 articles. Among them can be found sketches of the anonymous of the streets of New York (Hakutani, preface 9–10; introduction 31). For example, "Curious Shifts of the Poor," published in 1899 in *Demorest's* magazine, is a series of four sketches of the homeless in New York (rpt. *Selected Magazine* 180). These include an account of a "peculiar individual" who takes up a position at the corner of Broadway and Twenty-sixth Street in the evening. Like Crane, Dreiser deftly manipulates the expectations of what most readers can expect when he describes "a short, stocky-built solider, in a great cape-overcoat and soft felt hat" who is saluted by a passing policeman as the "Captain." The Captain has taken his place in the upscale theater section of the city, where "wealthy strollers, a gentleman in evening dress with a lady at his side, some clubmen, passing from one smoking room to another" pass by (170). In upscale Manhattan, the Captain in his uniform bears a degree of public authority. Is he from the Salvation Army? The reader is not told. The mystery is partly answered when he collects around him, as he does every evening, homeless men. He acknowledges them by noting:

> "Beds, eh, all of you?"
> There is a general shuffle and murmur of approval.
> "Well, line up here. I'll see what I can do. I haven't a cent myself."
> (171)

His lack of money is the first hint that he, too, may be homeless. The Captain begins his solicitations of the wealthy passersby: "Now, then, gentlemen, these men are without beds. They have got to have some place to sleep to-night. They can't lie out in the street. I need twelve cents to put one to bed. Who will give it me?" (172). Through the course of the evening he cajoles the passersby, sometimes without success, until finally he has collected enough to pay for the men lined up behind him. Then he leads his homeless company to a boarding house and pays their bill for the night. "When the last one has disappeared up the dingy stairway, he comes out, muffles his great coat closer in the cold air, pulls down his slouch brim, and tramps, a solitary, silent figure, into the night" (172).

By now one suspects that the Captain is also homeless. But this is never confirmed, and the reader is left confronting the inconclusive present, other than to acknowledge that good Samaritans can take many mysterious forms in which the mystery may not be unraveled.

A year later, when *Sister Carrie* was published, the sketches from "Curious Shifts of the Poor" appeared in chapter 45, the chapter title dubbed with the same name (*Sister Carrie* 403). Thus lodged in the heart of the canonical fiction is a reminder of phenomenalistic status that by its example subverts literary essentializing, much the way Stephen Crane's "Open Boat" did.

THE STRATEGIES employed by Stephen Crane, Lafcadio Hearn, Abraham Cahan, and Theodore Dreiser, among others, recall Steffens's advice to reporters "to get the news so completely and to report it so humanly that the reader will see himself in the other fellow's place" even if, as he acknowledged, the "fellow" was a murderer (*Autobiography* 317). Steffens anticipates by more than sixty years Truman Capote's *In Cold Blood* and Norman Mailer's *Executioner's Song,* which in their attempts to understand the subjectivities of convicted murderers became classics of the new journalism of the 1960s and 1970s, as well as allegories about the dark side of the American experience. Crane, Hearn, Cahan, and Dreiser also resist critical closure, or the distanced image of the absolute past, to confront the inconclusive present of an indeterminate world in the form of a mirror to phenomenal indeterminacy. In this, ultimately, we can detect a breakdown in class, racial, and ethnic structures.

Literary journalism's narrative ambition to narrow the gulf between subjectivity and the object also suggests why it was frequently associated with Populist and Progressive causes. When Crane experienced what it was like to be homeless, "or something near it," he moved beyond an epistemological problem, as did his readers imaginatively, to a social problem. This is reflected in the decision confronting Dreiser's Hurstwood. Initially neutralized by the epistemological problem posed by factual or objective news, when he confronts another, but phenomenal, reality, he is confronted with whether, as Kaplan noted, "to take sides. He must either be seen and attacked as a scab, join the strikers, or leave. There is no neutral position" (154). It should come as no surprise then that narrative literary journalists who did not "leave" their material but instead engaged their subjectivities in it found themselves having to take sides. Steffens's politics, for example, turned increasingly to the left (*Autobiography* 376–77). Cahan was a Socialist. Hutchins Hapgood increasingly took up the cause of trade unions (*Victorian* 355). Later, James Agee's 1947 *Let Us Now Praise Famous Men* proved to be one of the most compelling statements on the conditions of poor southern sharecroppers and was viewed as a call to social action (Fishkin 147). Sherwood Anderson would confront a similar epistemological and politicizing experience in his 1935 *Puzzled America,* as would Erskine Caldwell in *Some American People* of the same year. Ultimately, such a historical continuum can be traced up through the new journalism of the 1960s. Like Crane before them, these latter-day narrative literary journalists would seek to move beyond "a unit in the interesting sum of men slain" in order to engage another subjectivity in an indeterminate world.

Once it is understood why a modern narrative literary journalism emerged when it did, it is also sobering to realize, as the earlier discussion of Boswell and Johnson suggests, that it was not doing so in a historical vacuum. In reality, before the modern era there had always been some form of narrative literary journalism.

3 What Preceded

The Origins of Modern American
Literary Journalism

IN WHAT has become mythologized in the pantheon of American historical legend, John Smith recalls in his account of the founding of Jamestown and the settling of Virginia how Pocahontas saved his life: "Then as many could, layd hands on him, dragged him to them, and thereon laid his head, and being ready with their clubs, to beate out his braines, Pocahontas the Kings dearest daughter, when no entreaty could prevaile, got his head in her armes, and laid her owne upon his to save him from death: whereat the Emperour was contented he should live" (151).

The passage from Smith's 1624 *Generall Historie of Virginia, New-England, and the Summer Isles . . .* is remarkable because when Smith describes Pocahontas taking his head in her arms and placing hers upon his, he describes a scene of psychological tenderness and self-sacrifice. Today, such a rhetorical strategy—whether the Smith account is true or not since scholars have often debated the question—would be considered "novelistic" because it eschews the abstraction of careful and "modern" historical analysis. What the passage reveals is just how much such techniques as description mixed freely in a narrative whose fundamental intention, as the title implies, was to provide a history. Thus in the account can be detected two strains of rhetorical intention: on the one hand to provide a factual account, on the other to tell a story. Those two strains help to provide evidence of the origins generally of American journalistic practice and, more specifically, the origins of modern narrative literary journalism. Indeed, while the focus is on a "modern American" narrative literary journalism that emerges after the Civil War in reaction against the rise of objectified journalisms, it is fair to say that some kind of narrative literary journalism has long existed. The purpose of this chapter, then, is to provide a broad overview of that history, as well as of the relationship of the form to other nonfiction forms. The latter is important because comparative study of nonfiction forms, whether perceived as literary or not, remains to be conducted, and little if any exists that contextualizes narrative literary journalism of the premodern variety. Such an approach, really a reexamination, synthesis, and reinterpretation of what has preceded, will help to locate narrative literary journalism within a larger historical continuum.

Precursors to the modern form can be divided into three approximate historical time frames. The first early antecedents to the modern form can be traced back at least to the classical period in the Western tradition. The second period begins with the introduction of the printing press, when narrative prose, both nonfiction and fiction, evolves and takes on its modern complexion. Finally, immediate antecedents derive from the nineteenth century with the clear evolution of two kinds of journalism: Schudson's "story" and "information" models (89), or what more traditionally would be characterized as "narrative" and "discursive" modes, respectively. Moreover, the strains of the two models, reinforcing and challenging as they do ideological assumptions, foreshadow an ongoing—if futile—argument between an objectified discursive and a more subjective narrative journalism as to which most adequately accounts for the phenomenal world. Such an understanding helps to further account for why many modern narrative literary journalists would eventually take up Populist and Progressive political causes, challenging prevailing political, social, and cultural ideologies.

NARRATIVE LITERARY journalism, or at least its roots, likely extends as far back as there has been the perception that an accounting of phenomena in the temporal and spatial world had value to the individual and the community. Indeed, it is inaccurate to suggest that narrative literary journalism is an aberrant form that, like some tumor, grew out of the side of mainstream American journalistic practice that has primarily followed—and reified—the information or discursive model. Instead, it is more accurate to suggest that until recent times it usually was one variant interwoven to varying degrees with what today is often called objective news.

The origins of this rhetorical dichotomy can be illustrated with an ancient example: Plato, the adversary of poetry, nonetheless added literary embellishment to his account of the execution of Socrates in 399 B.C.E. In the account, Crito, who has come to administer the death sentence imposed by the Athenian authorities, tells Socrates: "Socrates, I shall not find fault with you, as I do with others, for being angry and cursing me, when at the behest of the authorities, I tell them to drink the poison. No, I have found you in all this time in every way the noblest and gentlest and best man who has ever come here. . . . Now, for you know the message I came to bring you, farewell and try to bear what you must as easily as you can." Crito's comments place the next few lines of the passage in literary context when Plato, the creative artist, writes of Crito: "And he burst into tears and turned and went away." That paradoxical gesture of turning away from the duty Crito must nonetheless fulfill captures the contradictions of human experience, contradictions made all the more poignant when Socrates responds, praising his executioner not as executioner, but as complex human: "How charming the man is! Ever since I have been here he has been coming to see me and talking with me from time to time, and has been the best of men, and now how nobly he weeps for me! But come, Crito, let us obey him, and let someone bring the poison, if it is ready" (9–10). In his Socratic wisdom, Socrates pays tribute to the paradoxical—and literary—nature of man as man *and* executioner. (That is if literature indeed ultimately escapes critical theory, as Mark Edmundson implies when he says that literature "resists being explained away" [31]. If literature then is forever teasing us "out of thought" or interpretation, the story of the execution of Socrates would qualify, given a paradoxical nature that is itself open to interpretation.)

What remains all the more remarkable is that Plato wrote the account not only in spite of being an adversary of poetry and thus more broadly literary art in its limited classical conception according to our contemporary perspective, but also because in advocating his abstract and totalized ideals he would foreshadow the informational or discursive model of journalism some twenty-two hundred years later. Such journalism is a model in the Platonic tradition because it aspires to an objective ideal, a perfectly abstracted report, ostensibly free of subjectivity, ideology, and the filtering and thus distorting nature of language—the result fundamentally Platonic in the attempt to transcend the contingent and Heraclitean nature of human experience. If a hypothetical classical journalist had been true to Plato's ideal, he would have provided the who, what, when, where, why, and how of the story. Such an account might read as follows, carefully abstracted in the attempt to eliminate emotional coloring and thus subtle evidence of a shaping consciousness that reflects subjectivity as one contributing means of production.

> Athens—Authorities executed Socrates the philosopher by poison yesterday.
>
> Crito, at the direction of the Athenian authorities, administered the poison the day after the sacred ship returned from Delos.
>
> Socrates drank the hemlock and died a few minutes later.
>
> He did not appear to be in great pain while the poison took effect.
>
> Socrates was executed after he was found guilty of corruption of the Athenian youth and neglect of the gods.
>
> The sentence had been delayed because no execution could take place until the sacred ship returned from Delos.

Lost is the literary resonance that teases us out of critical thought, expunged in the attempt to achieve the objective ideal. It was this that Lincoln Steffens detected when, looking back on his newspaper career, he observed that during the financial panic of 1893 while working as a Wall Street reporter he could not have reported a ruined financier weeping. More important, however, Plato's account of the death of Socrates suggests that distinctions between the rhetorical tropes of what we now call the information and story models were not as important then as they are today in reports of phenomenal experience.

Nonetheless, an awareness of such a concern did emerge in the Roman *acta,* or gazettes. The *acta senatus,* or acts of the Roman senate, possibly date as far back as 449 B.C.E., according to the Roman historian Suetonius. They, along with the *acta diurna,* or acts of the day, were first made public by Julius Caesar in 59 B.C.E., their purpose fundamentally informational or discursive (Stephens 64). It is of course from the *acta diurna* that our modern term journalism derives, and implicit in both gazettes is that there was a value to recording the official events in the passage of the contemporary "diurnal" period, or "day." At the same time, there were other precursors to the modern newspaper in ancient Rome that appealed more to a narrative or story model, one we would now characterize as human-interest journalism. In what would prove to be a forerunner of our modern tabloids, sensational, human-interest, and narrative literary journalisms, the Emperor Commodus directed late in the second century c.e. that "everything he did that was base or foul or cruel, or typical of a gladiator or procurer" be inserted in the *actis urbi,* or city gazette. Likewise, other *acta* "contained a rich supply of human interest stories" (65). For example, Pliny the Elder in his *Natural History* recalls the following anecdote recorded in the *acta populi Romani* in which a dog refused to leave the side of its executed master: "A dog belonging to one of them could not be driven away from him in prison and when he had been flung out on the Steps of Lamentation would not leave his body, uttering sorrowful howls to the vast concourse of the Roman public around, and when one of them threw it food it carried it to the mouth of its dead master; also when his corpse had been thrown into the Tiber it swam to it and tried to keep it afloat, a great crowd streaming out to view the animal's loyalty" (103).

Thus in the early Roman gazettes can be detected both story and informational modes of accounting for the phenomenal world, and while the informational may be dominant today as objective journalism, it by no means has a larger historical claim. Moreover, such a dichotomy implicitly provides a challenge to assumptions of how the phenomenal world should be perceived, given the conflicting claims of the specular nature of language, the subjective nature of cognition, and the embedding of ideological frames, all of which in their own ways filter, inform, and shape those accounts.

These issues of accountability help to explain why journalism in its varieties—whether openly discursive or narrative—has so frequently been drafted for ideological purposes as well as to challenge ideology. An early example in English letters of a narrative journalism drafted for unconcealed ideological or political purposes is the monk Oderic Vitalis's account of the death of William the Conqueror in 1087. The monk recounts how the dying king's lords and retainers gather around his deathbed, but the moment he expires, the lords depart for their estates to quell peasant unrest. Meanwhile, the retainers plunder the dead king's household: "The lesser attendants, seeing that their superiors had absconded, seized the arms, vessels, clothing, linen, and all the royal furnishings, and hurried away leaving the king's body almost naked on the floor of the house. . . . Each one of them, like a bird of prey, seized what he could of the royal trappings and made off at once with the booty" (103). The king's body thus abandoned, no one at first—including the king's family—will take responsibility for burying it. Finally, a knight comes forward and agrees to pay for the burial, but as the king's now-bloated body is placed into a sarcophagus of stone that proves too small, "the swollen bowels burst, and an intolerable stench assailed the nostrils of the bystanders and the whole crowd" that no amount of burning incense could mask. "So the priests made haste to conclude the funeral rites, and immediately returned, trembling, to their own houses" (107). To Vitalis, the king's death was a homily—a spiritual allegory—on the vanity of worldly position: "Behold, I beg you all, of what earthly loyalty is made. . . . So when the just ruler fell lawlessness broke loose, and first showed itself in the plunder of him who had been the avenger of plunder" (103).

At other times, however, we see the attempt to escape ideology, in a sense the distanced image of the absolute *ideological* past, and embrace the inconclusive present where ideology recedes to unconsciousness (given the critical assumption that ideology can never be *entirely* escaped; but at the same time implicit is that there is always the possibility to some degree of resistance to ideology). This can be detected in the late twelfth-century account of London by William FitzStephen, a clerk in the service of and a witness to the martyrdom of Thomas à Beckett in 1170. FitzStephen was also the author of the "Life of Beckett" to which his account of London was prefaced. The London portrait remains remarkable because of its scenes of everyday life. The descriptions are remarkable, too, because of the lack of any effort to moralize. For example, FitzStephen describes "battles on water" conducted by young men during the Easter holidays:

> A shield is hung upon a pole, fixed in the midst of the stream, a boat is prepared without oars, to be carried by the violence of the water, and in the fore part thereof standeth a young man, ready to give charge upon the shield with his lance; if so be he breaketh his lance, he runneth strongly against the shield, down he falleth into the water, for the boat is violently forced with the tide; but on each side of the shield ride two

boats, furnished with young men, which recover him that falleth as soon
as they may. Upon the bridge, wharfs, and houses, by the river's side,
stand great numbers to see and laugh thereat. (121–22)

As WITH much Western learning, we reach an important transition
with the invention and increasing use of the printing press in the second half of the fifteenth century. That and the introduction of paper
manufacturing, which made printed surfaces abundantly available, are
factors helping to mark a divide between older oral and scribal cultures
on the one hand, and a print culture on the other. Those consequences
are no less important for the evolution of narrative prose in the English
vernacular from which narrative literary journalism evolves. Understanding such an evolution is one way to understand the complex relationships between our modern narrative literary journalism and other
narrative prose forms, such as biography, travelogue, the novel, diary
and memoir, history, as well as narratives fundamentally sensational
in nature (and not necessarily exclusive of biography, travelogue, the
novel, diary, and history). Furthermore, throughout this evolution
these forms overlap. This is in part because the evolution of modern
narrative prose in the English vernacular is in many ways the story of
some of the epistemological concerns surrounding narrative literary
journalism. Moreover, a constant theme that serves as a critical backdrop to the evolution of prose is Bakhtin's position concerning the
difficult struggle to escape the image of the absolute critical past and
embrace the inconclusive present. Put differently, one can detect an
evolutionary change in which the boundaries of "reality" established
by a symbolic world, one rooted in, among other things, medieval
thinking and church precepts, shifted to one in which the boundaries
of reality *appeared* to be established in a phenomenal world. In this latter we also detect the rise of empiricism and ultimately the positivist
paradigm.

But the evolution was a slow one, much more in the nature of taking
two steps forward only to take one back, because frequently no sooner
had the phenomenal world been characterized than the characterizations were often reframed or reinscribed symbolically in critical reification, a process evident in the twentieth century's own modernism,
whether aesthetic or scientific. Ultimately, what we see at work in these

antecedents to a *modern* narrative literary journalism is the kind of critical volatilization Nietzsche identified, which to some degree must prove inescapable lest value-laden context and aesthetic patterning as a form of context be altogether eliminated and the result prove indecipherable. The issue here is one of emphasis, as the evolution of vernacular prose moves slowly away from the reality of a symbolic world, and toward the reality of a phenomenal, or temporal and spatial, world.

Such a critical construct can be illustrated by examining:

1. the shift to the use of vernacular in prose;
2. the transition in the ballad form from that of oral ballad to printed ballad in the sixteenth century;
3. the rise of printed sensational journalism in the sixteenth and seventeenth centuries;
4. accounts of voyages of discovery and colonization in the sixteenth and seventeenth centuries;
5. the transitional form of the character book, as well as biographies, histories, and diaries and memoirs of the seventeenth century;
6. the rise of social reporting in the seventeenth and eighteenth centuries; and
7. the rise of the fictional modern novel in the eighteenth century.

Throughout, one can detect occasional premodern examples of narrative literary journalism, in part because these forms overlap in their concerns. In terms of reading format, all but the modern novel are reflected in the broadsides, books, pamphlets or "news books," gazettes and corantos, and the newspapers that evolved after the wide-scale introduction of the printing press.

Latin, French, and Anglo-Norman were the favored languages for prose before the Renaissance. There were, certainly, accounts in Old and Middle English, but when it came to church and state affairs, documents were generally composed in these three official languages. As Dominica Legge has noted, Parliament and even everyday municipal affairs were conducted in French (279, 302, 309). In the thirteenth and fourteenth centuries there were, to be sure, vernacular texts, but invariably they were homiletic, devotional, didactic, or utilitarian and not inclined to challenge ideological assumptions (J. Bennett 347). This changes, however, by the fifteenth century: "Men who owed little or nothing to French or Latin were constantly attempting to put down their thoughts in a clear and unornamented fashion. . . . Their only endeavour was to state their ideas in a straightforward fashion" (H. Bennett 180). Guilds, for example, eschewed Latin and French for the vernacular. Why is the vernacular important to literary journalism? Because the language of the common people helped to make, if not respectable, at least acceptable, accounts of common life, unmediated by Medieval Latin and French, which were the official languages of church teaching and feudal responsibilities (again, variations on Bakhtin's "distanced image of the absolute past," in these cases religious and feudal critical pasts). The use especially of Latin, while a kind of international Esperanto for churchmen, scholars, and statesmen, was also an idealizing attempt to overcome the linguistic disarray reflected in the babel of European tongues. A variation on that babel is Bakhtin's conception of the inconclusive present, disconnected, unpredictable, and driven by phenomenal experience.

Essentially, then, the printing press, when combined with and supportive of the use of the vernacular, made modern prose possible. For example, the secrets of the artisan's guilds (often intentionally mysterious in order to preserve a guild's monopoly) that had been passed along orally between master and apprentice now became accessible to a vernacular-reading public (Eisenstein 2:559), or to a public listening to a reader. In a sense, the translation of the Bible into the vernacular by Martin Luther, William Tyndale, and others was not only the beginning of bringing the Word of God to the laity in print but also the beginning of acknowledging the phenomenal world unmediated by long-standing church teaching that the symbolic afterlife had a greater reality than our temporal world. Such an earlier church mediation is to be detected in Vitalis's homily on the death of William the Conqueror. To cite still another example, medieval mapmakers reflected a world that conformed to church teachings as well as widespread beliefs in the fantastic. The result was, as Susan Eisenstein has observed, an "inability to discriminate between Paradise and Atlantis on the one hand, Cathay and Jerusalem on the other, between unicorns and rhinoceroses, the fabulous and the factual" (1:227). This began to change as the result of accounts of the phenomenal—those of travel, war, and religion, for example. Indeed, we see the profane embraced for itself, when, for example, William Harrison in his contribution to *Holinshed's Chronicles,* an account of the customs and history of Great Britain published in 1586, provides his wife's recipe for brewing beer (Holinshed 285–86). Beer was examined for its own sake and for that reason existed in resistance to the kind of ideological symbolism that dominated much of "official" discourse. Ultimately, the vehicle for that resistance, the printing press, could reflect a vernacular-speaking world, one that in turn could be verified and improved upon through subsequent investigations.

Nonetheless, older forms and ways of viewing that reflected a symbolic world as reality were initially pressed into the service of the printing press. One anomaly (at least from a positivist perspective) is that, as Eisenstein intimates, the fabulous had as much "reality" to readers during this period as the phenomenal. As Lennard Davis notes in his discussion on "news/novels," which helps to account ultimately for the rise of the canonical fictional novel in the eighteenth century, "what is quite significant is that the news/novels discourse seems to make no real distinction between what we would call fact and fiction. That is, fictional tales seem to be considered [news] as readily as would an account of a sea battle or a foreign war" (51). Why is this so? Davis, who characterizes his critical method as "materialist"(86), maintains a distinction between what conventionally we characterize as "factual" and "fictional." Thus he dismisses belief in the fabulous in ballads as a belief derived from the "gullibility of ballad readers" (52). This discounts the idea, however, that to some readers such accounts did seem real, or did, to their own minds, have a phenomenalistic status. To cite a contemporary example, one need only look at the sensational accounts of the fabulous in tabloids.

In its first issue for the year 2000, one such tabloid, the *Weekly World News,* ran the following stories: "Face of Satan Seen over U.S. Capitol" (Mann 1, 46–47), "Ancient Scroll Provides a Description of Heaven" with a subheadline of "—And a Secret Formula for Resurrecting the Dead!" (Foster 6), "One in Four UFO Pilots Is Drunk!" (Sanford 13), "Demon's Body Found in Holy Land" (Foster 13), and "National Air Alert Issued by NTSB: Passenger Jet Reports Near Miss with Winged Entities at 40,000 Feet" with the caption "Angels appeared to float by a passenger jet flying at 40,000 feet" (Mann 40–41). We may character-

ize these as the beliefs of the gullible, but that does not preclude the
perception of such "events" by some as "real." Clearly there are those
who will read such examples of fabulation strictly for the entertainment
value of the stories, discounting that the stories have a phenomenalistic status. These readers are the skeptical with a sense of humor. But
though such stories strain credulity for skeptical readers, it would
equally strain credulity to suggest that all readers of tabloids such as
the *Weekly World News* fall into such a class and that there are not those
who, for whatever reasons, do believe such accounts are "real." These
latter may well exhibit the classic symptoms of choosing what they wish
to believe. But such a conclusion only confirms the critical stance that
perception determines what is conceived of as "reality."

This needs to be borne in mind not only for the printed ballad in
the period immediately after the introduction of the printing press but
also for other emergent forms claiming to provide accounts of the
phenomenal. Such later accounts include: "out of Suffolke and Es-
sex, where it rayned wheat the space of six or seven miles" in 1583;
"declaring the damnable life of Doctor Fian, a notable sorcerer, who
was burned at Edenborough in January last" in 1591; "of a prodigious
monster born in the township of Addlington" in 1613; "a true relation
of the strange appearance of a Man-Fish" in 1642; and, finally, in 1653,
"a perfect Mermaid . . . driven ashore nere Greenwich, with her combe
in one hande and her lookinge-glasse in the other" (Andrews 26, 39,
51). Ultimately, we should bear in mind that the fabulous has always
intermingled with events that have a demonstrable phenomenal status.
Davis is right in noting that little distinction is made between the two
by readers of early printed ballads. This is because to some there *is no
distinction* between the fabulous and the phenomenal, a critical stance
that can only be elided from a materialist perspective. The issue here,
however, is not that the clearly fabulous has a place in journalism,
whether it is objectified or literary, but rather that the emergence of
modern journalism is evolutionary and that at one time fabulation was
viewed as having as much "reality" as the phenomenally verifiable. The
irony, of course, is that in the second half of the twentieth century
deconstruction alone has assured that to some extent text is only a
poor mirror to phenomenon, and those texts are always to some degree only specular, or a form of distortion. There is always some de-

gree, then, of fiction or even fabulation in a text, even in the most objectified journalism. The writer of tabloids may be closer to the truth than the "objective" journalist would care to acknowledge.

This said, the printed ballad provides a useful point of departure for examining these forms precisely because it is transitional in nature. It was, of course, an evolutionary step beyond the oral ballad and medieval minstrelsy. On the one hand, printed ballads look to the past oral form with its emphasis on dramatic invention by the minstrel in which the ballads were poetic in order to be memorable. Moreover, they were framed according to dominant cultural ideologies in such forms as the romance or epic. The printed broadside ballads rooted in the earlier narrative ballads of the minstrelsy became popular in the sixteenth and seventeenth centuries (Shaaber 189–92). They were similarly subject to formulation and convention, and recall the constraints once again of Bakhtin's image of the absolute past. Despite this, they also look to the future because many ballads were narratives of historical events and rooted in the phenomenal. "To speak of the broadside ballad as a vehicle for news is perhaps misleading, and yet there are some ballads which are quite valuable for the information they impart and which must have served as news-reports when first published," notes M. A. Shaaber in his study of English journalism between 1476 and 1622 (193). One example is to be found in the early sixteenth-century "True Relation of the Life and Death of Sir Andrew Barton, a Pirate and Rover on the Seas," an anonymous ballad that recounts the capture of Barton by the English in 1511 (202). Still another is John Skelton's "Ballade of the Scottyshe Kynge," which describes the 1513 defeat and death of James IV of Scotland at the battle of Flodden Field (195). Shaaber notes, "Thus the public acts of the sovereign, the military successes of the English armies, and the discomfiture of the enemies of the realm are fully rehearsed in a long series of ballads" (195). As a result, such ballads remain valuable for news and historical content, even as they hearken back to an earlier discourse rooted ultimately in a highly symbolic oral tradition. Their affinity to a later literary journalism lies in their narrative nature. They are, in a sense, still another form of story journalism, albeit one invested with intentional invention and elaborate symbolism.

Because the broadside ballads looked back to a past when little distinction was made between fact and fiction, early narrative literary journalism eventually would have to repudiate fanciful invention. Before examining that repudiation, however, one needs to understand more fully what narrative prose accounts were confronting rhetorically in the sixteenth and seventeenth centuries, and to a lesser extent in the subsequent eighteenth and nineteenth centuries. With an increase in printed vernacular prose, an initial problem that arose at least among the learned (arbiters of rhetorical taste) was *how* prose was to be written. Under the influence of the new learning this resulted in a contest in the late sixteenth century. Should style take precedence over content? Or should content take precedence over style? Hidden in the argument is whether phenomenal experience should be framed according to a highly symbolic rhetorical politics. We see here the temporary popularity of euphuism, an artificiality of style that engages in excessive antithesis, simile, conceits, alliteration, and assonance, and that often contains classical and biblical references. Fundamentally, the problem with euphuism was one of rhetorical overkill. The issue is not that simile has its utility, or for that matter antithesis and alliteration, but rather that such figures were used to excess so that the result runs the risk of being only style, with little or no content. As a consequence, an elaborate symbolic reality took precedence over attempts to reflect a temporal reality, this, despite the rise of a vernacular prose. We have taken our two steps forward in the vernacular, only to take one (at least one!) back into an elaborate linguistic reality that bears little resemblance to the temporal world. Euphuism was not new; it had its classical roots. But it was practiced to the extreme by the late sixteenth-century writer John Lyly. For example, in Lyly's *Euphues: The Anatomy of Wyt,* Philautus discovers that his bosom friend Euphues (the source for "euphuism") has seduced Lucilla, the woman he loves:

> Why then did his pretended curtesie bewitch thee with such credulytie? shall my good will bee the cause of his ill wil? bicause I was content to be his friende, thought he mee meete to be made his foole? I see now that as the fish *Scolipidus* in the floud *Araris* [Ararat] at the waxinge of the *Moone* is as white as the driuen snow, and at the wayning as blacke as the burnt coale, so *Euphues,* which at the first encreasing of our familyaritie, *was* very zealous, is nowe at the last cast become most faythlesse. (232)

Alliteration and assonance abound. Every sentence contains antithesis. We can detect simile layered upon simile in reference to the fish *Scolipidus*. If Euphues is likened to the fish, does that mean he is also likened to the white swan and the black of an extinguished coal? Furthermore, the classical-biblical *Scolipidus* refers to the Latin *De Fluviis* (The Flood), an obscure account falsely attributed to Plutarch (Bond 243). As C. S. Lewis notes: "What constitutes euphuism is neither the structural devices nor the 'unnatural history' but the *unremitting* use of both. The excess is the novelty: the euphuism of any composition is a matter of degree" (313, emphasis added).

The problem of a "politically correct" rhetoric would continue to plague the evolution of vernacular prose, even after sixteenth-century euphuism was rejected by those who thought they could arrive at a better, and therefore more correct rhetoric, a circumstance evident in our own time in our many usage manuals. The issue of style is still one more variation on what could be characterized as "the distanced image of the absolute rhetorical past."

The issue of the distanced image of the absolute rhetorical past would be dealt with, incrementally, on different fronts. An example of an early challenge to prevailing assumptions of *how* the world should be perceived, and an attack on the artificiality of euphuism, is to be found in the oldest surviving feminist tract in English, a pamphlet published in 1589 by an unknown gentlewoman, *Jane Anger Her Protection for Women*. The pamphlet, an early form of journalism in English but in this instance largely informational or discursive in mode, challenges a still-earlier but now lost tract by a misogynist when "Jane Anger" calls his rhetoric to account in his attacks on women (A[nger] 22–29) (Lyly's *Euphues: The Anatomy of Wyt* was also largely a misogynist attack.) The rebuttal is important not only as a feminist protest but also because of the form the pseudonymous "Jane Anger" chose, journalism, or more broadly, a nonfiction prose form whose ultimate purpose is to hold the phenomenal world to account. In choosing a form that seeks for temporal accountability, she eschewed the dominant elitist genre among gentlefolk of her time, poetry, and the dominant ideology reflected in that poetry, the courtly love tradition of Sydney and Spenser that had so successfully marginalized gentlewomen (and by implication all women) from a fuller participation in civic affairs. "Jane Anger" did so by directly assaulting—and deconstructing—the inflated rhetorical posture of the misogynist's style: "The desire that every man has to show his true vein in writing is unspeakable, and their minds are so carried away with the manner, as no care at all is had of the matter. They run so into rhetoric as often times they overrun the bounds of their own wits and go they know not whither" (A[nger] 24). As A. Lynne Magnusson notes, "Anger" "represents men's verbal fluency not only as a signal of their disregard for truthful representation but also as their loss of control, as going 'they know not whither.' In this way, she caricatures and demystifies the claims some male writers make to divine inspiration," a divine inspiration, one might add, that was also reflected in the courtly love tradition of poetry (272).

Privileging substance over style and truthful representation over divine inspiration presents a challenge to prevailing ideological assumptions. Such a style that ultimately abandoned rhetorical flourish would come to be called the "plain style," a style ostensibly designed to hold the phenomenal world to account. "Anger's" statement then can be read as one historical marker of a transition taking place in English letters—and vernacular prose—that would have consequences for modern journalistic style. It is here that Jane Anger illustrates still another point when considering the evolution of nonfiction forms. While a new critical consciousness was reflected in the awareness of the nonfiction prose form called the "essay" when Francis Bacon first published his "Essays" in 1597, in reality he was only providing a name for the form that he borrowed from Montaigne (Bush 194–95). As the example of Jane Anger as well as other pamphlets of the period suggest, a proto-"essay" form had been long practiced, whether it reflected discussions of religious affairs or state affairs or, for that matter, agricultural issues, and it indeed has classical antecedents (Bush 193). It is safe to say that writers have long attempted "to essay" or "to assay" or to put evidence to a critical test, whether the evidence was metaphysical or phenomenal. But such essays reflective of human understanding are of course fundamentally discursive, or marked and framed by analytical reasoning, whether they tend more toward the expository or more toward the persuasive mode (since it is doubtful those two versions of discursiveness could be mutually exclusive). In being discursive, their virtue lies in the attempt at critical perspective on the part of the observer for the observed, or of one's subjectivity for the object. But therein lies such a form's liability, too, in that it reflects just how alienated the subject's consciousness has become. In any event, Bacon's "Essays" do reflect a critical consciousness about how analytical reasoning is expressed and thus provide an evolutionary step in understanding the development of modern nonfiction prose. More important, they reflect what will continue to be a slow but growing divide between discursive and narrative models. As a result, this concern over *how* to account for the world would be reflected in ideologically prescribed accounts of the phenomenal and countering challenges to those prescriptions, and the open conflict in the late nineteenth century between which style of news was more adequate to those tasks, the information or the story model.

Still another example in which ideology reflected in style is challenged is to be found in the 1600 pamphlet entitled *Nine Daies Wonder* by William Kemp. The style challenged in this instance is that of the ballad. Moreover, Kemp's account may be considered an early example of narrative literary journalism. He was a practitioner of the old English form of folk dancing known as Morris dancing in which the dancer wears bells on his legs. On a wager, Kemp danced for nine days from London to Norwich (a distance of more than seventy-five miles in a straight line) accompanied by a drummer. Kemp's purpose in writing his account was, as he said, "to satisfy his friends the truth, against all lying Ballad-makers" (5). Thus he took direct aim at the free invention practiced by ballad writers who based their ballads on true stories. Indeed, in his epistle dedicatory, Kemp notes that one ballad writer placed him dancing in the English town of New-Market, "which town I came neuer neere by the length of half the heath" (3). To "set the record straight," to indulge the well-established journalistic maxim, was his purpose then, although one cannot rule out that Kemp, too, sought profit from his feat as had the writers of broadside ballads.

We can also detect in Kemp his own struggles to escape rhetorical flourish when he indulges in a bit of overwrought alliteration and antithesis—some lingering influences of euphuism: "myselfe, thats I, otherwise called *Caualiero Kemp,* head-Master of Morrice-dauncers, high Head-borough of Heighs, and onely tricker of you Trill-lillies, and best bel-shangles betweened Sion and mount Surrey, began frolickly to foote it, from the right Honorable the Lord Mayors of London, towards the right worshipfull (and truely bountifull) Master Mayors of Norwich" (5). But as he proceeds with his narrative, Kemp largely abandons euphuism and the older rhetorical "reality" of a highly symbolic linguistic world, entering instead into the "reality" of a temporal or empirical world. Or as C. S. Lewis characterizes it: "Very soon the narrative develops a quite different interest; the details of the exploit, the entertainment at each resting place, the behaviour of the crowds, and the adventures of the road . . . [Kemp] makes me believe every word he writes" (417). Such is the endorsement of an early narrative literary journalism by the eminent sixteenth-century scholar. Kemp's common sense–appeal to the shared common senses points to his account as early literary journalism in the rich social portraiture written not only in the vernacular but also in a colloquial vein. For example, in Sudbury a butcher attempts to dance a mile with Kemp but gives it up, unequal to the task. Then, Kemp writes:

> As he and I were parting, a lusty Country lasse being among the people, cal'd him faint hearted lout: saying, if I had begun to daunce, I would haue held out one myle though it had cost my life. At which wordes many laughed. Nay saith she, if the Dauncer will lend me a leash of his belles, Ile venter to treade one mile with him my selfe. I lookt vpon her, saw mirth in her eies, heard boldnes in her words, and beheld her ready to tuck vp her russet petticoate, I fitted her with bels: which she merrily taking, garnisht her thicke short legs, and with a smooth brow bad the Tabrer [drummer] begin. The Drum strucke, forward marcht I with my merry Maydemarian: who shooke her fat sides: and footed it merrily to Melfoord, being a long myle. (14)

Except for the extended alliteration of the last sentence, the contrast with Lylian euphuism could hardly be more striking.

ANOTHER ANTECEDENT to our modern narrative literary journalism is the sensational narrative account. Indeed, it may not be too much to suggest that sensationalism is a necessary predecessor for narrative literary journalism. Sensationalism is not new of course. Clearly, the stench of William the Conqueror's body exploding is sensationalistic for purposes of illustrating a homily. Moreover, most sensational accounts written in the sixteenth and seventeenth centuries would still pay lip service to providing a moral. But another driving motive here for the writer and printer is familiar: profit that accompanied the rise of a middle class. Sensationalism always has been a good sell.

Typical were such pamphlets as those of Thomas Dekker. Largely recalled today as a dramatist, he was also a journalist recording the social scene in London in the early 1600s. On the one hand, while he embraced the inconclusive present of a phenomenal reality, he equally embraced the distanced image of the absolute past. If anything, that distanced image formally frames or directs the inconclusive present. For example, in *The Wonderfull Yeare, 1603* he recounts the reappearance of bubonic plague in England with sketches of ordinary (or in this case, extraordinary) life. In doing so, as Douglas Bush notes, "Dekker is much closer to the medieval and pictorial tradition of the Dance of Death" in his personification of death (41). Therein lies the distanced image of the absolute past or the means by which human mortality was metaphorically measured. For this reason it would be easy to dismiss Dekker and others like him as not being early literary journalists, and from a modern perspective this is understandable if the inconclusive present of phenomenal experience is to be the driving force behind narrative literary journalism. But to do so is to judge by a contemporary standard and ignore the literary sensibility of the period in which daily and symbolic realities are not separated but exist together, the daily usually framed by the symbolic. The symbolic world *was* reality then and a modern perspective fails to do such a narrative justice. In *The Wonderfull Yeare, 1603* that symbolic reality proved to be the danse macabre.

Moreover, is the symbolism ultimately so different from the metaphysical symbolism in, for example, "The Angels," the first chapter of Tom Wolfe's 1979 *The Right Stuff?* In it, America's space age heroes, the astronauts, are, as the chapter's title suggests, viewed as our modern equivalent of angels. Of course, in the chapter they keep crashing and dying, revealing human hubris in terms of their reification as heroes. In that, we see Wolfe's social satire. But social satire was what Dekker engaged in, too, and indeed the medieval concept of the danse macabre was fundamentally satire at the expense of humankind's hubris. Wolfe's, then, is merely a late twentieth-century version of an old

theme. In *The Wonderful Yeare, 1603,* for example, a wife suffering from
the plague and expecting to die confesses to her cobbler husband that
she has been unfaithful to him, bedding with the other husbands of
their community. She recovers, however, death having played its cat-
and-mouse game with her. Then there was a tinker who came to a town
where its residents were afraid to bury the corpse of a Londoner who
had died of the plague in a neighborhood tavern. The townspeople
pay the tinker a handsome sum to bury the corpse, and as he goes
about doing so he robs the purse on the corpse of the still more handsome sum of seven pounds. After the burial of the corpse is complete,
he returns to town singing, "Haue ye any more Londoners to bury, hey
downe, a downe, dery, haue ye any more Londoners to bury" (1:145).
The townspeople, seeing him and assuming he is infected with the
plague, flee as he marches away singing his song. These are, to be sure,
in the tradition of the medieval fabliaux, coarse and often cynical hu-
morous tales. In this instance the humor is framed by a personified
death's dance. But in death's distanced image of the absolute past can
also be detected the inconclusive present of the narrative journalism
of the era in the description, for example, of the tavern-keeper: "a
goodly fat Burger he was, with a belly Arching out like a Beere-barrell,
which made his legges (that were thicke & short, like two piles driuen
under *London*-bridge) to stradle halfe as wide as the toppe of Powles
[Saint Paul's Cathedral; the tavern-keeper was spread-legged for support because of his excessive weight]" (1:138). It can be detected again
when the tinker receives his undertaker's fee from the frightened
townspeople who fear to touch him because he has touched the corpse:

> Therefore ten shillings was saved leuyed out of hand, put into a rag,
> which was tyed to the ende of a long pole and deliuered (in sight of all
> the Parish, who stood aloofe stopping their noses) by the Headboroughs
> owene selfe in proper person, to the Tinker, who with one hand receiued
> the money, and with the other struck the boord, crying hey, a fresh
> double pot [of beer]. Which armour of proofe being fitted to his body,
> vp he hoists the Londoner on his backe (like a Schoole-boy) a Shouell
> and Pick-axe are standing ready for him: And thus furnished, into a field
> some good distance from the Towne he beares his deadly loade, and
> there throwes it downe, falling roundly to his tooles, vpon which the
> strong beere hauuing set an edge, they quickely cut out a lodging in the
> earth for the Citizen. (1:144)

The tinker proceeds to strip the Londoner of his clothes and money, and buries him.

As Bush notes of Dekker's journalism: "In general, the vicissitudes of a precarious existence [Dekker spent six years in debtor's prison] bore fruit in an extensive and peculiar knowledge of London and, without souring his zest for life, deepened his feeling for the submerged nine-tenths" (40). Still elsewhere Bush adds that Dekker portrays "an urban vignette of carts and coaches thundering, pots clinking, water-tankards running at tilt, porters sweating under burdens, merchants' men bearing bags of money" in what ultimately is a tapestry of urban life (41).

Dekker's *Wonderfull Yeare* also points to the highly sensational nature of such accounts openly framed by ideology, particularly moral pieties. The accounts were many and varied, and written on such topics as disasters, murders, voyages of exploration, witchcraft, and the just plain weird, all feeding an eager common—and vernacular—audience (Shaaber 141–65). Examples include "Mistres Turners Repentance, Who, about the poysoning of . . . Sir Thomas Ouverbury, was executed the fourteenth day of Nouember, last" in 1615 (142); "The forme and shape of a monstrous Child, borne at Maydstone in Kent . . . October, 1568" (155); and "The burnynge of Paules church in London . . . by lyghtnynge" in 1563 (163).

In accounts of murders one can detect forbears to *In Cold Blood* and *The Executioner's Song*, perennial modern favorites of narrative literary journalism. For example, in 1592, Thomas Kydde, better known as a dramatist and poet, wrote a pamphlet in which a wife murders her husband for the sake of her lover who eventually abandons her, pregnant. The plot may be hackneyed from our contemporary perspective. Nonetheless, in its descriptiveness and dialogue the account represents early narrative and sensational journalism such as in the scene where the wife poisons her husband:

> And by the time he [her husband] came againe she had made ready a messe of suger sops for him, one for herselfe, and another for a little boye which she brought with her, but her husbands she had poysoned as before: when he was come she gave her husband his messe, and she and the childe fell also to eathing of theirs. Within a pretty while after hee had eaten his, hee began to waxe very ill about the stomack, feeling also

a griuous griping of his inward partes, whereup he tould his wife he felt
himself not well: how so? quoth she; you were well before you went forth,
were you not? yes, indeed was I, said he: then he demaunded if she were
well; she answered, I; so likewise said the childe. Ah! quoth her husband,
now I feele my selfe sicke at the very heart; and immediatlie after he
began to vomet exceedlingly, with such straines as if his lungs would
burst in peeces. (10–11)

Her husband dies; eventually the murder is uncovered when her lover
abandons her; and the wife is burned at the stake while the former
lover is executed in front of her by hanging. The narrative is all the
more noteworthy because it recounts how the wife is tricked into con-
fessing the murder when she is told that her lover has implicated her,
anticipating the same strategy of eliciting a confession in *In Cold Blood*
several hundred years later.

Such accounts require further examination, however, in order to
understand the relationship between literary journalism and sensational journalism. What the two share in common is that both appeal
to the common sense–appeal of our shared common senses in the linguistic attempt to reflect the phenomenal world. The difference is that
narrative literary journalism attempts to provide insight into other subjectivities, while sensationalism attempts to reinforce the notion of the
marginalized as Other in order to elicit a response of terror or horror.
Still, given that both attempt to indulge the common sense–appeal of
the shared common senses, it is not too much to suggest that sensationalism is a necessary prerequisite for narrative literary journalism.

Most of these narratives (including Kydde's) are blatantly framed by
ideological concerns, whether religious, political, or some combination of the two. An example of the latter is John Foxe's late sixteenth-
century account of Anglican martyrs, commonly known as Foxe's *Book
of Martyrs,* inspirational readings framed by Anglican ideology. At the
same time, one can detect in it forerunners of narrative literary journalism and the fictional novel. Foxe's *Book of Martyrs* deserves further
examination if for no other reason than for its wide influence on English prose. After the Anglican Church had once and for all established
itself after the death of Queen Mary and the ascendancy of Queen Elizabeth, the *Book of Martyrs,* published in 1563, ranked at the time only
behind the English Bible and *The Book of Common Prayer* in its importance as a religious work in the state-sponsored church. "When pub-

lished it was an instant success; it went through four editions in its author's lifetime and through many more after his death, generation after generation for three hundred years. . . . Foxe had once been esteemed next to the Bible" (Williamson xi). For example, on publication of the twenty-three-hundred-page second edition (1570), a convocation of church officials directed that it be placed alongside the Bishop's Bible in every cathedral in England. One reason for its appeal was that its style was relatively simple and direct. But it is the sensational aspects of the text, particularly those based on eyewitness accounts and records, that also account for its success and anticipate modern literary journalism and the fictional novel. For example, "after his body was scorched with the fire and his left arm taken from him by the violence of the fire, the flesh being burnt to the white bone, at length he stooped over the chain and with the right hand, being somewhat starkened, knocked upon his breast softly, blood and matter issuing out of his mouth" (Foxe 360). And again: "They were first strangled, but the rope broke before they were dead, and the poor women fell in the fire. Perrotine, who was great with child, did fall on her side, where happened a rueful sight. . . . For as the belly of the woman brast asunder by the vehemency of the flame, the infant, a fair man child, fell into the fire, and being taken out of the fire by one W. House was laid upon the grass. Then was the child had to the provost, and from him to the bailiff, who gave censure that it should be carried back again and cast into the fire" (380).

The accounts are, clearly, grisly. But then that was their purpose, to prompt physical and emotional revulsion. The phenomenal world, because of its grisliness, was being granted an authority equal to the spiritual world. Moreover, it is Foxe's accounts of the laity that helped make the common respectable in the language that the commoner spoke. "Foxe's massive work was immensely popular partly because it enabled ordinary men and women to participate vicariously in a great historic epic," observes Eisenstein. "Successive editions of Foxe's *Book of Martyrs* were progressively enriched by dramatic accounts of fishermen, tailors, housewives and the like" (1:423).

ANOTHER PROSE strain that would eventually contribute to a modern narrative literary journalism and English nonfiction prose generally is to be found in the abundant accounts of voyages of exploration and colonization in the sixteenth and seventeenth centuries. That is, if such travelogues and accounts are not in fact early forms of narrative literary journalism, an issue explored in the introduction. Furthermore, such accounts were often sensationalistic if for no other reason than by virtue of their strangeness. Richard Haklyut's first edition of *Principall Navigations Voiages and Discoveries of the English Nation* appeared in 1589 and recounted the exploits of Englishmen at sea. Many of the narratives are simple chronological accounts, but occasionally they reflect description, especially sensationalistic. In the second expanded edition, for example, John Jane offers this account of the last ill-fated voyage of Thomas Cavendish:

> But after we came near unto the sun, our dried penguins began to corrupt, and there bred in them a most loathsome and ugly worm of an inch long. This worm did so mightily increase and devour our victuals that there was in reason no hope how we should avoid famine, but be devoured of these wicked creatures. There was nothing that they did not devour, only iron excepted; our clothes, boots, shoes, hats, shirts, stockings; and for the ship, they did so eat the timbers as that we greatly feared they would undo us by gnawing through the ship's side. (Jane 119)

An account of colonization that is more psychologically subtle is John Smith's 1624 narrative of Pocahontas saving his life. Assuming it is true (it was not included in Smith's initial account of the founding of the Virginia colony), it demonstrates the early use of techniques we now associate with narrative literary journalism.

Perhaps the most important contribution writers of travelogues made, however, to a future narrative literary journalism was to an evolving prose style, or the plain style, increasingly (but not immediately) unencumbered by Lylian rhetorical flourish. As Douglas Bush has observed of the seventeenth century: "Then, if we incline to regard this period as one of rhetorical and poetic prose, we should remember that the authors of records of travel were mostly plain men with utilitarian aims who produced a great deal of good plain prose without knowing it." Further, Bush notes, "travellers helped to enlarge the known world and actual knowledge and to emancipate their age from legend. As in the past, the spirit of travel and maritime discovery continued to affect every kind of imaginative and reflective literature" (190). The emancipation Bush discusses is one of emancipation from the distanced image of the absolute past by embracing the inconclusive present.

Such a literature of announced accountability to the phenomenal world—journalism—is reflected in William Bradford's journal of the founding of Plymouth Plantation, and in this we can see a further evolution of the plain style as well as a continuing challenge to the distanced image of the absolute past. Bradford's purpose in keeping the seventeenth-century journal was to document the realization of the Pilgrim God's plan on earth in the new colony. In undertaking the project, Bradford says, "I shall endeavour to manifest in a plain style, with singular regard unto the simple truth in all things; at least as near as my slender judgment can attain the same" (3). Bradford's preface is remarkable not only because of its claim to being written in a plain style but also because it so clearly reflects the evolving objective-subjective dichotomy and the interwoven threads of the informational and story models. The Pilgrim arrival in the New World came thirty-five years after Jane Anger's protest against the Renaissance cultural and linguistic conceits that had been impressed to marginalize women. Likewise, the Pilgrim and Puritan migration was in part a protest against a new generation of cultural, linguistic, and ultimately spiritual Cavalier conceits at the courts of James I and Charles I because at stake was no less than salvation. In order to justify the ways of man to God, Bradford undertook to record in his journal the realization of God's plan on earth far from the meddling of the secular and Cavalier authority. Bradford sets out to do so by means of a style free of Cavalier conceit-making and expressed "with singular regard unto the simple truth in all things." If he had stopped with the plain style he would have provided the cooked recipe for something akin to modern objective journalistic style. The problem is he must qualify his plain style with a "singular regard for the simple truth in all things," which can have at least two meanings. First, the plain style can be interpreted as a forerunner of the objective journalistic style, since such a "singular regard" implies a focused, clear, and unambiguous gaze on the particulars of the phenomenal world. But second, the singularity of the regard also implies one individual's perception of the world, opening the way for acknowledged subjectivity, which, by Bradford's next modifying clause, he can no longer avoid: "at least as near as my slender judgment can attain the same."

In "transcribing" God's divine plan on earth, Bradford has been defeated, by his own account, from the outset by his reflexivity. He was unwittingly acknowledging the impossibility of the divine inspiration that Jane Anger was assaulting in the previous century because of his own announced obligation—one based in his subjectivity—to the phenomenal. Thus the plain style was hardly plain but fraught with contradictions, as critic Hugh Kenner has noted: "Plain prose, the plain style, is the most disorienting form of discourse yet invented by man. . . . A man who doesn't make his language ornate cannot be deceiving us; so runs the hidden premise. Bishop Thomas Sprat extolled 'a close, naked, natural way of speaking' in 1667; it was the speech, he went on to say, of merchants and artisans, not of wits and scholars. Merchants and artisans are men who handle things and who presumably handle words with a similar probity" (183). As a consequence, Kenner notes, "journalism seemed guaranteed by the plain style. Handbooks and copy editors now teach journalists how to write plainly, that is, in such a manner that they will be trusted. You get yourself trusted by artifice" (187). The problem, of course, is that one man's plain style is another man's lush linguistic imagery, gorgeously reflexive. But if Bradford were defeated, it would be that defeat, epistemologically speaking, that many narrative literary journalists would later use as their attempted point of departure, often doing so with a similar humility as Bradford's: acknowledging the "I" in shaping how the world is perceived.

So THE struggle continued to grant phenomenal experience its own legitimacy outside of elaborate symbolisms founded on rhetoric, legend, and theology. Such a struggle would be reflected in the numerous histories, character books, biographies, annals, diaries, and memoirs of the seventeenth century, a grouping of nonfiction forms whose sheer breadth can only be explored in cursory fashion here. An etymological approach reveals that "history" long had had a place in the vernacular, according to the *Oxford English Dictionary* (*Compact Edition* 1:1515). On the other hand, "character book," "biography," "annals," "diary," and "memoir" took on meanings back in the seventeenth century which we largely accord them today. ("Autobiography" is of relatively recent usage, dating only to 1809 [*Compact Edition* 1:144].) Their meanings derive, at least in part, from the evolving critical consciousness that the

recording of phenomenal experience was a legitimate enterprise, one
that should not, as Francis Bacon observed in 1605 in his essay "Ad-
vancement of Learning," "vanish in the fumes of subtle or sublime
speculations" (297) but be founded on verifiable fact. It found expression still later in the century when Thomas Fuller, author of the 1662
Worthies of England, observed: "By *real,* I understand the commodities
and observables of every county" (2). Fuller, incidentally, was one of
the first to challenge (in his *Worthies*) the veracity of John Smith's account of the founding of the Virginia colony (75–76), additional evidence of the increasing expectation that accounts of the phenomenal
were to be factual.

By our contemporary standards the seventeenth-century character
books are a literary anomaly. This is because they consist of descriptions of idealized human personalities. However, they were not romantic, epic, or heroic idealizations. Instead, they were idealizations of
everyday types, such as the farmer, the milkmaid, the scholar, and so
forth. Thus, they reflected a kind of social—and phenomenal—portraiture. In this we see an early version of social science. The idealizing
of character was both the strength and weakness of the character
books. On the one hand, the brief descriptive essays attempted to reflect a "type," and in embracing mundane characters more reflective
of everyday life, that was two steps forward in the cause of reflecting
the inconclusive present. But it was one step back because the character sketches were ultimately only types, not individuals. Thus characters
were reinscribed in social symbolism, or the distanced image of the
absolute past, not necessarily of legend or Gospel but of emerging social classes. Nonetheless, the character books were important because
as they became more sophisticated they began to reflect psychological
depth. For example, John Earle, in his *Microcosmography,* describes a
"discontented man" as "one that is fallen out with the world and will be
revenged upon himself. . . . The root of his disease is a self-humouring
pride" (19). Unlike some of the earlier character writers such as
Thomas Overbury, Earle is credited "with sympathetic analysing of actions and motives. . . . Whether praising or blaming, Earle is not content to report what a character does or is, he asks why" (Bush 214). We
see, as a consequence, efforts at psychological verisimilitude.

The shortcomings of biography in this era offer a curious mirror to the shortcomings of the character books. If the character books were based on social stereotypes (and ultimately social ideology), the drawback to biography, as often as not, was that the individual—not the type—was usually praised or damned according to party or sectarian ideology, whether it was Anglican or Puritan, king or Parliament. One author of biography was Izaak Walton, better known for his meditation on angling, who was in his time an esteemed biographer of Anglican divines. "In all his writing he appears as one of those staunch and simple-minded Anglicans who saw history with the eyes of a bishop and could not regard other views as much better than perverse wickedness" (Bush 237). This begins to change, however, after the Glorious Revolution of 1688–89, when biography tends to be more factual. "By the close of the century the English reader was becoming accustomed . . . to being given the facts, however briefly, and whether they were exemplary or not" (Sutherland 248). The poet John Dryden is credited with introducing "biography" into the English language in 1683 with his "Life of Plutarch" (*Compact Edition* 1:218).

To the documentary literature of the age would be added accounts of sectarian differences and the English Civil War (Bush 47). Despite the times, narrative journalism could reflect a healthy humor. One royalist news sheet during the civil war reported the following confrontation between soldiers supporting Parliament and a newspaper hawker who sold the same royalist news sheet: "A hotte combat lately happened at the Salutation Taverne, in Holburne, where some of the Commonwealth vermin, called soldiers, had seized an Amazonian virago, named Mrs. Strosse, upon suspicion of being a loyalist and selling the *Man in the Moon;* but she, by applying beaten pepper to their eyes, disarmed them, and with their own swordes forced them to aske her forgiveness, and down on their marrybones, and pledge a health to the king and confusion to their masters; and so honorablie dismissed them" (*Man in the Moon* 102).

Although "diary" may have sixteenth-century antecedents in English (*Compact Edition* 1:718), it is perhaps more associated with the seventeenth because of two pre-eminent diarists, Samuel Pepys and John Evelyn. Neither of their diaries was available in print until the early nineteenth century. Nonetheless both contain descriptions that would qualify as early narrative literary journalism. For example, both wrote compelling eyewitness accounts of the great fire of London in 1666, or in effect accounts that are both history and memoir as we generally understand them (Pepys 7:267–89; Evelyn 2:20–26). In their descriptions of the inferno and resulting destruction we can see forerunners of John Hersey's 1946 *Hiroshima.*

Meanwhile, Evelyn and William Wycherley are credited with helping to introduce "memoir" as personal recollection into English during this period, a usage that appears to have largely replaced and perhaps evolved from "memorial" (*Compact Edition* 1:1767). In writing about one of his contemporaries, Evelyn cited "memoir" in his entry of 18 August 1673 (Old Style): "Nor could I forebear to note this extraordinary passage in these memoirs" (2:93). Meanwhile, in 1676 the dramatist William Wycherley cited memoir in the dedication to *The Plain Dealer*: "Your virtues deserve . . . a volume intire to give the World your Memoirs, or Life at large" (100). Wycherley's usage suggests that memoir could be not only self-written reminiscence or autobiography as we comprehend this latter—and etymologically later—term, but also biography. What Evelyn and Wycherley demonstrate then is just how fluid were generic boundaries during this period.

Boundaries could prove equally fluid for history. This is demonstrated in Sir Walter Raleigh's 1614 *A History of the World* which moves comfortably between both a profane world and a symbolic metaphysical world (Sutherland 224). Raleigh's announced purpose is to show, like Bradford, the workings of Providence from the beginning of time. However, a shift can be detected by the end of the seventeenth century, undoubtedly influenced in part by the founding of the Royal Society, to history based on historical method. Particularly noteworthy in this regard is the *History of the Rebellion* by Edward Hyde, Earl of Clarendon, which was available only in manuscript in the late seventeenth century but published in 1702–4. In a telling observation revealing the common origins of memoir and history, scholar James Sutherland notes, "*The History of the Rebellion* falls somewhere between formal history and memoir writing" because Hyde too wrote from personal knowledge (276). To some degree, into this aporia of competing discourses "between formal history and memoir" also falls a narrative literary journalism.

Also after the Restoration, efforts in mixed prose forms of biography *and* social portraiture become increasingly popular. One can detect in these early antecedents, if not examples of, narrative literary journalism. Among them was *Memoires of Monsieur Du Vall* by Walter Pope, published in 1670, which is an account of a handsome highwayman who ended on the gallows. Still another was *The Life and Death of Major Clancie, the Grandest Cheat of This Age* by Elkanah Settle, published in 1680. These were part of the developing literature of the rogue. They were also part of a popular literature widely available (*Memoires of Du Vall* sold ten thousand copies, a remarkable number for that period) to the popular reader who, as Sutherland observes, "could read numerous Lives of rogues and criminals, sensational in content, but in general plainly enough written" (248).

Settle's account of Irishman Dennis Clancie, who similarly went to the gallows, serves to illustrate why such accounts can also be viewed as a kind of early narrative literary journalism. Much as Truman Capote would go out of his way to claim that *In Cold Blood* was true (although evidence has since appeared that this was not always the case), Elkanah Settle adds an advertising subtitle to *Clancie* revealing similar intentions: "Wherein is set forth many of his Villainous Projects (Real matter of Fact) both in *England, Ireland, France, Spain and Italy*" (title page). It is the "matter of Fact" that will determine, at least according to authorial intention, the nature of "reality." Settle then is toying with the inconclusive present. *Clancie* tends to be more in the nature of a running account or chronology. Still, realistic technique associated with the modern novel is present. For example, Dennis Clancie is taken captive by the father of the young woman he loves. After Clancie wins his freedom, a servant

> brings Water, another the Towel, another his Hat: all waited upon him to Supper, and from thence to his Chamber. Next Morning, having his Horse and Arms delivered him in very good Order, he takes his Leave, particularly of the good Lady of the House, that procured him his Liberty.
>
> No sooner did he find himself without the Gate, mounted upon my Lords Gray Horse, and his Pistols fixt before him, but he turns towards the Door, and vows with a great imprecation, that no Body shall pass that way, but he will have his Life; unless they let him see his Mistress before he goes (25–26).

Here, then, in the literature of real-life rogues can be detected antecedents to *In Cold Blood*. On the one hand, *Clancie* is an early account of crime as a topical genre; on the other it is an example of narrative literary journalism as a modal genre. The "nonfiction novel" that Truman Capote claimed he invented was hardly new.

It is the contrast between such texts as *Clancie* and *Du Vall*, on the one hand, and the information or discursive model of news in the emerging newspaper, on the other, that helps to firmly locate the former as early narrative literary journalism or, at the least, as narrative journalism. This is the case even if *Clancie* and *Du Vall* tend to be more in the nature of running accounts lacking the "characterization" of extended description that has come to be associated with the modern form. Compare, for example, the above passage from *Clancie* with the following from the newspaper *Smith's Currant Intelligence,* also published in 1680: "We are told that our Troops are ordered to Rendezvouze about *Liege,* & that they will oblige the Hollanders to render *Masstricht* to the Spaniards, and *Hasselt* and *Maesryk* to the Elector of Cologne which they detain, contrary to the late Treaty of Peace" (1). Taking into account a different historical idiom, the passage is not all that different from the objectified information model that one might read in the press today: "The British Army was ordered to Liege to force the Dutch to give up Mastricht to the Spaniards, and Hasselt and Maesryk to the Elector of Cologne. The Dutch continue to control these towns despite the recent peace treaty." The difference from *Clancie* could hardly be more striking.

Equally important for our purposes in searching for the origins of American narrative literary journalism are the increasing number of accounts of the English colonies in North America. One of the most dramatic late seventeenth-century narrative accounts is Mary White Rowlandson's report of her captivity among Indians during King Phillip's War in 1676. Published in 1682, it proved to be among the most popular of American narratives from the seventeenth century. The narrative straddles the boundary between what today we would characterize as memoir and narrative literary journalism in that it is not only inward-directed (particularly in terms of Puritan piety) but also outward-directed in its social portraiture:

> Here one asked me to make a shirt for her Papoos, for which she gave me a mess of Broth, which was thickened with meal made of the Bark of

a Tree, and to make it the better, she had put into it about a handfull of Pease, and a few roasted Ground-nuts. I had not seen my son a pritty while, and here was an Indian of whom I made inquiry after him, and asked him when he saw him: he answered me, that such a time his master roasted him, and that himself did eat a piece of him, as big as his two fingers, and that he was very good meat. . . . In this place, on a cold night, as I lay by the fire, I removed a stick that kept the heat from me, a squaw moved it down again, at which I lookt up, and she threw a handfull of ashes in mine eyes. (140–41)

By the late seventeenth century, then, rough if imperfect patterns had been established for many modern narrative nonfiction forms, including history, biography, memoir, autobiography, travelogue, and finally, narrative literary journalism. Such forms were not mutually exclusive, and their boundaries readily overlapped. Indeed, I have suggested elsewhere this must always be the case with nonfiction because of its fluid epistemological nature (Hartsock 445–46). In the eighteenth century, however, it is not these now-established cousins to narrative literary journalism that require continued examination, but rather those of an emerging modern social reportage and the emerging novel.

The early eighteenth century sees a journalism of social concern come fully into its own, and indeed it is difficult sometimes to detect the difference between such a journalism and early narrative literary journalism. Moreover, it anticipates the influence of social investigation generally on American journalism practice in the late nineteenth century, which Michael Schudson has explored. However, to suggest that social reporting simply appeared is erroneous. Like most nonfiction forms it has its antecedents. After all, by stretching an understanding of the form, Vitalis's account of William the Conqueror's death has a social aspect given its homiletic nature: its intention was salvation for the body politic. In the sixteenth century "conny catching" pamphlets served as entertainment but also examined a distinctly urban problem, that of the rogue and pickpocket in London, or what today we call the "con-man" derived from "conny," which was rogue's slang for a victim and meant "rabbit." Elsewhere, John Taylor the "Water Poet" wrote in the seventeenth century about the livelihood of watermen being threatened by carters, and Henry Peacham wrote about a comparable rivalry in his *Coach and Sedan* in 1636. Similarly Dekker wrote from firsthand experience about prison life in the fifth edition of his *Lanthorn and Candlelight,* published in 1616 (Bush 40).

But with the approach of the eighteenth century we see a more fully developed narrative journalism with a social purpose in the form of Edward "Ned" Ward's sketches of London life, published in his *London Spy,* a monthly, from 1698 to 1700. "In an age when newsmen were little more than retailers of random information, Ward's paper proved him to be a master of anecdote and dialogue, an amazing reporter of the casual and picaresque. . . . His incisive portraits of vagrants, underworld characters, and alehouse patrons are comparable to Hogarth's later engravings" (Snyder and Morris 5). Ward thus sounds every bit a narrative literary journalist of the modern kind. The Hogarthian reference reveals Ward's interest in social conditions. For example, Ward toured Bridewell prison, recounting the condition of a debtor he found imprisoned there:

> Going from the Work-room to the Common-side . . . thro' the frightful Grates of which uncomfortable Appartment a Ghastly Skeleton stood peeping, that from his terrible Aspect, I thought some power Immortal had Imprisoned death, that the World might Live for ever. I could not speak to him without dread of danger, least when his lips open'd to give him an answer, he should poison the Air with his contagious Breath; and Communicate to me the same Pestilence which had brought his infected Body to a dismal Anatomy: Yet mov'd with pity towards so sad an Object, I began to enquire into the Causes of his sad appearance, who, after a Penitential Look that call'd for Mercy and Compassion, with much difficulty he rais'd his feeble Voice a degree above silence; and told me he had been Sick Six weeks under that sad Confinement, and had nothing to comfort him but Bread and Water, with now and then the refreshment of a little small-beer. ([Ward], April 1699, 10)

But Ward was also an early narrative literary journalist who could do more than write about abysmal social conditions. In this regard, what the passage above reveals is Ward's initial discomfort in engaging his subjectivity with that of the "Ghastly Skeleton": "I could not speak to him without dread of danger, least when his lips open'd to give him an answer, he should poison the Air with his contagious Breath." But then Ward overcomes his fear. Like Stephen Crane would attempt some two centuries later in learning about the homeless in "An Experiment in Misery," Ward risks his subjectivity in order to learn about the conditions of the imprisoned debtor.

Ward engages more fully in the kind of common sense–appeal of the shared common senses associated with narrative literary journalism in, for example, his reporting on the funeral of poet John Dryden in 1700, when the coaches of the "quality" block Chancery Lane in front of bawdy houses and the King's Head Tavern where Ward drank (and, it has been suggested, did some of his reporting):

> One Impudent Corrector of Jades Flesh, had run his Pole against the back Leather of a Forgoing coach to the great damage of a *Beau*'s reins, who peeping out at the Coach-Door, with at least a fifty Ounce Wig on, Swore[, "]Damn him, if he came out he would make as great a Slaughter amongst Hackney Rogues with his Sword, as ever *Samson* did amongst the *Philistines* with the Jaw Bone of an ass.["] Whilst he was thus Cursing and Swearing like an old Sinner in a fit of the Gout, his own Coachman flinging back the Thong of his Whip in striking at his Horses, gave him such a Cut over the Nose, that he Jirk'd in his Head as if he had been Shot, not knowing from whence the blow came, that he sat raving within his Leathern Territories, like a mad Gentleman Chain'd down to his Seat ... not daring to look out, for fear after the like manner he should a second time pay for his peeking. ([Ward], April 1700, 8)

Clearly, Ward did not hesitate to write at the expense of "quality." This accounts in part for why his were not considered "polite letters," the parent of a "high literature" that emerged in the nineteenth century. As the passage illustrates, Ward embraced the common and everyday. Ward scholar Howard William Troyer notes: "The uniqueness of Ward's method lay in turning the ordinary world, already familiar to his readers, into the extraordinary and the unusual" (35). What was taken for granted became the basis for fuller examination as Ward embraced the Other of the common that was often kept at arm's length. So popular were Ward's sketches that after he ceased publication other provincial papers reran them until as late as 1748, nearly fifty years later (Wiles 110, 335). Moreover, the popularity of the *London Spy* is attested to by the fact that it went through five editions between its appearance and 1718 (Troyer 252). But its perceived literary value is perhaps best reflected in that arbiter of canonical literature, the *Cam-*

bridge History of English Literature, in which scholar Charles Whibley observes: "After two centuries, it still keeps the fresh stamp of truth" (9:263). Even early narrative literary journalism had a staying power.

In the final analysis, what firmly establishes Ward as an early narrative literary journalist is his embracing in his method Bakhtin's "inconclusive present." As Troyer observes: "The *London Spy* is basically a trip about town . . . [achieved] by virtue of numerous interruptions, tangential excursions, and concern for trivia" (33). The interruptions, tangents, and trivia all point to a phenomenal world unshaped by "the distanced image of the absolute past." Moreover, Troyer, writing in 1946, anticipates what have become, in a sense, the ground rules for a narrative literary journalist: "Ward was less a reporter of news than a commentator. He selected his material. He colored his presentation as he chose" (50). He engaged his subjectivity, in other words, and without apologies.

Shortly after Ward discontinued the *London Spy* we find Joseph Addison and Richard Steele occupying somewhat anomalous positions in relation to narrative literary journalism. They are sometimes cited as early narrative literary journalists.[1] It is easy to understand why given their influence on the personal essay. But Addison and Steele, in their *Tatler* and *Spectator* columns, are largely discursive in their mode and only occasionally narrative. It is true that the strands of the information and story models still often weave comfortably together even as they tug in opposite directions. Nonetheless, that relationship has begun to unravel in the eighteenth century with Addison's polite essay on the one hand and Daniel Defoe's narrative forms on the other. When Addison does write in a narrative mode he often indulges in fictitious characters such as Tom Folio and Ned Softly. These formally fictional sketches are invariably framed in an Augustan rhetoric. Ultimately, their purpose is exposition and persuasion, not telling a story.

Steele, under his nom de plume Isaac Bickerstaff, acknowledges that exposition and persuasion are his purpose in the first issue of the *Tatler* in 1709. Of his readers, he says: "Now these Gentlemen, for the most Part, being Persons of strong Zeal and weak Intellects, It is both a Charitable and Necessary Work to offer something, whereby such worthy

---

1. See Applegate 3–4, 247–49.

and well-affected Members of the Commonwealth may be instructed, after their Reading, *what to think:* Which shall be the End and Purpose of this my Paper" (Bickerstaff 1). To that end, Steele's sketches usually illustrate a moral. For example, he provides in that first issue a sketch of a young man who suffers from love at first sight: "he was washing his Teeth at a Tavern Window in *Pall-Mall,* when a fine Equipage pass'd by, and in it a young Lady, who look'd up at him; away goes the Coach, and the young Gentleman pull'd off his Night-Cap, and instead of rub-bing his Gums, as he ought to do, out of the Window till about Four a Clock, he sits him down, and spoke not a Word till Twelve at Night; after which, he began to enquire, If any Body knew the Lady" (1). No one does, and after that his life deteriorates so that "his Attention to any Thing but his Passion, was utterly gone." He is lovesick. The moral of this story, according to Steele, is that the young man's "Passion has so extremely maul'd him." Steele concludes his homily: "our poor Lover has most Understanding when he's Drunk, and is least in his Senses when he is Sober" (1–2). In their didactic—and admittedly hu-morous—natures, the expository and persuasive modes framing the brief narrative are evident.

If anything, Addison is more discursive, and he too announces, in 1711, his expository and moralizing intentions in the *Spectator.* "As the great and only End of these my Speculations is to banish Vice and Igno-rance out of the Territories of *Great Britain,* I shall endeavour as much as possible to establish among us a Taste of polite Writing" (398). The call for polite writing, it should be added, was a thinly veiled call for an elitist literary style. In any event, if Addison and Steele have a place in literary journalism, it is rather more as practitioners of that discursive literary journalism commonly characterized as the "essay."

Daniel Defoe also occupies an ambiguous position in the evolution of modern narrative literary journalism. But unlike Addison and Steele he is a narrativist. His ambiguity arises from his indifference to bound-aries between fiction and nonfiction. For example, his *Journal of the Plague Year* is a sometime candidate as narrative literary journalism (Applegate 62). The problem with the 1722 account is that technically it is fiction: Defoe writes about an event that occurred in 1665; he was born in 1660. Still, *A Journal of the Plague Year* comes close to narrative literary journalism, revealing just how permeable boundaries could be

between fiction and nonfiction. As the eighteenth-century scholar Bonamy Dobrée observed of Defoe's *Journal:* "He warmed to the subject
of recreation; as you read, you felt it becoming ever more a personal
experience. Such *immersion* in the subject . . . fired his actualizing imagination" (427, emphasis added). By one measure, Dobrée has defined
at least part of the process for writing narrative literary journalism: "immersion" in subject matter. Immersion would prove to be one of the
defining characteristics identified by literary journalism scholar Norman Sims in "The Literary Journalists" (8–12), which appeared in
1984. Still earlier, Tom Wolfe would similarly identify "saturation" reporting as a characteristic of his form of narrative literary journalism,
the "new journalism," in his volume of that name. Thus from disparate
sectors, Wolfe as practitioner, Sims of the journalism academy, and
Dobrée of the English academy (Dobrée was also one of the general
editors, along with F. P. Wilson, of the distinguished Oxford History of
English Literature series) has come a recognition of how narrative literary journalists are similar.

If *A Journal of the Plague Year* does not quite qualify as narrative literary journalism, nonetheless Defoe did engage in narrative journalism
and narrative literary journalism. One example of the first was *The
Storm,* concerning an event of that nature that ravaged the English
coast in 1703. Whether it can be characterized as the kind of "literary"
journalism under discussion here is open to debate. But at the least
it is "narrative." The account, published in 1704, consists largely of
correspondence from throughout the kingdom from witnesses to the
storm. Defoe's role is largely as editor. When he is author his approach
is usually discursive in tying together his correspondents. However, on
occasion he provides his own narrative voice. For example, he describes the response of the townspeople of Deale, England, on the
coast, to shipwrecked mariners who amid the storm find refuge on a
sandbar at low tide, a sandbar that will disappear with the incoming
storm tide:

> It was, without doubt, a sad Spectacle to behold the poor Seamen walk-
> ing too and fro upon the Sands, to view their Postures, and the Signals
> they made for help, which, by the Assistance of [spy]Glasses was Easily
> seen from the Shore.
>   Here they had a few Hours Reprieve, but had neither Present Refresh-

> ment, nor any hopes of Life, for they were sure to be all wash'd into
> another World at the Reflux of the Tide. Some Boats are said to come
> very near them in quest of Booty, and in search of Plunder [from ship-
> wrecks], and to carry off what they could get, but no Body concern'd
> themselves for the Lives of these miserable Creatures. (199–200)

Finally, the mayor of Deale commandeers boats from the community
and rescues two hundred stranded seamen before the tide comes in
and drowns an undetermined number still on the sandbar. Like Settle's
account of the rogue Dennis Clancie, Defoe's description lacks lush
description and characterization. Once again, we detect what is largely
a chronological account.

However, an example of what has been characterized as a "pioneer"
of narrative literary journalism (Kerrane and Yagoda 21) is to be found
in Defoe's *True and Genuine Account of the Life and Actions of the Late Jonathan Wild,* published in 1725 and part of the continuing true-life literature of roguery. Indeed, the real-life Wild would eventually provide the
inspiration for Henry Fielding's novel based on the character of the
same name. But Defoe insists, as did Settle with *Major Clancie,* in an
advertising subtitle that his account of Wild is "Not made up of *Fiction*
and *Fable,* but taken from his Own Mouth, and collected from PAPERS
of his Own Writing." The need to insist, then, that an account is factual
has a very old pedigree and reflects in the emerging Augustan age a
faith in language as a mirror to phenomenon.

Like his authored sections of *The Storm,* much of Defoe's forty-page
pamphlet on Wild is often simply chronological. But on one occasion
Defoe engages in the kind of common sense–appeal to the shared common senses that is often associated with the realistic novel. In it, Wild,
who is in collusion with the thieves, undertakes to have stolen property
returned to a woman on condition of a reward, which was one of his
favorite methods of cheating people:

> Upon the Lady's going along . . . *Street,* a *Ticket-Porter,* with his Hat in his
> Hand, shows himself by the Coach-side, and the Lady taking the Hint,
> stops her Coach and lets down the Glass, and speaking to the Fellow,
> says, Would you speak with me Friend?
>   The Fellow says not a Word, but delivers into her Hand the [stolen]
> Watch with all the Trinkits and Dimonds perfectly safe; and when she
> had look'd upon it a little, gives her a Note, wherein was written nothing
> but thus in Words at length, *Eighteen Guineas.* (28)

So the real-life Jonathan Wild pursued his trade.

Taken collectively, what can be detected in the *Journal of the Plague Year, The Storm,* and *Jonathan Wild* is Defoe's wide-ranging if ambiguous exploration and probing of the not-so-clear boundaries between what we conventionally view as fiction and nonfiction, and in that sense Defoe is indeed a pioneer. As Dobrée further observes of Defoe, in what sounds like the literary journalist's litmus test, "his imagination was creative in the world of actuality. . . . It was always as a reporting journalist [that Defoe wrote], but one whose interest in facts was burningly eager, and whose imagination was like a magnifying glass to make the dim vivid" (34). For his own era he was indeed something of a narrative literary journalist.

It has become a commonplace that Defoe ushers in the modern novel with the publication of *The Life and Strange Surprising Adventures of Robinson Crusoe* in 1719. Thus he provides a convenient entrée into the influence of the modern novel on modern narrative literary journalism, at least if we conceive of modern narrative literary journalism as the adoption after the American Civil War of techniques *now* associated with the realistic novel. He did probe and explore at length those not-so-clear boundaries between fiction and nonfiction. But the relations between the two are complex, and it may be more apt to suggest that the boundaries between the modern novel and narrative literary journalism are instead firming up during the early eighteenth century (as firm as any boundaries can prove in narrative prose that aspires to the inconclusive present) in what conventionally we characterize as fiction and nonfiction (or what might, less conventionally, be characterized in the same order as overt and covert fictions given the specular nature of any mediated communication that makes of it a "fiction"). After all, narrative literary journalism of a premodern variety, such as Kemp's *Nine Daies Wonder,* takes advantage of those techniques that were slowly refined in the sixteenth and seventeenth centuries and whose antecedents can be traced back at least as far as Plato's account of the death of Socrates.

What is perhaps more important is that to some degree a reversal of stature can be detected in the fortunes of the novel and early narrative literary journalism that helps situate the two in relation to each other and other prose forms. Although some seventeenth-century narrative prose accounts approach the "threshold of the realistic middle-class novel" that emerges with Defoe in the early eighteenth century, none-theless the "dominant tradition was that of the chivalric, courtly, or pastoral romance" (Bush 53). In other words, the fictional novel before Defoe consisted largely of texts frozen timelessly in Bakhtin's distanced image of the absolute past. This changes by the time of Defoe; he takes as his overtly fictional subject the colloquial (although, in another in-stance of taking two steps forward and one step back, Defoe reinscribes his material in the distanced image of an absolute *moral* past bearing the mark of his latter-day Puritan faith in redemption through peni-tence). The fictional novel, then, in a repudiation of its critical past, has discovered the inconclusive present, something the nonfictional narrative was long indulging. As a result, it may be more appropriate to conclude that the modern fictional novel borrowed technique from nonfictional narratives and not the other way around. Nor was the rep-utation of the fictional novel up to this point very high. This is reflected in Defoe's attempt to pass off *Robinson Crusoe* as a journalism—a true, relatively contemporary account—rather than a fiction. In other words, characterizing a story as true gave it a legitimacy that the early and overtly fictional novel did not have. This practice reached well back into the seventeenth century: "At a time when rogue biographies and secret histories were much in fashion, the real or supposed authen-ticity of a story was an asset to the writer of fiction" (Sutherland 214). Consider the advertising subtitles to Settle's *Major Clancie* and Defoe's *Jonathan Wild*. Yet in what must stand as one of the great ironies in the development of narrative prose, by the second half of the eighteenth century the reverse was true, if remarks by and concerning James Bos-well, journalist, biographer, and true-life storyteller, are any indication. Samuel Johnson observed that Boswell desired to write a true-life "novel" of a notable's life (*Letters of Johnson* 290), and Boswell indicated the novel's influence on his style in keeping his journal ("Memoirs" 206). The remarks reflect the ascendancy of the fictional novel, im-plying that true-life accounts should imitate fiction. Boswell would real-ize such a "novelization" (how different from the "novelization" to be found in the earlier novels of chivalric romance!) in, among other works, his travelogue, *The Journal of a Tour to the Hebrides with Samuel Johnson LL.D.* (1786), and his biography, the *Life of Samuel Johnson* (1791). But one can detect in such a perception the early beginnings of an erroneous understanding about the relationship between narrative literary journalism and the novel, one that would be magnified and perpetuated two hundred years later by no less than the eminent new journalist of the 1960s Tom Wolfe. In his examination of the form, he notes: "The introduction of detailed realism into English Literature in the eighteenth century was like the introduction of electricity into machine technology" ("New Journalism," preface n. pag.). In fact, with the exception of interior monologue, "detailed realism" was long a part of the premodern variety of narrative literary journalism and it was the novel that borrowed from it. But Wolfe can be forgiven his misunderstanding because he was repeating what was all but assumed.

This, however, is not to belittle Defoe's overt fictions because we do see in them the early signs of interior monologue, and this provides an important distinction between the fictional novel and narrative literary journalism. When, for example, Robinson Crusoe observes a ship wrecked on the rocks of his island, he reflects:

> I cannot explain by any possible Energy of Words what a strange longing or hankering of Desires I felt in my Soul upon this Sight; breaking out sometimes thus; O that there had been but one or two; nay, or but one Soul sav'd out of this Ship, to have escap'd to me, that I might but have had one Companion, one Fellow-Creature to have spoken to me, and to have conver'd with! In all the Time of my solitary Life, I never felt so earnest, so strong a Desire after the Society of my Fellow-Creatures, or so deep a Regret at the want of it. (217)

Crusoe's reflections are perhaps not interior monologue as we have come to know it. Nonetheless, they are reflections of the feelings and thoughts he had at that moment even if recalled from the distance of time: he did have the "Desires" he struggles to describe. As it would evolve, interior monologue is a technique of the fictional novelist that can only be envied by the narrative literary journalist who must be reduced, if he or she is to remain true to being a strict "nonfictionist," to being *told* what thoughts take place in other people's minds. When one is *told*, one is already removed at least one step from the "reality" of another's consciousness (the specular, mediating nature of language is itself still another remove). On the other hand, the solace of the narrative literary journalist is that unconcealed fiction is an unabashed fake and can never make the claim that it is true to life. It is in that epistemological stalemate that unconcealed fiction and narrative literary journalism must exist.

In addition, one can detect in Boswell's example that true-life accounts could benefit from the techniques associated with the emergent modern fictional novel a critical acknowledgment that such material gains from the subjectivity of what conventionally would be called creative artistry, or what Weber calls the "shaping consciousness." As Boswell scholar Frederick A. Pottle observes of the *London Journal*, "Boswell generally knows his story something as a novelist does" (12). The result is that "great power of imaginative realization can make up for a lack of [fictional] invention" (14). With "imaginative realization" at the heart of a narrative literary journalism, we see here that the strands are separating still a little more between the information and story models, a tendency that intensifies in the next century with the evolution of journalistic style in the American newspaper.

Meanwhile, across the Atlantic, narrative accounts continued to multiply, many more than can be covered here. But among some noteworthy ones that serve as a kind of premodern narrative literary journalism could be included Sarah Kemble Knight's account of her five-months journey from Boston to New York and back in 1704 and 1705. Although Knight's account would not be published until 1825, its significance (as with the earlier account by Rowlandson of her Indian captivity) lies in its going beyond the inward-directed examinations of autobiography to provide rich sketches of contemporary colonial society, sketches fundamentally outward-directed in their social portraiture not unlike much of modern narrative literary journalism. For example, Knight recounts an argument in a tavern between drunkards so that it is impossible for her to fall asleep (reminding us perhaps of the budget motels with too-thin walls that have dotted the American traveler's landscape in recent years). Finally, one of the drunkards speaks "with such a Roreing voice and Thundering blows with the fist of wickedness on the Table, that it pierced my very head. I heartily fretted, and wish't 'um tongue tyed. . . . They kept calling for tother Gill [a four-ounce measure of liquor], which while they were swallowing, was some Intermission; But presently, like Oyle to fire, encreased the flame. I set my Candle on a chest by the bedside, and setting up, fell to me old way of composing my Resentments":

> I ask thy Aid, O Potent Rum!
> To Charm these wrangling Topers Dum.
> Thou Hast their Giddy Brains possest—
> The man confounded with the Beast—
> And I, poor I, can get no rest.
> Intoxicate them with thy fumes;
> O still their Tongues till morning comes!

"And I know not but my wishes took effect; for the dispute soon ended with t'other Dram; and so Good night!" (18–19).

What can be said of Knight's and Rowlandson's social portraiture can also be applied to Hector St. John de Crèvecoeur's *Letters from an American Farmer,* published in 1782. Although much of what Crèvecoeur writes is discursive, nonetheless he too indulges in narrative. In particular, his account of a black slave in South Carolina left to die in a cage after having killed the overseer of a plantation is as compelling as any in narrative literary journalism:

> I perceived at about six rods distance something resembling a cage, sus-
> pended to the limbs of a tree; all the branches of which appeared cov-
> ered with large birds of prey, fluttering about, and anxiously endeavour-
> ing to perch on the cage. Actuated by an involuntary motion of my
> hands, more than by any design of my mind, I fired at them; they all flew
> to a short distance, with a most hideous noise: when, horrid to think and
> painful to repeat, I perceived a negro, suspended in the cage, and left
> there to expire! I shudder when I recollect that the birds had already
> picked out his eyes, his cheek bones were bare; his arms had been at-
> tacked in several places, and his body seemed covered with a multitude
> of wounds. From the edges of the hollow sockets and from the lacera-
> tions with which he was disfigured, the blood slowly dropped, and tinged
> the ground beneath. . . . The living spectre, though deprived of his eyes,
> could still distinctly hear, and in his uncouth dialect begged me to give
> him some water to allay his thirst. . . . [Crèvecoeur offers a vessel of water
> to the slave:] with trembling hands I guided it to the quivering lips of
> the wretched sufferer. . . . He endeavored to meet it, as he instinctively
> guessed its approach by the noise it made passing through the bars of
> the cage. "Tankè, you whitè man, tankè you, putè somè poison and givè
> me." "How long have you been hanging there?" I asked him. "Two days,
> and me no die; the birds, the birds; aaah me!" (172–73)

LARZAR ZIFF, among others, notes that two dominant styles of journalism had emerged by the 1890s. One was a more recent style that

attempted a neutrality in tone, or what we now call objective reporting (146). Likewise, he identifies a "personal journalism," or a journalism of acknowledged subjectivity (147). The choice of words in the last is noteworthy given that the new journalism of the 1960s and 1970s was also often called personal journalism, among other names (Weber, "Some Sort" 20). That evolution, the separation of the information and story models, is one that can be traced from early in the nineteenth century, thus ushering in what I call the immediate antecedents to modern narrative literary journalism. From the perspective of modern journalism history, the two strains divided during the nineteenth century, partly in response to that period's positivist spirit and scientific materialism. But while an emerging objective journalism embraced that spirit, narrative literary journalism paradoxically would embrace it, then, in the end, repudiate it. The development of the two strains can be traced in part to the appearance in the 1830s of the mass-circulation newspaper and the eventual demise of the elitist partisan press.

Among the most important events, in 1833 Benjamin H. Day started the first successful penny newspaper in New York, the *Sun*. As Frank Luther Mott notes, new steam-driven presses and methods of paper-making made the penny paper possible because more issues could be printed faster and more cheaply (215, 220). Before the penny press, newspapers were largely partisan in their reports. Earlier newspapers were expensive to produce and found their audience largely among propertied classes who could afford them and which the newspapers catered to in terms of ideological sentiment. Providing a sound economic basis for the production of a mass-circulation paper that could be made available cheaply to nonpropertied classes spelled the beginning of the end for the elitist partisan press. Day's concern was to provide a news product that would appeal to lower classes, and among other efforts to that end he copied the example of the London *Morning Herald* by making police reports about assault, prostitution, drunkenness, and assorted mayhem a mainstay of the newspaper, precisely the kind of news that propertied and more genteel classes would condemn. Day, in effect, was following the advice of the Emperor Commodus some seventeen hundred years earlier. Thus yellow or sensational journalism began its ascendancy, even as partisan political reporting was deemphasized. "In short, the *Sun* broke sharply with the traditional American news concept, and began to print whatever was interesting and readable regardless of its wide significance or recognized importance. This does not mean that the paper did not treat serious subjects, but even these were not allowed the great length and heaviness which they were likely to have in the six-cent [partisan] papers" (Mott 224). In short, Day sold newspapers, pandering to the tastes of a wider audience. Thus the hold of the elitist partisan press began to loosen.

That hold was loosened still further in 1835 when James Gordon Bennett founded the *New York Herald* and in so doing enunciated a policy of political independence that, while practiced more in the breach than in reality, helped to establish the principle of the "independent press" and, more important for our purposes, an independent or "neutral" news style to suit. In the first issue, the *Herald* announced: "We shall endeavor to record facts on every public and proper subject, stripped of verbiage and coloring, with comments when suitable, just, independent, fearless, and good-tempered" (F. Hudson 433). In the "facts" one can detect precision, and in the stripping of "verbiage and coloring" one can detect conciseness, two stylistic requirements that are still offered to beginning news writers in at least one contemporary journalism textbook (Fedler 143–44). The problem is that while conciseness would propel the development of an objectified news style, the recording of facts would continue to be problematic: one man's objectified plain facts are another man's lush linguistic facts, gorgeously reflexive. Although the partisan press would remain robust up through the Civil War—one notable example is Horace Greeley's *New York Tribune*—nonetheless their time was passing. What also passed with them, however, was that in openly acknowledging their ideological slant, their publishers acknowledged their subjectivity. Whatever the faults of partisan journalism, its virtue was the possibility of a more open reflexivity. Such a reflexivity reflected in partisanship was becoming, for its time, politically incorrect.

Another measure that reflects the passing of the "traditional American news concept" can be detected in Charles Dana's statement of principles when he and other investors bought the *Sun* in 1868. The paper would "study condensation, clearness, point, and will endeavor to present its daily photography of the whole world's doings in the most luminous and lively manner" (O'Brien 199). Dana's "condensation," "clearness," and "point" are part of an early effort to present reports that are concise and precise (or specific), like the certitude of transcription seemingly assured by the photograph, even though the perception of that certitude tends to elide the photographer's subjective eye that framed the photograph in the first place.

What further emerges then is the formula for modern objective journalism, which in a reversal of narrative storytelling places the most important information in what is called the summary news lead. The summary news lead, as well as the inverted pyramid style of writing in which information is ideally presented in descending order of importance, was the result in part of the invention of the telegraph and its use during the Civil War. "It came about because correspondents could not always be sure their entire dispatch would find its way through the precarious telegraph system, and so they tried to make sure that the essential facts would arrive if the rest of the story were cut off" (Tebbel 206). Still another factor in the development of a factual or objective journalism in the post–Civil War period was that "an increased number of [newspaper] editions caused pressure for more rapid handling of local news, and the summary lead gained favor as a means of condensing stories" (Emery 228).

The summary lead is still extant today in the journalism profession and remains a standard in contemporary journalism textbooks, its chief characteristic to sum up the story while including the most important details in that summary (Fedler 139, 214). Thus we see the emergence of a journalistic formula that depends on a concise-precise stylistic balance. The summary lead fulfills the requirements of Schudson's information model because its purpose is not to tell a story but rather to provide information that is persuasively beyond dispute. As Fred Fedler acknowledges, "the lead immediately reveals every major detail" (214). The aspiration of the summary lead, then, is to answer all major questions. But by doing so its tendency is to deny questioning and thus involvement on the part of the reader, unlike the narrative, or story, which attracts the reader by what the reader does not know and can only question. In the development of the objective style, the epistemological gulf has widened between reader and a hypothetically objectified world, a chasm that has two consequences. First, the style pretends that the world can be objectified, eliding such issues as subjectivity and the filtering nature of language. Second, because it engages in summarization, it engages in the elimination or distilling out of distinctive differences implicit in the randomness of the phenomenal world, or as Nietzsche characterized it, volatilization. In a manner of speaking, then, objective objectified news style is aspiring to the Platonic ideal. But one political or ideological consequence, as Trachtenberg has observed, was that in making life a distant and unattainable object, it disempowered the reader from experience (*Incorporation* 124–25). As a result, such a style had a hidden if unconscious political agenda. As Schudson suggests, the development of a factual objectified news style was based in part on the belief that the world could be reported factually, a result of the prevailing positivist belief that science could cure society's ills (71–72). Ultimately, that is an ideological position.

A consequence of the ascendancy of the objective objectified style is that by 1912 and the sinking of the *Titanic* such objectification had achieved a level of dispassion in the extreme, so alienated had the reader's subjectivity become from perception of the phenomenal: "The admission that the *Titanic,* the biggest steamship in the world, had been sunk by an iceberg and had gone to the bottom of the Atlantic, probably carrying more than 1,400 of her passengers and crew with her, was made at the White Star Line offices, 9 Broadway, at 8:20 o'clock last night" ("Titanic Sinks"). The "admission" speaks of course to the mediation by language in comprehending the phenomenal. But in that linguistic gulf can be detected the wide divide between objectified phenomenon permitted to be perceived only at a distance. The admission, at 9 Broadway, at 8:20 o'clock in the evening can only diminish the original incident as beyond subjective appreciation and is in sharp contrast, for example, to Thomas Hardy's own imaginative—and subjective—visit to the *Titanic*'s grave at the bottom of the Atlantic when he says that "Over mirrors Meant / To glass the opulent / The sea-worm crawls—grotesque, slimed, dumb, indifferent" (7). Hardy's rhetorical strategy could not help but elicit subjective reaction when human ambition, and indeed hubris given that the *Titanic* was believed unsinkable, has been reduced to one in which the sea-worm of the dark depths is indifferent. While the indifference of a factual or objective objectified news style, derived from 9 Broadway in this instance, is numbing to consciousness, the indifference of the imagined sea-worm crawling across the human vanity of a looking glass is sobering if not chilling in and to the existential deep. Such is the difference between an objective news and literature, and it speaks to the shortcomings of objectification and to what narrative literary journalists ultimately oppose.

WHILE AN objective objectified news style on the order of the information model—the plainest of the plain style—was developing in nineteenth-century American journalism practice, a more subjective style was reflected in the developing feature story. By the end of the nineteenth century it may have been overshadowed by an ascendant factual objectified style; nonetheless it was the latest variation on an ancient theme that demonstrated a more flagrant shaping consciousness. At the same time, a narrative literary journalism continued to be written in its own right.

Precursors to the modern feature story are to be found in the anecdotes of police news that Day ran in the *Sun*:

> Wm. Luvoy got drunk because yesterday was so devilish warm. Drank nine glasses of brandy and water, and swore he'd be cursed if he wouldn't drink nine more as quick as he could raise the money to buy it with. He would like to know what right the magistrate had to interfere with his private affairs. Fined $1—forgot his pocketbook, and was sent over to bridewell.
>
> Bridget McMunn got drunk and threw a pitcher at Mr. Ellis, of 53 Ludlow st. Bridget said she was the mother of three little orphans—God Bless their dear souls—and if she went to prison they would choke to death for want of something to eat. Committed. ("Police Office" n. pag.)

Aside from their sensational nature, the accounts are fundamentally stories because they do not begin with a summary of the outcome of the trials. Instead, the accounts begin at the beginning of the story, drunkenness in these cases, and the reader initially must question what will be the conclusion. In their own modest way, then, such sketches engage reader subjectivity with what the reader does not know. In the case of the penny press, such reports might be socially lowbrow but if nothing else they indicate the durability of highly colored (and thus more openly subjective) storytelling in true accounts. The conclusion in these examples from the *Sun* may become formulaically predictable because all the accused are "Committed," but there is a difference between predictability of a conclusion the reader does not know and telling the reader the conclusion at the beginning by summing up a factual or objective story. For example, in the objective style the McMunn passage might be written as follows:

> Manhattan—A judge jailed Bridget McMunn yesterday after she was found guilty of public drunkenness and assault.
>
> She pleaded for leniency, saying that if she were sent to prison there would be no one to take care of her three children.
>
> The judge found her guilty of public intoxication and throwing a pitcher at Mr. Ellis, of 53 Ludlow St.
>
> McMunn warned the judge that her children, whom she characterized as "orphans," could starve to death if she were incarcerated.

The emergence of the fully developed feature story is often credited to Charles A. Dana. As managing editor at Horace Greeley's *New York Tribune,* and later, after he bought the *Sun,* Dana "added two improvements. One was what came to be called the 'human interest story,' which he virtually invented. The other was a sharpened sense of news value" (Tebbel 220). The first was the "personal journalism" observed by Ziff that was "devotedly echoed" in newspapers around the country (147). We can detect once again that boundaries between feature stories and a narrative literary journalism are indeed extremely fine. As Ziff notes, "personal journalism encouraged the picturing of . . . incidents in an individually colorful style" (151). Such a prescription, of course, can be applied whole to narrative literary journalism.

Thus the emerging feature story was one influence on narrative literary journalism. However, throughout the nineteenth century nonfiction as artful narrative was being practiced as part of an unbroken tradition. One example is Augustus Baldwin Longstreet's Georgia sketches, which first appeared in Georgia newspapers in the 1830s. When they were collected in his *Georgia Scenes, Characters, Incidents, &c.* and published in 1840, his intention was clearly literary *and* journalistic when in his preface, he noted: "I used some little art in order to recommend them to the readers of my own times," while also noting, "some of the scenes are as literally true as the frailties of memory would allow them to be" (iii). Not all are true, but those stories that are true are clearly a narrative literary journalism, appearing as they did before the human-interest feature story emerged in the 1860s. What is evident is that writers such as Longstreet passed comfortably and indifferently between fictional and nonfictional modes whose division can be viewed largely as a modern invention. Another example of this confusion be-tween fiction and nonfiction is reflected in Herman Melville's South Sea account *Typee*. The uncertainty is reflected today in those two arbi-ters of canonical American literature, *The Oxford Companion to American Literature* and the *Norton Anthology of American Literature*. The *Oxford Com-panion* characterizes *Typee* as a "fictional narrative" (Hart 681), whereas the *Norton Anthology* characterizes the account as "the story of his [Mel-ville's] captivity by a Polynesian tribe" (Baym et. al. 1:2146).

Melville's account does point to the extensive travel literature that reflects more broadly a healthy narrative journalism for the era. Among them is the now-obscure *Travels through the South of France . . .* by the all-but-forgotten American "Lt. Col. Pinkney" published in 1809 ("Fete Champetre" 674). Similar to antecedents in the seventeenth and eighteenth centuries such as Crèvecoeur, Rowlandson, and Brad-ford, Pinkney frames what he sees according to generalizing precepts, when he notes, for example, that French women were marked by "more fancy, more taste, and more elegance" than English women but that English women were more "handsome" (676). In a sense, by mak-ing conclusive judgments, such generalizations reflect the "distanced image of the absolute past" and recall—and indeed are descendants of—the sketches in the popular character books of the seventeenth century by John Earle and Thomas Overbury. Whether it was the ana-lytical generalization of a Pinkney or the didactic and religious general-izations of a Rowlandson and Bradford, writers were still attaching the ship of their lives to totalizations that were to determine how they were supposed to view the world. But of course phenomena always provide the exception. So even as Pinkney generalizes about human types, he is confronted with phenomenal ambiguity and acknowledges as much in a statement that anticipates literary realism, literary naturalism, and modern narrative literary journalism. In the same sketch where he characterizes French ladies during a fete, he also describes a peasant boy who is a self-taught artist. The local senator greatly admires the boy for his talent and takes him into his household, promising to give him a formal education in art. Yet the same boy is described, when having been thrown accidentally from a horse, of taking a knife from his pocket and repeatedly stabbing the beast. As Pinkney notes, "How inconsistent is what is called character!" That of course is the point of the literary realist's characterizations: that they are inconsistent, or ambiguous, reflecting the fluidity and open-endedness of life and not presenting the generalizations of the seventeenth-century character book. This can also be detected in Plato's account of Crito as both executioner and humane individual.

Noteworthy among other journalistic narratives in the mid-nineteenth century are Henry David Thoreau's four sketches about Cape Cod published in *Putnam's Monthly Magazine* in 1855. Thoreau announces his intention to narrow the gulf between himself and, in this case, a natural world that is as much metaphor as substance when he says in the first line, "Wishing to get a better view than I had yet had of the ocean . . . I made a visit to Cape Cod" (3). But the sketches are not solely a transcendental interpretation, because they are filled with scene construction, character development, dialogue, and what those three point to, a social allegory. Of the opening shipwreck, Thoreau writes:

> A little further on a crowd of men was collected around the mate of the *St. John,* who was telling his story. He was a slim-looking youth, who spoke of the captain as the master, and seemed a little excited. He was saying that when they jumped into the boat, she filled, and, the vessel lurching, the weight of the water in the boat caused the painter to break, and so they were separated. Whereat one man came away, saying:—
>
> "Well, I don't see but he tells a straight story enough. You see, the weight of the water in the boat broke the painter. A boat full of water is very heavy,"—and so on, in a loud and impertinently earnest tone, as if he had a bet depending on it, but had no humane interest in the matter.
>
> Another, a large man, stood near by upon a rock, gazing into the sea, and chewing large quids of tobacco, as if that habit were forever confirmed with him. (10–11)

The mate is "a little excited," the speaker following him talks in a "loud and impertinently earnest tone," and the "large man" as he stares into the sea chews his tobacco as if the "habit were forever confirmed with him." Thus they are characterized. Indeed, the middle speaker is reminiscent some forty years later of an account by Stephen Crane in which he describes a simple street scene in New York where a man passes out in public, perhaps from an epileptic fit, and a crowd gathers: "Meanwhile others with magnificent passions for abstract statistical information were questioning the boy. 'What's his name?' 'Where does he live?'" ("When Man Falls a Crowd Gathers" 106). Both Crane and Thoreau are providing social allegories about those who deflect trauma by, in the one case, evaluating what is abstractly statistical and, in the other, acting as if he had a bet depending on it but had no humane interest in the matter. By means of such irony Thoreau and Crane confront their readers with the issue of subjectivities that avoid engaging with the objectified Other. Such characterizations present oppositionally one allegory of what so much narrative literary journalism is about: the attempt to engage subjectivities.

This also helps to explain in part why serialization of the manuscript in *Putnam's* ceased abruptly after chapter 4. Thoreau's editor (and friend) George William Curtis feared that subsequent chapters would offend Cape Cod residents, and Thoreau, refusing to agree to changes, withdrew the remainder of the chapters from publication (Theroux xii–xiii). Among his characterizations, he notes an imbecile's mutterings, rejects portions of a breakfast contaminated with tobacco juice by his spitting host, and vomits after eating clams, much to the amusement of that host (104–14). Clearly, to the genteel sensibility of Brahmin society, such profane matters of the open-ended present were disagreeable.

Moreover, such "traveling" journalists were being moved to social action as would those later in the century. For example, Richard Henry Dana Jr. in his *Two Years before the Mast* recounts life at sea, departing in 1834 to sail around Cape Horn to California, and then after spending a year gathering seal skins there, returning again by way of the Horn to the East Coast in 1836. *Two Years before the Mast* was published in 1840, and Dana's acknowledged purpose was to present "the life of a common sailor at sea as it is,—the light and the dark together" (xvi). Thus like modern literary journalists, his intention was to gain insight into the social Other, no small matter given that Dana was a Boston blueblood. The extent of his success is reflected in a review in the seminal *Cyclopaedia of American Literature* published in 1855 by the Duyckinck brothers, the most comprehensive work on the subject up to that time. As the review notes of the book, "It is life itself,—a passage of intense unexaggerated reality" (620). "Dark" insight Dana does indeed gain, witnessing fellow seaman flogged, and as a consequence he vows in *Two Years before the Mast* "to redress the grievances and relieve the sufferings of that class of beings with whom my lot had so long been cast" (108). Like many narrative literary journalists who would follow after, he was politicized by the experience and indeed would publish in the *American Jurist* his article "Cruelty to Seamen" in 1839, the year he graduated from Harvard Law School. Two years later he published *The Seaman's Friend,* which instructed seamen on their legal rights. Ultimately, such were the consequences of engaging his blueblood subjectivity with ordinary seamen.

BY THE 1890s the journalist in America would find him- or herself caught in a conflict between the two journalistic models, or between a stylistic requirement to present the news as concisely and neutrally as possible, and a requirement inherent in the journalist's mission— namely that if there were to be a full accounting, it would have to be as fully and colorfully detailed as possible. Therein lies an unbroken tradition. But the problem with this last—a mission requiring a "full" accounting—is that it begs the epistemological question, How can one be fully detailed? Once the question is asked, the author's subjectivity emerges from background to foreground in the recognition that given a phenomenological world's infinite indeterminacy, any selection of the details involves selection that can ultimately and only be the consequence of individual cognition, something reflected in still-earlier versions of narrative journalism such as Bradford's and Longstreet's. This is true of both modern journalistic models, of course, but to differing degrees. It is the insistence, whether conscious or not, of a more openly shaping consciousness in the story or narrative model that helps to distinguish it from the information or discursive model. Within that story model also lies the conventional feature story, the older tradition of narrative journalism, and sensational versions of true-life narratives. The difference is that a modern narrative literary journalism attempts to avoid formulaic emotion and the emphasis on differences between people, whether cultural, racial, or social. As Connery noted of the relationship between conventional feature stories and narrative literary journalism, "although some literary journalism bore a striking resemblance to what was coming to be known as newspaper feature writing, it eschewed the evolving formula of that article type, with its predictability and clichés" ("Third Way" 6).

In any event, caught between the demands of factual objectified news and a more subjective version, we know the choices narrative literary journalists made. The story or narrative model has a long and venerable history, which is important for establishing the pedigree of narrative literary journalism among the different narrative models. In fact, in an uncanny historical echo of the *acta populi Romani* some eighteen hundred years later, John B. Bogart, city editor of the *Sun* from 1873 to 1890, would give advice to a young reporter that has become legend: "When a dog bites a man, that is not news, because it happens so often. But if a man bites a dog, that is news" (O'Brien 241). The advice is similar to the account in the *acta populi Romani* of the dog that follows its executed master's body out into the Tiber River. The personification of the Roman dog's behavior and the "caninization" of the American man's behavior in Bogart's advice both point to the shaping consciousness that narrative literary journalists would openly embrace.

In addition, we can see at work in the two strains of journalism the kinds of ideological concerns that would eventually be reflected in the development of objective objectified news and narrative literary journalism, and that raise a fundamental epistemological question, How best can one account for the phenomenal world? In principle, objective news would seem to serve the purpose better because of its announced intention to exclude partisanship. But as several critics have noted, objective news paradoxically disempowers readers by excluding their participation in such discourse. Narrative literary journalism offers more of an opportunity for reader engagement precisely because its purpose is to narrow the distance between subjectivity and the object, not divorce them. By such a means then, or by vicariously experiencing the life of the disenfranchised Other, narrative literary journalists not infrequently moved from an epistemological problem to a social one and found themselves politicized as they challenged the disenfranchisement posed by prevailing political, economic, and social ideologies, among others. Thus they were able to resist the critical closure imposed by the taken-for-granted assumptions of those ideologies, not unlike Governor Bradford of Plymouth Plantation, who unwittingly found himself beyond the spiritual closure of God's latter-day Eden on Earth. This is not to suggest that objective news is incapable of challenging prevailing ideologies. But its strength is also its liability because in "neutering" its readers, they become disempowered. Nor is this to suggest that one form of journalism is superior to the other. That has been precisely the problem in the historic privileging of the information or discursive model over the story model, and more specifically of objective news over narrative literary journalism in our own century. Rather, given that the strengths of both are also their liabilities, such a conclusion argues in favor of a diversity of journalisms in the problematic attempt to interpret the phenomenal world. This was something Plato the objectifying and idealizing philosopher understood when he lowered his eye from the ideal and established his gaze on the phenomenal as a sometime narrative literary journalist.

In the late nineteenth century, Lafcadio Hearn, Stephen Crane, Hutchins Hapgood, and Lincoln Steffens, among others, were eschewing Platonic abstraction and what was becoming the journalistic ideal in favor of the concrete particular. Indeed, Hapgood and Steffens had formally repudiated the neo-Platonic ideal. In the 1880s Steffens and in the early 1890s Hapgood had gone to Germany to study latter-day Platonism in the forms of Hegelian ethics and aesthetics. Instead, they discovered the sensationalism of a bohemian lifestyle. The danger, however, for such future narrative literary journalists during this period, or as a future advocate of the form as in the case of Steffens, was that they would lose their way solely in sensationalism, because sensationalism is still another version of objectification, which is explored in greater detail in the next chapter.

4 Narrative Literary Journalism, Sensational Journalism, and Muckraking

ALAN TRACHTENBERG'S examination of Stephen Crane's city sketches, which has achieved all but canonical status among scholars of narrative literary journalism, establishes an opposition between Crane's work, which he suggests results in an "exchange of subjectivities," and Jacob Riis's *How the Other Half Lives,* which Trachtenberg lumps among "sensational" journalistic accounts because "the reader is not permitted to cross into the inner world of the slums—into its own point of view" ("Experiments" 273, 271–72). Yet *A Sourcebook of American Literary Journalism: Representative Writers in an Emerging Genre* includes critical articles on both Crane (Robertson 69–80) and Riis (Good 81–90) as practitioners of literary journalism. Moreover, the *Sourcebook*'s editor, Thomas B. Connery, cites Trachtenberg's examination of Crane in his introductory essay to the collection (5). The question is, then, do Riis and Crane belong in the same league as Connery's collection would suggest? Or does Riis engage in sensationalism? Or is he a mere muckraker, whereas Crane provides profound insight into the human condition, at least by one standard reflected in Crane's election to the traditional literary canon?

Such problems are not unique to Crane and Riis. One scholar has suggested that Jack London's *People of the Abyss* qualifies as narrative literary journalism because of the use of techniques associated with realistic fiction and the "intentional injection" of the reporter's subjectivity into the report (R. Hudson 1, 4). Yet on the same page he acknowledges that London's account of the life of the poor and unemployed in the East End of London at the turn of the century reflects "muckraker indignation." Thus does it also qualify as muckraking journalism? Moreover, does *The People of the Abyss* also qualify as yellow sensationalism, as I suggest, given the sweeping and patronizing generalizations London engages in in the service of his public commitment to Socialism: "It is incontrovertible that the [city] children grow up into rotten adults, without virility or stamina, a weak-kneed, narrow-chested, listless breed, that crumples up and goes down in the brute struggle for life with the invading hordes from the country" (31). Clearly, the resident of the slum has no chance. Is such a passage narrative literary journalism? Hudson would suggest yes because he cites the passage in support of that claim (19). Is it also muckraking? Or sensationalism? All? Some of each?

In this journalistic stew of similar and different discourses, where one leaves off and the other begins is not always clear: sensational journalism can clearly bear a resemblance to and thus "soil" the aesthetic ambitions of narrative literary journalism. Narrative literary journalism can bear a resemblance to muckraking, and muckraking can clearly bear a resemblance to sensational journalism. Furthermore, narrative literary journalism has been working at a disadvantage since its modern emergence during the post–Civil War period, if only by virtue of the fact that as an area of scholarly study it is the most recent, having been largely ignored by scholars until the impressionistic new journalism of the 1960s. Thus any consideration of it takes place in the substantial shadows cast by the weightier scholarship on sensational and muckraking journalisms.

As a consequence, if narrative literary journalism is not to be mistaken for sensational or muckraking journalism there is a need to understand what makes it distinctive among these journalistic discourses as well as other nonfiction discourses. But equally important is a need to understand the overlapping and mutual concerns of these discourses if we are to better establish a historical site for the form that despite increasing recognition still "remains largely unexplored by scholars" (Connery, "Research Review" 1). This chapter attempts to better situate narrative literary journalism as rhetorical practice among

these other nonfiction prose forms, as well as in its relationship to the
more traditional and discursive essay. It also attempts to establish more
fully why sensational yellow journalism is in its own way an objectified
journalism and how the emergence of modern narrative literary journalism after the Civil War was not only a reaction against factual or objective journalism but also a reaction against yellow journalism. These
efforts are necessary not only because such competing journalistic
forms were prominent in turn-of-the-century publications but also because they continue to play prominent roles—if the content of the *National Enquirer,* the *New Yorker,* and award-winning muckraking investigations in recent times are any indication.

In this chapter, I explore the form's relationship to traditional rhetorical modes and the more traditional discursive essay, examine narrative literary journalism's relationship to sensational yellow journalism,
and probe its ambiguous relationship to muckraking.

One means for understanding the similarities and differences between narrative literary journalism and other nonfiction forms is to
locate them among different—and adapted—modes of discourse not
only because narrative literary journalism is a problematic terminology
but also because not all nonfiction forms operate in the same mode. I
simplify the four traditional modes of discourse (exposition, argument,
narration, and description) into two, discursive (including exposition
and argument) and narrative (including temporal narration and spatial description). In doing so, however, I do not mean to reinscribe
their status as separate classifications as was the practice when they
were formulated in their basic modern form by Alexander Bain in
1866 (Connors 362–64). Instead, I simplify the modes into two because such categories help to make one initial and preliminary distinction in separating different nonfictional forms.

One of the problems with the designation narrative literary journalism for the texts under discussion here and used by scholars such as
Connery, Kerrane, and Yagoda is that it tends to move to the margins
such writers as the essayist H. L. Mencken, who can be said to have
engaged in still another form of literary journalism reflected in the
more traditional discursive essay. Such a distinction is important because while an argument can be made that the discursive essay is also
literary journalism, to do so runs two risks. First, it risks critical rebuke

from elitist literary circles for reducing to the lowly level of a journalism what has, or at least once was viewed as having, a pedigree and lineage worthy of poetry and drama, and one that was viewed in the eighteenth and first half of the nineteenth centuries as being the "dominating form" above the novel, the genre of a rising middle class (Pattee, *History* 417). Second, and as a corollary to the first, placing literary journalism as the kind examined here next to its better-known discursive sibling runs the risk of continuing to marginalize it in the larger shadow of the scholarship of that sibling.

Ultimately, the issue is one of distinguishing between discursive and narrative modes. This is not to suggest that such boundaries are hard and fast. Indeed, literary journalism as narrative is often freely discursive. And the discursive mode known conventionally as the reflective "essay" does not hesitate to draft for use narrative techniques of the kind derived from realistic novel-writing. Although Mencken is a largely discursive writer, he freely utilizes concrete imagery commonly associated with novel-writing in, for example, the following assault on literary critics who have established themselves as a critical aristocracy: "It would ruin him equally to wear celluloid collars, or to move to Union Hill, N.J., or to serve ham and cabbage at his table. And it would ruin him, too, to drink coffee from his saucer, or to marry a chambermaid with a gold tooth" (68). The auxiliary function of "would," the past tense of the verb "will," converts the concrete images of celluloid collars, ham and cabbage, drinking coffee with a saucer, and marrying a chambermaid with a gold tooth to a conditional result from which Mencken can draw his discursive conclusions. This would be in a narrative mode if the images were cast in the active voice of the simple past tense: "It ruined him to wear."

The issue is one of modal emphasis, and a writer who comfortably straddles the messy boundary between discursive and narrative modes is E. B. White. In one of his 1938 articles during his brief sojourn at *Harper's Magazine* he describes shingling his roof at his Maine farm and in doing so engages in the kind of description associated with novel-writing:

> Long before the coming of the cold I was on the barn roof, laying clear cedar shingles, five inches to the weather. My neighbors' roofs all showed signs of activity, so I built some staging and mounted my own beanstalk

to see what I could see. It seems a long while ago that I was up there, hanging on by the seat of my pants: those clear days at the edge of frost, with a view of pasture, woods, sea, hills, and my pumpkin patch stretched out below in serene abundance. I stayed on the barn, steadily laying shingles, all during the days when Mr. Chamberlain, M. Daladier, the Duce and the Führer were arranging their horse trade. (20)

As White mends his roof, he finds a vantage point from which to meditate on world affairs, and in so doing he moves from a narrative to a discursive mode. Throughout the article he continues to traverse back and forth between the two modes.

Distinguishing between a mode—discursive—that Mencken largely engages in, versus a mode—narrative—that, say, a Stephen Crane largely engaged in is not to suggest that what Mencken wrote is not a literary journalism. This has been part of the problem with much recent critical usage of the terminology, which has been applied largely to narrative texts—whether Crane's New York City sketches of the 1890s or more recent fare such as Truman Capote's *In Cold Blood*. Instead, it may be more appropriate to suggest that there exist a narrative literary journalism *and* a discursive literary journalism, or a literary narrative journalism and a literary discursive journalism if the critical examination of the latter two emphasizes modalities, a discussion that thus far has been largely absent from scholarly considerations of literary journalism. Nor should such modal categories be viewed as having hard and fast boundaries. As reflections of strategies for negotiating meaning, they might be better viewed as being in ongoing negotiation with each other. Therefore, the issue of identifying texts by Crane and Mencken is one that comes down to discovering which modalities predominate—with writers like E. B. White proving frustratingly challenging to the traditional rhetorician tied to a rigid canon of modes. Such an understanding should help distinguish between the more traditional essay and narrative nonfiction and journalism.

While narrative literary journalism, sensational journalism, and muckraking can draft for use the techniques of novel-writing, clearly the latter two are not bound to do so. Instead, they can adhere more closely to a discursive mode that to varying degrees bears a closer relationship to Schudson's "information model" of news (89). Conventionally we would call such examples of muckraking journalism objective news because they persuade by virtue of the presentation of facts, or as Walter Benjamin has described the problem, such news persuades because "information . . . lays claim to prompt verifiability" ("Story-teller" 88–89). Such is also the case with yellow or sensational journal-ism when the *style* of the information model is discursively *mimicked*. One notorious example of this is the incendiary report in William Ran-dolph Hearst's *New York Journal* on the sinking of the battleship USS *Maine* in 1898:

> Assistant Secretary of the Navy Theodore Roosevelt says he is convinced that the destruction of the Maine in Havana Harbor was not an accident.
>
> The Journal offers a reward of $50,000 for exclusive evidence that will convict the person, persons or Government criminally responsible for the destruction of the American battle ship and the death of 258 of its crew.
>
> The suspicion that the Maine was deliberately blown up grows stronger every hour. Not a single fact to the contrary has been produced.
>
> Captain Sigsbee, of the Maine, and Consul-General Lee both urge that public opinion be suspended until they have completed their inves-tigation. They are taking the course of tactful men who are convinced that there has been treachery.
>
> Washington reports very late that Captain Sigsbee had feared some such event as a hidden mine. The English cipher code was used all day yesterday by the naval officers in cabling instead of the usual American code. (Zalinski 1)

Clearly, the rhetorical choices are designed to incite outrage or to sensationalize: even as American officials are reported to caution "that public opinion be suspended until they have completed their investiga-tion," the officials are cited by the *Journal* as "men who are convinced that there has been treachery." Throughout, the article reflects a wounded editorial self-righteousness gratuitously transferred to the American officials. In an appeal to the information model that mimics Benjamin's notion of "prompt verifiability," the author indeed appeals to "facts" by noting that "not a single fact to the contrary has been produced." Ultimately, what is conveniently elided is that not a single fact has been produced to support the claim that the USS *Maine* was "deliberately blown up." Guilt, clearly, has been assumed before trial.

Similarly revealing is the conclusion of the banner headline and how it was arrived at: "Destruction of the war ship Maine was the work of an enemy." One man, Roosevelt, was "convinced" of what then becomes a general "suspicion" that "grows stronger every hour" because "not a single fact to the contrary has been produced" so that "tactful" officials are equally convinced "there has been treachery." The result, since there are no supporting facts, is the assumption of guilt, or that the sinking "*was* the work of an enemy" (emphasis added). But while the front-page report was sensational, it mimicked the attributes of the information model, even if the information was tainted, because it was discursive rather than narrative. It is here that the four older, more traditional rhetorical modalities prove helpful in revealing a negotiation taking place between exposition and argument. Schudson's suggested information model is fundamentally expository, its rhetorical intention exposition of verifiable experience. However, the *Maine* example is tainted strongly by the argumentative mode in its attempt to incite emotional outrage and induce emotional persuasion.

The information or discursive emphasis can be reflected similarly in muckraking journalism as Lincoln Steffens would do, for example, in his 1903 exposé of political corruption in Minneapolis. This was just one of his "Shame of the Cities" muckraking investigations, and the article's largely discursive mode is reflected in its lead: "Wherever anything extraordinary is done in American municipal politics, whether for good or for evil, you can trace it almost invariably to one man. The people do not do it. Neither do the 'gangs,' 'combines,' or political parties. These are but instruments by which bosses (not leaders; we Americans are not led, but driven) rule the people, and commonly sell them out" (42). Steffens then proceeds to an exposition of the facts in support of his thesis, namely that the mayor of Minneapolis was receiving payoffs from criminals. Although the lead reflects an argumentative mode (as does, in principle, any thesis that is making a claim that must yet be demonstrated) with its sweeping generalization about "American municipal politics" and "Americans," the exposé is ultimately expository in marshaling phenomenal evidence such as the famous "Big Mitt Ledger" Steffens obtained that revealed payoffs to the mayor (*Autobiography* 381). In this instance, the expository and argumentative modes are engaged in a negotiation, but the verified substance of the exposé gives it largely an expository nature that places it in Schudson's information model.

Sensational journalism and muckraking, then, can occupy a modal space outside the boundaries of literary journalism of the narrative kind when they are largely discursive. But that leaves untouched those discourses that utilize largely (but not necessarily exclusively) a narrative mode, or as Connery has said, a text that "is shaped and transformed into a story or sketch by use of narrative and rhetorical techniques generally associated with fiction" (*Sourcebook* xiv). It is in a consideration of what narrative literary journalism attempts to do epistemologically as opposed to sensational journalism that such discourses can be further distinguished, even if in some instances they share the narrative mode. This is because narrative literary journalism attempts to narrow the distance between the subjectivity of the journalist and reader on the one hand and an objectified world on the other. From another vantage point, such reportage prompts an emotional response as a result of descriptive tropes that reader, journalist, and objectified human can generally be expected to have in common.

Such an epistemological intention to close the distance between subjectivity and an objectified world serves to illustrate what separates literary journalism from sensational journalism in the latter's varieties. Even though sensationalism can incorporate the techniques of novel-writing, its purpose is not to overcome the epistemological gulf between one's subjectivity and what has been objectified as Other. As critic, photographer, and writer John Berger has noted, sensational photography engages in "the reducing of the experience of the other into a pure framed spectacle from which the viewer, as a safe and separate spectator, obtains a thrill or a shock" ("Another Way" 63). The same can be applied to yellow sensational journalism and is appropriate in that both mediums—photography and narrative text—attempt to draw on the common sense–appeal of the shared common senses. The example of the sinking of the *Maine* illustrates the discursive point. Berger's definition of sensational photography can be applied to the fundamentally argumentative report. Similarly, such observations can apply to journalism in a narrative mode. For example, June Howard notes that in a sketch by Frank Norris from 1897 the conception of the "brute" was reinforced as Other (80). The title and subject of Norris's article illustrates the narrative point. Called "Brute," it is an account of a common laborer going home at the end of the day:

> He had been working all day in a squalid neighborhood by the gas works and coal yards, surrounded by lifting cranes, pile drivers, dredging ma-

chines, engines of colossal, brutal strength, where all about him were immense blocks of granite, tons of pig iron; everything had been enormous, crude, had been huge in weight, tremendous in power, gigantic in size.

By long association with such things he had become like them, huge, hard, brutal, strong with a crude, blind strength, stupid, unreasoning. (81)

In describing the workman as "crude," "stupid," "hard," "unreasoning," and "brutal," Norris has failed to close the distance between his (and by implication his reader's) subjectivity and the Other as object. Thus Norris has reduced the experience of the Other into a spectacle from which the viewer, as a safe and separate spectator, can obtain a thrill or shock. Norris's condescending treatment, in a sense, reenacts an elitist conceit and is in sharp contrast to other narrative literary journalism, such as Lafcadio Hearn's empathetic sketches of African American life on the Cincinnati levee.

Such differences between sensational journalism and narrative literary journalism notwithstanding, it is not inconceivable that writers may at times be more successful in overcoming by degree the separation from Other, while at other times they may consciously or unconsciously reinforce differences between self and the object. One example of the former is Norris's account of detectives awaiting the arrival of a sailing vessel carrying a man wanted in Australia for murder: "There were four beds made up on the floor of the room, and Conroy was dozing in one, pretending to read 'Phra the Phoenician,' the whiles. The other detectives sat about a gas stove, smoking. They were for the most part big, burly men, with red faces, very jovial and not at all like the sleuths you expected to see" (*Frank Norris* 120). In this example, Norris mutes the tendency to engage in the kind of rhetoric that so thoroughly reduced the character in "Brute" to the brutish Other. Instead Norris has imaginatively engaged readers with what their own common senses can generally tell them while for the most part avoiding value-laden adjectives that would diminish the detectives as cardboard cutouts. Indeed, Norris consciously takes issue with the sensationalizing stereotypes a reader of the 1890s might expect to have of "sleuths." The "brutalizing" of the Other has been kept to a relative minimum.

Even Norris's sketch "Brute" could have been redeemable, at least

in part, as narrative literary journalism. After Norris frames the workman as "hard," "brutal," "crude," "stupid," and "unreasoning," he describes the workman's actions: "He was on his way home now, his immense hands dangling half-open at his sides." The workman discovers
a violet as he is walking, stoops down, and plucks it. "It was a beautiful
thing, redolent with the scent of the woods, suggestive of everything
pretty and delicate." When the workman appears to be uncertain as to
what to make of the violet, "instinctively his hand carried it to his
mouth; he ground it between his huge teeth and slowly ate it. It was
the only way he knew." It is the gratuitous and, more important, patronizing valuation of the final sentence of the sketch that reinscribes
the Other in the established value-laden frame of the brute: "It was the
only way he knew." Either the workman is to be pitied or simply dismissed as a brute. In any event, the workman remains the Other. If
Norris had exercised the kind of rhetorical understatement that an Ernest Hemingway or a Stephen Crane was famous for by cutting the last
sentence, he would have opened up the conclusion to a resonance of
meanings: "instinctively his hand carried it to his mouth; he ground it
between his huge teeth and slowly ate it." While of course the workman
could still be viewed as a "brute" or someone to be pitied, he could
equally be viewed as someone who takes delight in the offerings of nature at the end of a long workday, made all the more poignant by its
taking place in an urban setting seemingly hostile to nature. It is not
unlike the way children in the forest might break a branch of sassafras
or pluck a sprig of mint to chew or grind between their teeth. Indeed,
perhaps unknown to Norris is that violets are edible and historically
have been used as breath fresheners, expectorants, and antiseptics, as
well as garnishes for soups and punches, and their petals can be sug-
ared for decorating pastries or for adding "verve" to jams ("Violet"
498–99). Such an empathic understanding is what narrative literary
journalism is about, and indeed the "brute" may have known something Norris did not.

BERGER'S DISTINCTION, then, helps to differentiate clearly between
sensationalism and literary journalism in narrative modes. However,
the relationship between these two forms and muckraking is more ambiguous. Part of the problem is that muckraking journalism has always

been tainted by sensationalism, as one contemporary journalism history notes: "Some, like *McClure's* [magazine], were investigative magazines containing well-researched articles based on fact. Others jumped on the bandwagon with sensational stories lacking in research and detail" (Folkerts and Teeter 323). There is, of course, an important biographical connection here, too. Lincoln Steffens was instrumental in encouraging a narrative literary journalism at the *Commercial Advertiser*, what he called in his autobiography the "descriptive sketch" (242); he moved on to muckraking, taking a position as a reporter and managing editor at *McClure's Magazine* where in October 1902 he published "Tweed Days in St. Louis," an exposé of corruption in that city. His article would be followed a month later by Ida Tarbell's "History of the Standard Oil Company" in the same publication; the two are often credited with ushering in the era of "muckraking" journalism.[1] They receive the credit even though Steffens would acknowledge that muckraking long had been practiced by journalists (*Autobiography* 357).

What remains significant is the perceived *qualitative* difference between what was published in *McClure's* and other magazines clearly engaged in muckraking. The emphasis on sound news gathering, as Folkerts and Teeter characterized it, is reflected in editorial treatment of a muckraking article Steffens wrote for *McClure's Magazine* on corruption in Pittsburgh. In writing to his colleague and fellow shareholder in *McClure's*, John S. Philips, publisher Sam McClure said: "I wish to go over the Pittsburgh article very carefully before it is published. . . . I think that the article to begin with should be free from bias, just the same as a news article or newspaper." In a similar vein, McClure wrote to Willa Cather, one of his editors, concerning the reporting of another reporter: "If Turner has any defect in writing it is a defect that almost all writers lean towards, that is a certain distaste towards documentation" (qtd. in H. Wilson 192). Within Folkerts and Teeter's judgment that *McClure's* published "well-researched articles based on fact" while other publications "jumped on the bandwagon with sensational stories lacking in research and detail" can be detected further the peculiar relationship between muckraking and sensational journalism in a largely narrative mode: muckraking can be either sensational or responsible.

---

1. See Emery and Emery 271; and Tebbel 284–86.

In effect, muckraking can overlap with narrative sensational journalism or narrative literary journalism. There is no reason why journalistic texts cannot claim to be both muckraking and literary journalism in a narrative mode, or muckraking and sensational yellow journalism in a narrative mode. The one exception, clearly, is that narrative literary journalism because of its epistemological concerns provides an antithesis to sensational journalism even if sensational journalism is fundamentally narrative in mode.

One example of a narrative journalism that could qualify as both narrative literary journalism and muckraking is Stephen Crane's "In the Depths of a Coal Mine," which appeared in *McClure's Magazine* in 1894 and supports Steffens's position that there were journalists who had been practicing some form of muckraking before Steffens went to *McClure's*. The sketch is an exposé of conditions in a coal mine in the Wilkes Barre–Scranton area of Pennsylvania. Even a cursory glance reveals that it is fundamentally narrative in mode and not discursive. Of the forty-six paragraphs, perhaps five could be characterized as fundamentally discursive. Of them, four are formally a digression about the life of mules underground in the mines (598–99). The fifth is the paragraph that provides a discursive climax for the piece when Crane digresses and comments on the significance of what he sees underground: "Great and mystically dreadful is the earth from a mine's depth" (599). However, two of the four paragraphs on the lives of mules are only formally discursive. While it is true that their purpose is to consider, as digression, the fate of mules underground, in those two paragraphs the digression reinscribes itself once again fundamentally as narrative when Crane relates two anecdotes he was told by miners about mules.

It is also true that some of the adjectives Crane uses to characterize his visit to the coal mine run the risk of sensationalism, such as when he says he was "appalled" by the mud and that in wet mines "gruesome" fungi grew (599). But the larger issue is how Crane shapes his exposé, a shape that by and large does not attempt to shock or elicit a thrill by emphasizing the difference between the life of miners and those who make their living on the surface. Rather, he attempts to solicit an empathic response. He reveals that strategy at the beginning of the narrative: "The [coal] breakers squatted upon the hillsides and in the valley like enormous preying monsters eating of the sunshine, the grass, the green leaves. The smoke from their nostrils had ravaged the air of coolness and fragrance. All that remained of the vegetation looked dark, miserable, half-strangled. Along the summit-line of the mountain, a few unhappy trees were etched upon the clouds. Overhead stretched a sky of imperial blue, incredibly far away from the sombre land" (590). The passage provides an initial disruption to most readers' experience when Crane lands them in the disorienting world of "enormous preying monsters," "ravaged" air, and "half-strangled" vegetation. The result might be sensational, especially with such value-laden adjectives as "miserable" and "ravaged," except that as readers follow the vertical sweep of what they see from the valley to the "summit-line of the mountains," they discover what begins to be more of a symbolically shared experience, "a few unhappy trees etched" or silhouetted upon what readers are familiar with, clouds. Rising through the clouds, the reader arrives at the imperial blue of the sky, "incredibly far away from the sombre land." In other words, readers find themselves looking back at what they are familiar with as a visual point of reference *and* departure. Yet where they are remains a land of "ravaged" and "half-strangled" vegetation. Furthermore, from such a vantage they will begin their symbolic descent into the mines before they have the opportunity to recover the familiarity of the blue sky.

The passage, then, provides foreshadowing of what will come. Generally, it escapes sensationalism—with perhaps the exception of "miserable," which is fundamentally emotive, unlike "ravaged" and "half-strangled," which can be equally descriptive—in referring the reader back to what the reader can be expected to be familiar with by means of the scanning or sweeping naked eye. The portrait is one of ontological complexity, depth, and ambiguity in its visual contrasts, where both dark and light, good and bad, and shades in between coexist for better or worse, instead of a sensationalized portrait composed to illustrate a didactic point in the name of exposing unhealthy working conditions in the coal mines.

That complexity of ontological experience, its ambiguous nature, is reflected in Crane's treatment of the miners in whom he finds a camaraderie that surprises him: "The tiny lamps on their hats made a trembling light that left weirdly shrouded the movements of their limbs

and bodies. We might have been confronting terrible spectres" (594).
If Crane had concluded his description at that, the passage might prove
sensational: difference from a normative experience will have been reinforced to elicit a thrill or shock. Instead, Crane continues: "But they
said 'Hello, Jim' to our conductor. Their mouths expanded in smiles—
wide and startling smiles" (595). Thus the miners are welcoming in
their unexpected gesture of friendliness, unexpected because they
were first perceived as spectres of the symbolic lower depths, clearly a
common theme in the literary naturalism of the time and of which
Crane was one of its most prominent contributors. Such ambiguity of
phenomenal experience is explored further when Crane provides the
dialogue between his guide and the miners. The strategy is significant
because Crane avoids a conventional journalist's intrusive interviewing
techniques that would reduce the passage to the digression of an inter-
viewee being removed from his natural locale. Instead, Crane is attempting to be an observant fly on the wall of the coal mines:

> He who worked at the drill engaged in conversation with our guide. He
> looked back over his shoulder, continuing to poke away. "When are yeh
> goin' t' measure this up, Jim?" he demanded. "Do yeh wanta git me
> killed?"
>
>   "Well, I'd measure it up t'-day, on'y I ain't got me tape," replied the
> other.
>
>   "Well, when will yeh? Yeh wanta hurry up," said the miner. "I don't
> wanta git killed."
>
>   "Oh, I'll be down on Monday."
>
>   "Humph!"
>
> They engaged in a sort of altercation in which they made jests.
>
>   "You'll be carried out o'there feet first before long."
>
>   "Will I?"
>
> Yet one had to look closely to understand that they were not about to
> spring at each other's throats. The vague illumination created all the
> effect of the snarling of two wolves. (595)

The passage is noteworthy for several reasons. First, Crane describes
what he hears and sees but does not intrude as the interviewing and
thus digressive journalist. Colloquially, he provides a "slice of life." Second, the exchange takes place in the figurative illumination and thus
psychological resonance cast by the earlier smiles, "wide and startling,"
that greeted Crane's guide. In that illumination of the white smile amid

the dark, it is no wonder Crane concluded that the "altercation" was, at least in part, in "jest." Third, Crane acknowledges that he "had to look closely to understand that they were not about to spring at each other's throats." A sensationalizing journalist who wanted to maintain that the miners were the spectral Other, not men capable of smiling and playfully jesting despite the hardship of the mines, would avoid looking too closely in order to justify emphasizing differences (and not commonalties) so the reader could be shocked. Crane is keenly aware of this when he reveals his journalistic intention, noting that the poor light "created" only the "effect" of the snarling of two wolves.

The result is a portrait of ambiguity, one of primarily dark hues, but one nonetheless with its redeeming moments. The ambiguity is not unlike Lafcadio Hearn's in his accounts of African American life in Cincinnati. Crane's narrative literary journalism resonates, then, because he indulges in paradox in his portrait of ontological complexity. It is a paradox that sharpens when Crane notes in the next paragraph after the reference to the "snarling of two wolves" that elsewhere in the mines "there was the same effect of strangely satanic smiles and eyeballs wild and glittering in the pale glow of the lamps" (595). Alone, "satanic smiles" clearly would be sensationalizing. But those smiles were mitigated earlier when they were offered as friendly gestures, as well as by the playful jests and the realization that how the miners look is only an effect of the light. The result is a fundamental humanness despite what could have been characterized as Other. If the miners are indeed satanic, they are more on the order of Milton's terribly human Satan. Crane has aspired then in his muckraking journalism to at least one (if canonical) measure of literature.

To be sure, Crane's treatment of the coal mines is not without potential sensationalizing flaws, perhaps the most flagrant the last clause of the last sentence to the article, when digressively and didactically he observes: "Of that sinister struggle far below there came no sound, no suggestion save the loaded cars that emerged one after another in eternal procession and were sent creaking up the incline that their contents might be fed into the mouth of the breaker, imperturbably cruel and insatiate, black emblem of greed, and of the gods of this labor" (600). The passage might have worked better as narrative if it had ended earlier and more ambiguously with "insatiate," much as Norris's

"Brute" could have benefitted from understatement. The conclusion would then read: "Of the sinister struggle far below there came no sound, no suggestion save the heavily loaded cars that emerged one after another with terrific monotony and were sent creaking up to feed the insatiate breaker" (607). Except for the lingering and sensationalizing "sinister," this last passage is relatively free of such judgments designed to reinforce reader shock and their differences with the humanized satans beneath the earth. Instead, the reader is left with interpretive possibilities, such as that the mechanical "insatiate breaker" is a metaphor for something larger, possibly the inexorability of life or the breaking of men's souls. These possibilities speak more compellingly—if not more profoundly—than the didactic message that accompanied the published story. Such a conclusion would speak more compellingly precisely because it engages the reader with what the reader does not know. Unfortunately, Crane's own intentions only made the situation worse. For a conclusion, he attacked in much stronger terms the coal mine owners. But that passage was cut by editors at *McClure's Magazine* as "too caustic of big business" (Stallman and Hagemann, *New York City Sketches* 289). More to the point is that the success of a piece of writing as narrative literary journalism is reflected, in part, in the overall ability of the writer to overcome the desire solely to shock, and instead convey understanding of the subjectivities of the Other.

Such an examination suggests why London's *People of the Abyss* is indeed muckraking but also fundamentally sensationalism and fundamentally not narrative literary journalism. Certainly it mimics the superficial attributes of narrative literary journalism in drafting the techniques of novel-writing and in invoking the subjectivity of the author. But it is the outrage of the author's subjectivity in the service of his Socialist cause that prohibits narrowing the distance between subjectivity and the object. When Jack London said that "it is incontrovertible that the [city] children grow up into rotten adults, without stamina, a weak-kneed, narrow-chested, listless breed, that crumples up and goes down in the brute struggle for life with the invading hordes from the country," clearly he has reinscribed their status as other, as irredeemable (31). Similarly when the country immigrant comes to the city: "If nothing else, the air he breathes, and from which he never escapes, is sufficient to weaken him mentally and physically, so that he becomes unable to compete with the fresh virile life from the country hastening on to London Town to destroy and be destroyed" (31). Such are the meek who shall never inherit the earth, forever condemned by a totalizing ideology. Such didacticism by London can only serve one sensationalizing (if in these instances a fundamentally discursive) purpose: to scare the hell out of the reader not unlike what a hell-fire sermon attempts.

Nor are London's efforts limited only to discursive passages. Consider his description of a ship's stoker: "A young sot; a premature wreck; physical inability to do a stoker's work, the gutter or the workhouse; and the end,—he saw it all, as clearly as I, but it held no terrors for him. From the moment of his birth, all the forces of his environment had tended to harden him, and he viewed his wretched inevitable future with a callousness and unconcern I could not shake" (27). Here the individual, not the laboring masses, are incapable of redemption, if only to see a violet growing in an urban scape and to pluck it as if finding something redeeming in life. Indeed, so incapable is London of overcoming his aversion to the Other's life in London's East End that he all but concedes his defeat—his inability to understand empathically the subjectivities of the Other in that region—when in his correspondence he writes from the East End: "I've read of misery, and seen a bit; but this beats anything I could have imagined. . . . I have my book over one-quarter done and am bowling along in a rush to finish it & get out of here. I think I should die if I had to live two years in the East End of London" ("To George and Caroline Sterling" 306). Jack London is fleeing from the Other or at the least is not embracing it. This latter point he all but acknowledges elsewhere when in a letter to his confidant Anna Strunsky he reveals his motivation for undertaking *People of the Abyss*: "This book I am plunging through with, will not be a great book. In two weeks and a couple of days I have done almost half of it. It is written, first, for money; second, in its own small way, for the human good" (309). Money, then, is his first motivation. London's experience, his flight from the Other, is in contrast to, for example, that of James Agee some thirty years later who went to live with poor white southern sharecroppers in Alabama and could not write the kind of formulaic article *Fortune* magazine wanted him to write (Fishkin

145). The result was the much more intimate *Let Us Now Praise Famous Men* because Agee dared to descend emotionally into those lower depths. He dared to risk his own emotions, something London could not do.

ULTIMATELY, THEN, the issue is not whether a Riis is in the same league as a Crane or a London. Instead, it is how well he and these other writers utilize rhetorical strategies to close the distance between subjectivity and the object—or how well they do not. The rhetorical success of overcoming the difference between self and Other, of avoiding reinforcing difference and showing commonalties instead, can represent one of the measures for determining what qualifies as narrative literary journalism and separates it from sensational journalism. It is a measure, of course, that in its application is open to considerable debate among scholars. But it is a debate that can only help to further refine our understanding of the discourse and its site in journalism and literary histories.

As for muckraking journalism, it can reenact the same epistemological problems of literary or sensational journalisms in a narrative mode, reinforcing the differences between subject and object, or attempting to close the distance between them. If the latter, it overlaps with narrative literary journalism. I suggest this is the case in Crane's coal mine article. He has for the most part succeeded in narrowing that distance, and the few discursive passages and the occasional lapses into sensationalizing value judgments are offset by the overall rhetorical weight of his "looking closely" in order to distinguish between "effect" and our more ambiguous human reality. This would prove to be the ambition of narrative literary journalists in the newly born twentieth century and up through the new journalism of the 1960s and 1970s.

5 What Followed

Narrative Literary Journalism from
1910 to the "New" Journalism

Turning and turning in the widening gyre
The falcon cannot hear the falconer;
Things fall apart; the center cannot hold;
Mere anarchy is loosed upon the world,
The blood-dimmed tide is loosed, and everywhere
The ceremony of innocence is drowned. . . .
A shape with lion body and the head of a man,
A gaze blank and pitiless as the sun,
Is moving its slow thighs.

W. B. YEATS, "The Second Coming"

IN HER preface to *Slouching towards Bethlehem,* Joan Didion makes two statements that reflect her critical attitude toward her version of narrative literary journalism. First, she observes that "since I am neither a camera eye nor much given to writing pieces which do not interest me, whatever I do write reflects, sometimes gratuitously, how I feel" (xv). Second, she notes that "this book is called *Slouching towards Bethlehem* because for several years now certain lines from the Yeats poem . . . have reverberated in my inner ear as if they were surgically implanted there. The widening gyre, the falcon which does not hear the falconer, the gaze blank and pitiless as the sun; those have been my points of reference, the only images against which much of what I was seeing and hearing and thinking seemed to make any pattern" (xiii).

Her remarks are revealing. First, because she cannot bring the scientific eye of a camera free of subjectivity to bear on her subjects (as of course no camera can), and because she does not care to write about subjects she has no interest in, or is, in effect, alienated from, she falls back on her subjectivity and what *it* selects as *its* focus, even if gratuitously or critically unearned, in attempting to understand the phenomenal world she is reporting on. Didion is attempting then to close the gulf between herself and an objectified world and her method of doing so is what comes closest to home: her subjectivity. Second, her subjectivity has led her to conclusions about the phenomenal world that in her particular interpretation happen to be like Yeats's widening gyre in which a bird of prey is caught, indifferent to the calls of its master. In the lack of pity, in the indifference, Didion concludes that "the center cannot hold." In the end she resists critical closure if she is true to her points of reference. The problematic natures of subjectivity and language alone have assured that, if not the problematic nature of phenomenon as well (assuming in this last that our subjective and linguistic frames of reference can be dispensed with). In the end Didion is reduced to rhetorical pattern-making—telling a story—at the direction of her subjectivity and language.

This has been much the history of narrative literary journalism in the twentieth century, and Didion's understanding of the role of her subjectivity in her reporting, as well as her resistance to closure, suggests a prism through which that history can be viewed. Using that prism—an interpretive historical frame—I follow the course of narrative literary journalism during this period as an attempt on the part of journalists, as a professional class, to narrow the gulf between subjectivity and the phenomenal world in reaction against mainstream, objectifying journalisms that were attempting to widen the gulf. Moreover, I examine, as a consequence, the resistance to critical closure in such attempts.

In doing so I continue drawing in part from the historiographic template proposed by scholar Thomas B. Connery, the three important periods of modern narrative literary journalism in the United States: the 1890s and first decade of this century; the 1930s and 1940s; and the new journalism of the 1960s and 1970s (preface xii–xiii). In this chapter I focus on the time frame from approximately 1910 to the 1970s, examining the two latter major periods within that chronology, as well as the lulls between those two periods. In doing so I take into account those rare historicizing efforts that further help to define narrative literary journalism during its second major period in the 1930s and 1940s, and conclude with linkages to the new journalism of the 1960s. I examine writers of the new journalism only briefly because that territory is one that has been well covered and delineated by the outpouring of critical response since its appearance. Rather, my focus is on the linkages from the earlier periods up to the 1960s and 1970s in order to emphasize the historical continuum of the form.

In his 1915 *History of American Literature,* Fred Lewis Pattee indirectly offers a reason for why narrative literary journalism, as practiced by journalists, had begun to go into a decline by the end of the first decade of the twentieth century: a shift in critical opinion increasingly denied that journalistic endeavor could be "literary." In his history, Pattee conflates journalism and literary naturalism in his discussion of writers who were journalists and promoters of naturalism: "During the closing years of the [nineteenth] century there came into American literature, suddenly and unheralded, a group of young men, journalists for the most part, who for a time seemed to promise revolution" (396). Among them he includes Frank Norris, Hamlin Garland, Stephen Crane, and Richard Harding Davis. Pattee continues, "The group was a passing phenomenon. Many of its members were dead . . . and the others, like R. H. Davis, for instance, turned at length to historical romance and other conventional fields" (396–97). In the critical condescension can be detected the declining fortunes of narrative literary journalism after its first robust period.

But if journalism was being repudiated by literature, the opposite was also true: journalism was repudiating literature. This can be detected in the departure of Steffens and Hapgood from the *Commercial Advertiser* in the first years of the new century, in part because managing editor H. J. Wright proved unsympathetic toward a narrative literary journalism, preferring instead "objective pictures of the news" (Hapgood, *Victorian* 172). Moreover, the mutual separation between journalism and literature would be reflected after World War I in reaction against the patriotic if not jingoistic tone of mainstream, factual objectified news during World War I, when newspapers were carefully monitored and censored under the Espionage Act of 1917 and the Sedition Act of 1918 (Emery and Emery 329–31), as well as because many journalists became willing propagandists for the war effort (Schudson 141–42). As a result, "in the war and after, journalists began to see *everything* as illusion, since ["factual" reporting] was so evidently the product of self-conscious artists of illusion" (Schudson 142, Schudson's emphasis). The response, in part, after the Armistice was to intensify efforts to write "objective" news, a style that yet prevails today. The concept of objective news was theorized by, among others, Walter Lippmann, who has been characterized as "the most wise and forceful spokesman for the ideal of objectivity" (Schudson 151). In an article he coauthored with Charles Merz, an editor of the *New York World,* the two noted that "the greater the indictment against the reliability of human witnesses, the more urgent is a constant testing, as objectively as possible, of these results" ("'A Test of the News'" 33). Such a conception of journalistic prose meant that an inherently more subjective literary journalism could only be the loser.

But if the first major period of narrative literary journalism had passed, the form was still practiced and published during the teens and twenties. The issue of a subjectivity attempting to engage the phenomenal world—whether the subjectivity of the journalist or the reader—is reflected in different ways and degrees, but nonetheless exists in the rhetorical choices writers made in pressing into service the kinds of tropes associated with novelistic color. Among writers of this first "lull" are Hard and Lardner. Others include Richard Harding Davis, John Reed, Elizabeth Cochrane, Damon Runyon in the teens and twenties, and Dorothy Day, E. E. Cummings, Morris Markey, Ben Hecht, and Ernest Hemingway in the twenties, thirties, and later.[1] Some, of course, such as Reed and Day, were engaged in open and conspicuous ideological causes that clearly influence their work. Cochrane, known by her nom de plume of "Nellie Bly," is largely remembered as an early muckraker, but she also wrote compelling accounts of World War I from the Eastern Front that could qualify as narrative literary journalism

---

1. See Humphrey on Reed; Applegate on Cochrane; Pauly on Runyon ("Damon Runyon"); Roberts on Day; Kerrane and Yagoda on Markey and Hecht; and Weber on Hemingway ("Hemingway's Permanent Records").

(Kroeger 400, 406–7, 410). Runyon wrote on sports and the wider social picture. Markey was one of the first writer's at the *New Yorker*, founded in 1925, a publication that served as an important mainstay for the form. Not all can be explored in depth. But the work of several will illustrate that some journalists continued to value a subjective approach.

Davis's accounts of the beginning of World War I appeared around the time of Pattee's dismissal of Davis as a historical romancer, thus effectively excising Davis from history as a literary journalist. In fact, Davis had been a narrative literary journalist ever since he became one of America's most famous war correspondents in the 1890s (Bradley 55, 60). Indeed, he is perhaps best known as a narrative literary journalist for his sketch "The Death of Rodriguez," an account of the execution of a Cuban patriot by the Spanish military authorities just before the outbreak of the Spanish-American War. Davis was also the model for the Gilded Age's gentlemanly Gibson man (Rogers 337) and was a close friend of Stephen Crane. Davis's sense of genteel honor prompted him once to defend Crane's honor when the latter was defamed by an acquaintance of Davis (Churchill 195). Davis continued to write narrative literary journalism until shortly before his death in 1916, thus helping to bridge the lull in the fortunes of the form during this period.

One example is his report to the London *News Chronicle* of the German army entering Brussels in 1914. Another is his volume *With the Allies,* which was based on those initial newspaper dispatches. Eschewing historical romance, at which he had become so adept, Davis foregrounds the issue of subjectivity when in the first sentence of the *News Chronicle* account he writes, "The entrance of the German army into Brussels has lost the human quality" ("German Army Marches" 445). His method for attempting to close the gulf between what can't be described and his—and by implication the reader's—subjectivities is instructive. In the next sentence, he adds, "It was lost as soon as the three soldiers who led the army bicycled into the Boulevard du Regent and asked the way to the Gare du Nord. When they passed the human note passed with them" (445). What Davis does is describe a pedestrian scene, as if the three German soldiers were on a bicycle outing for the weekend and having gotten lost are politely asking directions to the railroad station. But the civility of the occasion that the average reader can expect to know in their own realm of experience is undercut by what is implied, that the soldiers are dressed in battle fatigues of field gray and are presumably carrying their Mausers across their backs as they trundle into Brussels. With them passed the human note that readers could comprehend, the passing foreshadowed by the presumed uniforms and carbines. Having established that basis of understanding, that illusion of the "exchange of subjectivities" as Trachtenberg calls it, Davis then ushers readers into what he finds he cannot describe: "What came after them, and twenty-four hours later is still coming, is not men marching, but a force of nature like a tidal wave, an avalanche or a river flooding its banks. At this minute it is rolling through Brussels as the swollen waters of the Conemaugh Valley swept through Johnstown. . . . It held the mystery and menace of fog rolling toward you across the sea" (446).

In his attempt to describe the German inundation, Davis is reduced to extravagant simile and metaphor-making because his own subjectivity has difficulty comprehending what he sees. He appeals to what he can expect his readers to know, the great Johnstown flood of 1889 and the "mystery" and "menace" of a fog rolling in direct appeal toward "you," the reader, from out of the sea. Moreover, in invoking the Johnstown flood he is appealing to his own experience, or rather the experience of his subjectivity to that event: as a young cub reporter he had covered the catastrophe for a Philadelphia newspaper (Ziff 176).

Davis then describes the details of the German army that creates the impression of the metaphoric tidal wave or of the wall of water that descended on the Conemaugh Valley when the upstream dam broke: the sea of gray uniforms, the mechanical, inexorable, precision marching, and the general efficiency of the vast enterprise marching and sometimes singing in unison: "The men of the infantry sang 'Fatherland, My Fatherland.' Between each line of song they took three steps. . . . When the melody gave way the silence was broken only by the stamp of iron-shod boots, and then again the song rose" (447). Davis has drafted rhetorical tropes that utilize the common sense–appeal of what the common senses detect. Finally, he concludes the piece with, once again, metaphors of that for which he cannot account: "But now for twenty-six hours the grey army has rumbled by with the mystery of fog and pertinacity of a steam roller" (448). Implicitly in the clash of the mixed metaphors his subjectivity has acknowledged the impossibility of coming to closure.

Similarly, in an effort to draw the readers' subjectivities into an acknowledgment of an unaccountable universe, Davis uses, in *With the Allies,* contrast between what he can expect his readers to be familiar with, in this case the everyday pedestrian evidence of life, and what he cannot describe. One example is Davis's description of the burning of the great medieval library of the university in Louvain, Belgium, and the summary executions of many of that city's citizens in a calculated campaign of terror by the German army. In a passage that would be strikingly if not suspiciously echoed by Ernest Hemingway more than a decade later, Davis describes white walls surrounding gardens: "Over those that faced south had been trained pear-trees, their branches, heavy with fruit, spread out against the walls like branches of a candelabra" (*With the Allies* 89). (In "Italy, 1927," which appeared in the *New Republic,* Hemingway wrote, "Against the walls of the houses there were pear trees, their branches candelabraed against the white walls" [350].) Then, after having located his readers in the familiar, Davis attempts to remove them from the ordinary course of life to the unfamiliar and unaccountable: "It was all like a scene upon the stage, unreal, inhuman. You felt that the curtain of fire, purring and crackling and sending up hot sparks to meet the kind, calm stars, was only a painted backdrop; that the reports of rifles from the dark ruins came from blank cartridges, and that these trembling shopkeepers and peasants ringed in bayonets would not in a few minutes really die, but that they themselves and their homes would be restored to their wives and children" (95).

The last clause of the passage perhaps runs the risk of sentimentality, a charge that has been leveled against Davis's writing by others (Bradley 64). But if it suffers from sentimentality, it nonetheless reflects a journalist's subjectivity attempting to fend off in its longing for a more civil and pedestrian life what will prove inevitable, the execution of hostages and the destruction of one of the great medieval libraries. Davis, the hardened war correspondent, the model of the debonair Gibson man cool under fire, long a defender of the genteel values of nineteenth-century idealism (62), has been reduced to acknowledging the pain of his own subjectivity, or as one scholar has put it of the former Gibson man:

> It was as if, finally, Davis had grown up. His final work indicated that his assumptions about the world had been shaken. . . . He was seeing civilized nations conduct a war without rules, a war that threatened to overwhelm everything that had gone before. He had to put away the idea of his age that history was the working out of what was best.
>
> The war, however, pushed him to produce his most mature work as a writer, challenging the preconceived notions that had weakened his work for decades. (Bradley 65)

Davis reflexively acknowledges the role of his subjectivity in a passage resonant with meaning when he announces his break with objectified news altogether, opting instead for a version of more open subjectivity. Shortly after the fall of Brussels he was arrested by the German army and charged with being a spy. Like the shopkeepers and peasants of Louvain, he faced the prospect of summary execution. Fortunately for him the U.S. ambassador in Brussels intervened. But Davis opens his account of the experience with the following passage that has wider epistemological implications: "This story is a personal experience, but is told in spite of that fact and because it illustrates a side of war that is unfamiliar. It is unfamiliar for the reason that it is seamy and uninviting. With bayonet charges, bugle-calls, and aviators it has nothing in common" (*With the Allies* 31). Davis's choice of language is revealing. There is the open acknowledgment of subjectivity in the personal experience, which he tells "in spite of that fact" in a direct challenge to reporting based on "facts" that preclude overt expressions of subjectivity. He also eschews the élan of military heroics, which he seems to intuit will die in the trenches of the coming Western Front. He sees through the sham of such posing, this from the man who offered the pose of the swashbuckling war correspondent (Ziff 174, 180) and defended a genteel idealism in his earlier literary journalism during the fin de siècle. (Indeed, much of that work has been characterized as "chauvinistic and imperialistic" [Bradley 56].) Near the end of his life, Davis was undergoing a conversion and like many literary journalists was being politicized by the experience. This is reflected first in the title of the book: he is "with the Allies." It is reflected again at the end of "The Burning of Louvain" when, after he longs to see the Louvain hostages "restored to their wives and children," he collapses in the despair of a subjectivity incapable of making sense of their coming dark: "You felt it was only a nightmare, cruel and uncivilized. And then you remembered that the German Emperor has told us what it is. It is his Holy War" (*With the Allies* 95). A holy war, by definition, should be redemptive, not the cruel and arbitrary nightmare of a contingent world it has become for the doomed residents of Louvain. There can be no critical closure of a Hegelian history marching inexorably to a happy conclusion, singing *Vaterland, Mein Vaterland,* or for that matter, *Deutschland Über Alles,* Germany (among other totalitarian totalizations) "above all."

Other examples of the form that appear during the lull in the fortunes of narrative literary journalism between 1910 and the Depression era are the sketches of the young journalist Ben Hecht, perhaps better known as the coauthor of the play *The Front Page.* In the early 1920s he wrote a column for the *Chicago Daily News.* As with many newspaper columnists, he moved indifferently between discursive and narrative prose. Those like Hecht who worked for large cosmopolitan newspapers were working in a tradition that can be traced back to Ned Ward's sketches of late seventeenth-century London, lacking only in Ward's vulgarisms. This was especially true when they were largely narrative in mode. But in the case of Hecht, the comparisons don't end there. His narrative sketches have been likened to the work of the grotesque humorist and Slavic author Nikolai Gogol (Kerrane and Yagoda 407). Hecht acknowledged in his autobiography, *A Child of the Century,* the influence of Gogol—as well as of Bret Harte, Richard Harding Davis, Nathaniel Hawthorne, Maxim Gorky, Honoré de Balzac, Guy de Maupassant, Edgar Allan Poe, William Makepeace Thackeray, and "a man of marvels named [Alexandre] Dumas" (84). Thus he came to the business of writing journalism with a literary disposition. But the Gogol comparison is particularly apt because Hecht went so far as to name his French poodle "Googie" for Gogol.

Hecht, self-taught in his literary studies and always partial to Russian literature (*Child* 69), in part because of his family's (and his second wife's) Russian-Jewish heritage, can also be Chekhovian at times. For example, in "The Dagger Venus" Hecht recounts the story of the "great

Salvini," a knife-thrower on the vaudeville circuit. During his act the target of his knives is the outline of his wife, Lucia, who stands against the target as he throws. The problem for Salvini is that his wife has been gaining weight. In the knife-thrower's hotel room, Hecht describes the sound of exercise instructions and music ("one, two, one, two, higher, two") on a phonograph in a neighboring room where she is exercising in an attempt to lose weight. But Salvini bemoans that her exercise has been to no avail because of her uncontrollable appetite. As she has grown larger, he finds it difficult not to hit her in their act: "Because for eight years I have thrown at a target of 150 pounds. And my art cannot change" (192). Meanwhile, the phonograph music becomes an obsessive reminder to Salvini of what he anticipates will be his ultimate failure: mortally striking his wife with a knife. At that prospect, he says in a moment of shaky bravado: "Some day she will be sorry. Yes, some day she will understand what she is doing to me. She will eat, eat until she grow so fat that it is all my target that I mastered." And then, the knife-thrower says, the "great Salvini" will be ruined. The story concludes:

> "I will tell you. Why does she eat, eat, eat? Why does she grow fat? Because she no longer loves me. No, she do it on purpose to ruin me."
> And the great Salvini covered his ears with his hands as the phonograph continued relentlessly, "one, two, one, two, higher, two." (192)

Clearly, there is humor here. Equally clearly it is grotesque humor. Nor is it necessarily at the expense of Salvini's overweight wife. The grotesque quality derives from something darker, namely Salvini who, like the self-centered "artist" he reveals himself to be, never tries to consider why his wife has an appetite she can never satisfy. Would he be obsessive about eating if he spent his life, year after year, the target of his spouse's knives? Or is there some other reason? Hecht never says. Instead, in a Chekhovian note he concludes with the simple, understated evidence of the moment (albeit a decidedly dark evidence) that resonates with larger possibilities of meaning: "And the great Salvini covered his ears with his hands as the phonograph continued relentlessly, 'one, two, one, two, higher, two.'" Hecht teases us out of thought with the inconclusive present.

Something of an anomaly during this period is Edward Estlin Cum-

mings's 1922 *The Enormous Room*. His account of being imprisoned in
a French detention center during World War I is anomalous for several
reasons. First, it was one of Cummings's few attempts at a true-life narrative before becoming better known as the orthographically lower-
cased poet e. e. cummings, who would dispense with capitalization and
other standards of typography. The work is also anomalous because
Cummings was never a journalist, thus providing the exception to the
rule that most of the authors examined here at one time or another
had been journalists for pay. Thus, he provides a reminder of the dangers of adhering to too rigid a classification scheme. Third, the work
can clearly be viewed as both memoir and narrative literary journalism. On the one hand, it is inward directed by virtue of being Cummings's reminiscences about himself. On the other hand, he engages
in outward-directed social portraiture of the kind associated with narrative literary journalism, describing the lives of his fellow inmates in the
"Enormous Room" that serves as their prison (90). Thus *The Enormous
Room* is a reminder of just how porous the boundaries are between memoir and narrative literary journalism, as well as other nonfiction forms.

Among the work's characteristics, it anticipates Hunter Thompson's
gonzo journalism of the 1960s and 1970s without the hallucinatory
drugs. Like Thompson, Cummings is irreverent in his responses to his
surroundings and circumstances. A picaro at heart, he welcomes his
arrest on suspicion of engaging in seditious correspondence as an opportunity to escape the mud and banal bureaucracy at the war front
where he is a volunteer working for an American Red Cross ambulance
corps, or *section sanitaire*. For example, after his arrest he engages in
an exchange with his English driver, followed by his musings on the
circumstances:

> "Did y' do something to get pinched?"
> "Probably," I answered importantly and vaguely, feeling a new dignity.
> "Well, if you didn't, maybe B— [a companion also arrested] did."
> "Maybe," I countered, trying not to appear enthusiastic. As a matter
> of fact I was never so excited and proud. I was, to be sure, a criminal!
> Well, well, thank God that settled one question for good and all—no
> more *section sanitaire* for me! No more Mr. A. and his daily lectures on
> cleanliness, deportment, etc. In spite of myself I started to sing (9).

Still elsewhere, Cummings flippantly describes the morning routine of emptying buckets of inmate urine in a sewer: "Here the full pails were dumped: with the exception, occasionally, of one or two pails of urine which the *Surveillant* [chief assistant] might direct to be thrown on the [prison] *Directeur's* little garden in which it was rumoured he was growing a rose for his daughter" (87).

Moreover, as Thompson would some fifty years later, Cummings engages in mock allegory, parodying John Bunyan's *Pilgrim's Progress* with chapter titles inspired by the latter: "I Begin a Pilgrimage," "A Pilgrim's Progress," "An Approach to the Delectable Mountains," and "Apollyon." A foul fiend in *Pilgrim's Progress,* Apollyon in *Enormous Room* is the designation Cummings gives to the prison director whose rose garden is the recipient of the prisoners' urine buckets at the direction of the *surveillant.* Much as Cummings characterizes his several-month stay in the prison as a pilgrimage, Hunter Thompson would later characterize his *Fear and Loathing in Las Vegas* as a quest, subtitled *A Savage Journey to the Heart of the American Dream.* His account reads as a glib, drug-induced mock heroic in the picaresque tradition in which ultimately the American dream is found to be empty. Cummings and Thompson, then, help to constitute a tradition within the history of narrative literary journalism.

During this period Ernest Hemingway was developing his literary voice, and he did so through his narrative literary journalism. Like Davis and Hecht, Hemingway spanned several periods, writing during the first lull, during the form's second major period, and into the 1950s when once again there was a lull in its practice. One early example from the 1920s is "Italy, 1927," which Hemingway wrote for the *New Republic.* A first-person account of Fascist Italy, "Italy, 1927" is notable in part because Hemingway would later anthologize it in his collected short stories as a fiction called "Che Ti Dice la Patria" (Fatherland, what are you saying?). But what remains remarkable is that at the time of its first publication it appeared in a journal dedicated largely to news analysis, or rather an analysis, much like objective news, that sought to present an authoritative interpretation that transcended subjectivity. "Italy, 1927" finds itself sandwiched between two such articles, posing a kind of challenge to the prevailing journalistic paradigm of the era. In the article, Hemingway and his traveling companion are fined by a petty Fascist apparatchik in what amounts to a shakedown because their car's license plate is ostensibly dirty. The Fascist fines them again when Hemingway disputes the charge and complains that if there is any dirt on the license plate it is because of the state of Italian roads (313). After the incident, Hemingway observes ironically, "We drove for two hours after it was dark and slept in Mentone that night. It seemed very cheerful and clean and sane and lovely. . . . Naturally, in such a short trip, we had no opportunity to see how things were with the country or the people" (353).

In the irony Hemingway denies the kind of objectifying generalization that conventional journalistic "takeouts," as such efforts to capture the mood of a community or country are commonly called, engage in. In doing so, he resists coming to critical closure. Clearly, as a slice of diurnal life, the anecdote utilizes techniques such as description and dialogue ("He wrote in indelible pencil, tore out the slip and handed it to me. I read it. 'This is for twenty-five lire'" [353]) in the attempt to narrow the gulf between subjectivity and an objectified world. Moreover, as diurnal slices of life reflecting a heightened or more evident subjectivity when contrasted to objective news, such slices recall Hamlin Garland's position on naturalism, that it "is an individual thing,— the question of one man facing certain facts and telling his individual relations to them." Hemingway is working, then, within the tradition of literary naturalism, as had many of his forebears in literary journalism. And the consequence of Hemingway telling his individual relations to the incident is that there can be no omniscient closure, which is reflected in the irony of the conclusion: he cannot engage in the epistemological conceit of drawing conclusions about the state of an entire country or its people. Rather, he can only hint at it in the evidence of a petty Fascist official shaking him down. Like the Socratic question, one is left to question what the inconclusive future will bring from the one example.

Hemingway does not foreground his subjectivity to the degree that many literary journalists do; nonetheless it is evident for at least two reasons. First, through the choice of tropes commonly associated with novel-writing "the writer makes his presence and his shaping consciousness known" (Weber, "Some Sort" 20). To be sure, all writing, including

objective news, reflects a shaping consciousness. The difference is one
of degree, and in contrast to narrative literary journalism, objective
news reflects an attempt to *deny* a shaping consciousness by means of
the pose of objectivity reflected in distilled and abstracted language.
Objective journalism attempts to transcend or elide subjectivity as one
contributing means of production. Second, the impact of what Hemingway does is heightened by the contrast his article provides to those
preceding and following his. They are written in a distilled and abstracted language. For example, in the preceding article, "Mexico's Bid
for Supremacy in Central America," Linton Wells writes: "In fact, for
twenty-four hours, the radical element could have overthrown, and assumed control of, the government—but it didn't grasp the fact until
afterwards, and then it was too late. American soldiers occupied Pan-
ama City and settled the affair in their own efficient way. Several persons were killed; a number deported. Peace and order were restored,
but the matter hasn't ended" (350). The "radical element," the failure
to "grasp the fact," "American soldiers" who "settled the affair in their
own efficient way," the "several persons . . . killed; a number deported,"
and "peace and order . . . restored," reflect the kind of linguistic distillation—Nietzsche's volatilization—that objective mainstream journalism engages in, resulting in the widening gulf of a subjectivity alienated from objectified death, among other abstractions. The writing
recalls Stephen Crane's observation that objectified mortality in mainstream journalism becomes ultimately little more than "a unit in the
interesting sum of men slain" ("Regulars Get No Glory" 171). Hemingway's "felt detail" is in sharp contrast to Linton Wells's "grasp" of abstract facts. The same analysis could be applied to the article that follows Hemingway's, a report on the lack of leadership in the U.S. Senate
("Washington Notes" 353).

Moreover, "Italy, 1927" reveals one of Hemingway's early encounters
with Fascism. Eventually, his antipathy toward Fascism would be reflected in his reportage on behalf of the Republican side during the
Spanish Civil War and in the novel *For Whom the Bell Tolls*. The experience he describes in "Italy, 1927" contributes, then, to his being politicized because of the engagement of his subjectivity.

Meanwhile, during this period there were less successful efforts at a
narrative literary journalism drafting the tropes of novel-writing, such

as Lowell Thomas's *With Lawrence in Arabia*. They make up a more popular class of pseudoliterary journalism because they mimic the attributes of literary journalism. In the case of Thomas this should come as
no surprise; he has never been fully respectable as a journalist, being
something of a grandstander more interested in self-promotion. In a
sense, he is the P. T. Barnum of American journalism, and he is rarely
taken into account in journalism histories. Indeed, one journalism historian characterizes him as a mere "patterer" adept at empty chatter
(A. Lee 564). *With Lawrence* is a pseudoliterary journalism because
Thomas writes historical romance framed by "the distanced image of
the absolute past." On recounting his first meeting with T. E. Lawrence,
Thomas acknowledges that his intention is historical romance when he
gushes, "And that was how I first made the acquaintance of one of the
most picturesque personalities of modern times, a man who will be
blazoned on the romantic pages of history with Raleigh, Drake, Clive,
and Gordon" (6). Nor does Thomas stop there. He claims that "two
remarkable figures appeared" during World War I, Lawrence and Gen.
Edmund H. H. Allenby. "The dashing adventures and anecdotes of
their careers will furnish golden themes to writers of the future, as the
lives of Ulysses, King Arthur, and Richard the Lion-Hearted did to poets, troubadours, and chroniclers of other days." At the end of the book
Thomas compares Lawrence to Marco Polo as well (408). Clearly the
author has framed himself as a chronicler of romantic historical epics
and is subject to the ideologies they imply: they are a way of framing
how the world should be viewed, and Thomas is seeking for critical
closure, not Bakhtin's "inconclusive present" in which such closure is
unattainable.

The gush is in sharp contrast to Lawrence's own *Revolt in the Desert*,
excerpted from his *Seven Pillars of Wisdom*. While Lawrence writes discursively, he also provides the kind of novelistic scene construction that
is common to literary journalism and that does not seek for closure:

> When at last we anchored in Jeddah's outer harbour, off the white town
> hung between the blazing sky and its reflection in the mirage which
> swept and rolled over the wide lagoon, then the heat of Arabia came out
> like a drawn sword and struck us speechless. . . . There were only lights
> and shadow, the white houses and black gaps of streets: in front, the
> pallid lustre of the haze shimmering upon the inner harbour: behind,

the dazzle of league after league of featureless sand, running up to an
edge of low hills, faintly suggested in the far away mist of heat. (1)

Lawrence's style is relatively free of the gushing valuations of a grand-
standing, attention-seeking Thomas, of whom Lawrence, in a slight,
makes no mention in *Revolt in the Desert*. It was against that kind of romantic gush, which is perhaps one form of sensationalism as well as
ideological tyranny, that narrative literary journalism rebelled, and
would continue to rebel against even more vociferously during the
Great Depression.

THE ADVENT of the Great Depression prompted a reevaluation of journalistic practice. As a result some journalists would once again eschew
the objective model for a much more subjective one. The observation
is important because what emerges is that in times of social transformation and crisis an objectified rhetoric proves even more inadequate.
Instead, a greater need emerges for a rhetoric that attempts to help
one understand other subjectivities, particularly subjectivities at the
heart of such transformation and crisis: narrative literary journalism in
short. Too, such a subjective model would once again find itself not
infrequently aligned with Progressive politics. Moreover, the political
implications of the separation of subjectivity from an objectified world
would be reflected in the low regard to which newspapers had fallen
in the opinion of the average American in the 1930s.

As James Boylan notes, many newspapers "defaulted" in their reporting on the Great Depression, downplaying it in response to calls
by politicians and leaders not to panic the American public (159). One
of those more prominent calls was made by President Herbert Hoover
in 1929 in the aftermath of the collapse of Wall Street: "If we overdo
our job we may create a sense that the situation is more serious than it
really is; . . . if you could confine yourselves merely to the statement of
things that actually happen; that when the government and municipali-
ties and various sources report that they have gone out to do something, that would be the most helpful form of news on the subject"
(Hoover 401). Hoover is not only pressuring journalists to exercise re-
straint in their reporting but also urging them to report only the posi-
tive side of government relief efforts. Hoover's mention of the "sub-

ject" is of course in hindsight ironic. Furthermore, his call to journalists to "confine yourselves merely to the statement of things that actually happen" veils a call for a dispassionate journalism that makes "things" of subjective experience or that objectifies experience as "objective" news. As Boylan notes of U.S. newspapers during the period, "Most appeared ready to maintain discreet silence until the depression blew over" (161). So divorced had many American newspapers become from the daily evidence of the Depression that one angry but brave newspaper editor from the *Toledo Blade*, at the 1933 meeting of the American Society of Newspaper Editors, "introduced a resolution charging that newspapers had lulled the public into an 'unreal and false economic security' and had 'tended to keep from readers the truth about economic and financial status in various local situations'" (qtd. in Boylan 162). That prompted an editor of the *Philadelphia Bulletin* to defend his colleagues because "they had used discretion and had not told people all the facts that they know" about possible bank failures (162). The resolution was tabled, and the society authorized its board of directors to censor the transcript of the proceedings, which it declined to do. In fact, American newspapers had become so identified with big business "that editors had been proud to receive the encomiums of bankers' associations for 'steadying the social, economic and business structures of the communities they serve' and for their 'refusal to become vehicles for hysteria'" (161). The consequences were perhaps predictable. "Public opinion polls in the late thirties suggested that 30 million Americans, nearly one adult in three, doubted the honesty of the American press" (Stott 79). One repudiation of the mainstream press was reflected in President Roosevelt's reelection campaign in 1936 when "more than 80 per cent of the press opposed Roosevelt, and he won by the highest percentage ever" (Stott 79).

In a telling observation that reveals why a narrative literary journalism found an opening during this period, William Stott notes that "for many people in the thirties the newspaper form itself was apparently compromised. . . . The newspaper's indirectness—the gap between an event and the published report—left too much room for tampering" (83). Implicitly, that is what objectification in objective news does, turning experience into an object and tampering with it by neutering it as subjective experience.

It would be largely in the magazine press that a narrative literary journalism would find a more active voice in an attempt to provide "news on the subject," but a different "subject" from what President Hoover had hoped for. The narrative literary journalism of this period was often called "literary reportage." The terminology was promoted by Alfred Kazin in his 1941 study of American literary realism *On Native Grounds*. In it, Kazin proved to be one of the few critical voices of the era that came to the form's defense (491). But the term "reportage" was already in use in the 1930s. "Reportage is three-dimensional reporting. The writer not only condenses reality, he helps the reader feel the fact. The finest writers of reportage are artists in the fullest sense of the term. They do their editorializing through their imagery" (North 121). At the time he wrote that, Joseph North was editor of the *New Masses,* a prominent leftist publication. In the editorializing can be detected the shaping consciousness of the journalist, while in the imagery lies the common sense–appeal of our shared common senses.

As Boylan notes, the "documentary [reportage] of the early 1930s . . . was designed to upset the status quo" (175). Hemingway, Edmund Wilson, Sherwood Anderson, Erskine Caldwell, and James Agee are among those who took up the Progressive protest. When their narrative ambition in their literary journalism attempted to more openly acknowledge the relationship between subjectivity and a phenomenal world, they found they could not stay detached (no small matter in Hemingway's case given the emotional detachment in his fiction that paradoxically made him famous)—and that would make activists of them.

Not all writers or publications became social advocates, however. One of the conspicuous exceptions was the work that appeared in the *New Yorker,* which from its founding in 1925 was an early and consistent champion of a narrative literary journalism while largely eschewing open political positions in its sketches. A major influence on the magazine's literary reportage was the hiring of its future editor William Shawn in 1933 to write the "Notes and Comments" column. "The institutional conditions were ripe for literary journalism" because reporters were given the time by Shawn to develop their articles (Sims, "Joseph Mitchell" 84). Many of the *New Yorker*'s reporters came from the *New York Herald Tribune* where they were feature writers. The *Herald Tribune*'s city editor at the time, Stanley Walker, encouraged his reporters to write more in-depth features than most papers permitted. But as Norman Sims notes, the daily deadlines made such endeavors difficult, and many saw in the *New Yorker* an opportunity to write the kind of features that had not been possible ("Joseph Mitchell" 84). A more subjective journalism was indeed Harold Ross's intention when he founded the *New Yorker*. The publication, he said, "will be interpretive rather than stenographic" (qtd. in Kramer 61). In addition to Morris Markey, the *New Yorker* attracted E. B. White, Joseph Mitchell, Lillian Ross, A. J. Liebling, John McNulty, and St. Clair McKelway, all of whom would prove to be mainstays of the form from the 1930s through the 1960s. Nor does such a list include prominent freelancers such as John Hersey.

Moreover, columnists continued their version of narrative literary journalism, enjoying the wider freedom the column format provided. One example is that of Meyer Berger who contributed to the *New Yorker* and *Life* but who is perhaps best recalled for his column "About New York" in the *New York Times* (acknowledgments xi). His work on New York includes vivid portraits of metropolitan life. For example, in one story, he recalls how Al Capone snubs "de Lawd," which is also the title of the piece. In it, an elderly African American actor—Richard Berry Harrison—who plays "de Lawd" in playwright Marc Connelly's *Green Pastures*, is offered the opportunity to meet and have a photograph taken with "Public Enemy Number One" through a go-between while Capone is on his way to trial in a federal court house. They are introduced but Capone snubs Harrison when he sees that he is black: "Capone's face went dark. Rudely he brushed de Lawd aside. 'Go the hell o' my way,' [Capone] snarled." Turning to Harrison, Berger observes: "The old man's eyes were moist with pain and humiliation. His hands gripped his old hat tightly. He stared after the receding gunman. 'He didn't have to go for to do that,' he said" (180–81). Berger is recalling this three years later at Harrison's funeral under the arching and vaulted roof of the Cathedral of Saint John the Divine. Some seven thousand adoring mourners have turned out for the elderly black man who had played "de Lawd" in the widely acclaimed play that appealed to both blacks and whites. And as his fellow actors carry Harrison's coffin down the cathedral steps, Berger writes, "a lane opened before the pallbearers on the long stone flight and the cleavage of the human

tide recalled Marc Connelly's most powerful line: 'Gangway! Gangway
for de Lawd God Jehovah'" (185). Thus as Berger intimates, the humil-
iated shall inherit both the earth and the heavenly kingdom. Whether
the same can be said of Capone is another matter.

Meanwhile, the topical genres of travel, sports, and crime narratives
had taken on their modern form during the interwar period. They are
important to acknowledge because of their overlap with a modal form
such as narrative literary journalism. Mostly what is examined here is
a narrative literary journalism that takes as its subject a broad social
portraiture difficult to define topically. But narrative sports-reporting,
such as that of Ring Lardner, is, modally at least, a form of narrative
literary journalism. Another writer of sports narrative (as well as general columns) from the mid-1920s through the 1930s was Westwood
Pegler, a sometime member of the Chicago school who wrote for the
Chicago Tribune. Travel narratives from the 1920s and 1930s also included the Latin American travelogues by Carleton Beals and those of
Arabia by Freya Madeline Stark. And then there were narratives about
true crime. Again, what Truman Capote did was not new, despite his
self-promotion. One example is Hickman Powell's *Ninety Times Guilty,*
published in 1939, about mob infiltration of the New York City prostitution racket (Kerrane and Yagoda 97).

Whether narrative literary journalists were overtly or covertly ideological, what all shared in common was a more open acknowledgment
of the place of subjectivity in the report. At the beginning of the thirties, the attempt to narrow the gulf between subjectivities is reflected
in a comparison of narrative literary journalism to objective objectified versions of the same event. One example is a piece Edmund Wilson did for the *New Republic* in 1931 compared to a report of the same
event, a Communist protest march in Manhattan, that appeared in the
New York Times. In the unsigned *Times* piece (in itself evidence of a disengaged subjectivity), the reporter writes: "Sympathy was obviously
with the police. Small articles and bags of water were cast on the rioters'
heads from the windows of nearby buildings" ("2,000 Reds" 1). Of the
same incident, Wilson wrote in his signed article (his signature's appearance at the end reminiscent of the more familiar and by implication subjective epistolary form) that appeared in the *New Republic* on
February 11: "Somebody from a high floor of the Sun Building drops

a paper bag full of water down into the swarm around the statue. The bag comes apart in the air and people watch the whirls of water fall" ("Communists and Cops" 346). As Boylan notes of these two passages, "the *Times* reporter saw the falling bag(s) and locked up their meaning securely with a conclusion about political sentiment in the upper floors. Wilson let the bag fall bearing only its own message" (171). Boylan's analysis deserves further examination. First, the bag's "bearing only its own message" hints suggestively at one of the conclusions of an overt writing-subjectivity: the bag's "own message" is indeterminate. Put another way, the more heightened the subjectivity, the more aware or reflexive it must be of its own limitations in imposing "a conclusion about political sentiment," unlike the *Times*' reporter who betrays in considerably greater degree the alienation of his own subjectivity from an abstract objectification and ultimately reification of ostensible sentiment.

Furthermore, Wilson begins the attempt to close the gulf between subjectivity and objectification when he directly addresses the reader in the first paragraph, thus involving him or her in the activity, by noting that "*you* can't get anywhere near the building without running the gauntlet of the cops and presenting unimpeachable credentials" ("Communists and Cops," 344, emphasis added). Elsewhere, he conflates office workers, who are "out to lunch," with Communists by comparing them as one group to policemen who "seem the only healthy full-sized people" (345). While perhaps unflattering to the office workers—that they are by implication "unhealthy"—nonetheless at some subjective level they can let out a collective sigh of relief in finding that the Other, the brutish Communists, do after all have some human qualities similar to themselves. But that is their undoing because in the collective conflation, the subjectivity of the ranks of the bourgeoisie has been joined with that of the proletariat into a combined and symbolic body politic that finds itself separated, because of the "rigorously guarded park," from "the men's wear shops, Schrafft's soda fountains, Ligett's drug stores and cafeterias of Nassau Street and Broadway" (346). Thus Wilson first conflates the office workers with the proletariat by finding what they have in common, their diminutive size compared to police officers. So reduced to diminished circumstances like the proletariat, the office workers are separated by Wilson from the

world they are most familiar with, men's wear shops, Schrafft's soda
fountains, Ligett's drug stores, and cafeterias. It is part of his strategy
to get the office workers to try on another subjectivity, that of being an
unemployed proletarian who can only long for a world once-familiar
but now placed out of reach because of unemployment or a rigorously
guarded park, a world made a distant object by denied desire. Indeed,
Wilson all but suggests that this conflation is part of a Communist plan
when he says of the physical space into which office workers and Communists have been placed: "In that cramped and inhospitable arena,
the Communists produce simply confusion—a confusion which gets
worse and worse" (346). For the office worker too, one might add.

Clearly, in his attempt to manipulate subjectivity, Wilson has an ideological agenda. But then he is engaged in a form whose purpose is to
subjectively engage. Wilson has done so and attempts to get his reader
to do so. The ideological hand is heavy at times, so that Wilson crosses
over that fine line that separates narrative literary journalism from sensationalism and the reinscription of the Other as brute. He does so in
the following passage in which he strains for balance in distinguishing
between two kinds of police officers, but still concludes with one type
as a brutish caricature: "The policemen seem to fall into two classes:
the husky good-natured kind who accomplish their disciplinary duties,
though with satisfaction, without heat, and the more stupid staring-eye
type hired frankly as mobilizeable brutes" (345). Wilson has failed to
meet the "stated ideal" of literary journalism, as suggested by Lincoln
Steffens, to examine the "mobilizeable brutes" and report about them
"so humanly that the reader will see himself in the other fellow's place"
(Steffens, *Autobiography* 317). Wilson's purpose may be to serve an
ideological cause, to move one to political action, but in doing so this
section of the article tends to shortchange the remainder of the piece
as narrative literary journalism. Nonetheless, there is still another un-
dercurrent to the passage that serves as something of a corrective to
the ideology of the brute. As June Howard suggests, the Other is "the
sexual, the violent, the unaware, the uncontrolled and uncontrollable,
the proletarian, the criminal, and above all—the brute" (80). Wilson,
in effect, has deftly reversed roles, playing on stereotypes of the brute
that had accumulated in the American cultural psyche, so that repre-
sentatives of authority—the police—are reduced to being the brute.

Despite the heavy hand of ideology, Wilson never entirely loses sight of his subjectivity and what it ultimately concludes with, when seemingly apropos of nothing, he observes immediately following the passage in which the "confusion . . . gets worse and worse": "From the other side of the park, a dreadful woman's scream is heard" (346). There is no explanation. It bears, as Boylan says, only its own message. Is the scream that of a Communist faithful slugged with a police truncheon? In the conflated confusion, is it that of an office worker who has found herself among Communists, or even worse, one who has discovered that she has shared her subjectivity (and potentially her psychic bed?) with a Communist? Or is it simply what David Bromwich calls, in a consideration of critic Irving Howe's position on the matter, "gratuitous" or "irrelevant" details? "The detail we call irrelevant or gratuitous has a way of seeming peculiarly right, so that we think it belongs just where it occurs, though strictly speaking it lacks any formal or dramatic warrant" (7). It is easy to overlook still another possible meaning to the sentence: is the woman a "dreadful" woman and her scream benign? Are any or all of these the answers to the questions? Wilson does not tell us; he leaves us confronting the indeterminate, the product of a subjectivity that in its limited cognition does not attempt to make something out of that of which it has no knowledge, unlike the abstract objectification of a "conclusion about a political sentiment" in the *Times* article. The reader is confronting Bakhtin's inconclusive present. Furthermore, unlike the questions beginning journalists are advised to ask as part of a ritualized mantra for objectively reporting an objectified world—who, what, when, where, why, and how—in order to find answers suggesting that there can be closure, Wilson refuses the reader answers to the questions, thus inviting questioning and engagement of the reader's subjectivity. Such engagement with the inconclusive present, as Cathy N. Davidson has noted in her interpretation of Bakhtin, "empowers the hitherto powerless individual, at least imaginatively, by authorizing necessarily private responses to texts" (303).

SUCH WOULD be the continuing ambition of a narrative literary journalism during the 1930s. Other practitioners during this period include Martha Gellhorn and Ernest Hemingway, with their reporting on the Spanish Civil War. William Stott observes that the challenges such reportage posed to the social, cultural, and economic status quo would become less pronounced, and eventually would be co-opted (at least in part) by the government as the thirties progressed. When "the New Deal came to power, it institutionalized documentary; it made the weapon that undermined the establishment part of the establishment" (92). As a consequence, he suggests, there were two kinds of what he calls "documentary reportage," subversive and officially sanctioned. The officially sanctioned was sponsored by the Federal Writers' Project (FWP), which came under the umbrella of the Works Progress Administration and operated from 1935 to 1941. Employing writers, journalists, and editors, as well as unemployed Ph.D.'s and students for research purposes, it was one more effort on the part of the Roosevelt administration to get Americans back to work during the Depression. Their subject, broadly speaking, was the "reaffirmation of national values" (Penkower vii) reflected in, among other projects, the writing of local and cultural histories, ethnic studies, the gathering of folklore, and the writing of the American Guide Series for each of the states.

The Federal Writers' Project employed as many as sixty-six hundred writers at one time. Just how much of what was written can be characterized as narrative literary journalism is yet to be determined. But the project's writers had considerable latitude and indeed were encouraged to write colorfully and in a personal voice. The guide series, for example, was more than just a collection of travel instructions. Such instructions were indeed a part of the series, but at the same time writers contributed essays on folklore and personal descriptions of communities and of the workers in different industries. It was, in its own way, a form of American social realism. Until more excavation is conducted, at best what can be detected in it are traces of narrative literary journalism. For example, the novelist Zora Neale Hurston is usually recalled for *Their Eyes Were Watching God,* published in 1937 and an early feminist novel. But she also worked for the Federal Writers' Project collecting black folklore in the South (she had trained as an anthropologist) and wrote accounts for the Florida guide that could qualify as narrative literary journalism. In fact, she would incorporate a passage that describes migrant workers originally written for the FWP into *Their Eyes Were Watching God* (Bordelon 122).

Among her contributions to the Florida guidebook is the following

description, of her hometown, "Eatonville When You Look at It," popu-
lated by working-class blacks. As its title implies, one must take the time
to look in order to understand a community: "Maitland is Maitland
until it gets to Hurst's corner, and then it is Eatonville. Right in front
of Willie Sewell's yellow-painted house the hard road quits being the
hard road for a generous mile and becomes the heart of Eatonville. Or
from a stranger's point of view, you could say that the road just bursts
through on its way from Highway #17 to #441 scattering Eatonville
right and left" (124). In addition to the "lyrical" quality of the prose,
as scholar Pamela Bordelon notes (123), Hurston also uses what has
become by now a common approach in narrative literary journalism,
that of placing the reader, imaginatively, in a location of which he or
she might normally not take note. Eatonville, with a population of only
136, would likely otherwise be ignored. And yet its location between
Jacksonville and the Winter Park–Orlando area is one that travelers
must pass through. It is a black community without a paved road, one
that might appear to strangers as simply "scattered right and left." But
for Hurston it was much more.

> After the shop you come to Widow Dash's orange grove, her screened
> porch, "double hips," and her new husband. . . . Take the left side of the
> road and except for the Macedonia Baptist church people just live along
> that side and play croquet in Armetta Jones's backyard behind the huge
> camphor tree. . . . There are back streets on both sides of the road. The
> two back streets on the right side are full of little houses squatting under
> hovering oaks. These houses are old and were made out of the town's
> first dreams. . . . They call the tree-shaded land that runs past the school-
> house West Street and it goes past several minor groves until it passes Jim
> Steele's fine orange grove and dips itself in Lake Belle, which is the home
> of Eatonville's most celebrated resident, the world's largest alligator.
> (124–25)

Nor does Hurston ignore her own subjectivity, but notes "the big
barn on the lake" where she lives, thus implicitly acknowledging once
again what Hamlin Garland observed in *Crumbling Idols* that applies so
aptly to narrative literary journalism: "Write of those things of which
you know most, and for which you care most. By so doing you will be
true to yourself, true to your locality, and true to your time" (35). In
the familiarity of the community, of Widow Dash's "new husband," of

the shade of the camphor tree in Armetta Jones's backyard where residents play croquet, of the little houses "made out of the town's first dreams," and of "Eatonville's most celebrated resident, the world's largest alligator," Hurston almost evokes a magical realism, one clearly imbued with the character of her own folklore studies of the African American experience in Florida. It is a land of the biblical camphor, a land of dreams, and a land of an alligator of epic and mythical proportions worthy of Grendel in the white, Anglo-Saxon folk tradition. At whatever level of consciousness, this was Hurston's method of getting a predominantly white society to try on a different and African American subjectivity, one that appeals to the deepest of mythic archetypes. In Hurston's case, this should come as no surprise. In addition to her work recording folklore, she wrote *Moses: Man of the Mountain,* an African American folk interpretation of the biblical Jews, published in 1939.

But it remains unclear just how much of the work of the Federal Writers' Project can be considered narrative literary journalism. What may be more important is that the project engaged in and fostered a larger national reexamination in literary terms. As Alfred Kazin asked: "Why is it that so much of the literature of the thirties and early forties must seem in retrospect a literature of Fact?" ("Imagination" 490–91). One example that stands out before the "co-option" of the national reexamination by federal and state efforts is that of novelist, poet, historian, folklorist, and literary journalist Carl Carmer. The last three characterizations illustrate Kazin's point. Originally from New York, Carmer served as an English professor at the University of Alabama in the 1920s. In 1934 he published *Stars Fell on Alabama,* which recounts, as narrative, the different cultures he found in that state, including black, white, and Cajun—as well as the Ku Klux Klan in its heyday. Carmer describes life in Tuscaloosa, a country dance, a camp revival meeting, turpentiners, plantation life, a Cajun "hell-raising," and a lynching, knowledge of which plantation whites attempted to keep from Carmer.

As the contents of *Stars Fell on Alabama* suggest, it would be a mistake to think that in the national reexamination most if not all the narrative literary journalism from this period was openly ideological. Stott proposes that two kinds of documentary reportage emerged, one that was "instrumental" in attempting to prompt social action, and another more "conservative" strain he calls "descriptive" (238, 240). Because instrumental reportage was driven largely by unconcealed ideological concerns, Stott suggests, some critics began to see the need for a more ideologically neutral (although not necessarily objective objectified) reportage. As Nathan Asch observed in a 1935 review, a journalism was emerging that would leave it "up to the reader to draw his own conclusions" (108). This, to some degree, was what Wilson was attempting to do when he described the falling paper bag of water bearing its own message, even though Wilson's leftist sympathies would, to a greater degree, get the better of him. In line with the national reexamination taking place during the Depression, such a descriptive reportage often went "in search of America," which would be the subtitle of a book Asch published in 1937 called *The Road: In Search of America.* The book described a cross-country trip he took by car in the mid-thirties. Generally critics considered the book a failure because of its didacticism (Stott 250). Nonetheless, Asch had tapped into what became a popular subgenre, which Sherwood Anderson is credited with having started as columns for the then new news-weekly *Today.* They were collected and published in 1935 as *Puzzled America* (Stott 245–46).

The idea for Anderson's columns came from Raymond Moley, one of President Roosevelt's brain trusters and the editor of *Today.* Moley suggested that Anderson travel across country, talk to people, and write up their views. As Moley told him, "the people must explain too, and be heard. The President and those in high office hear flattery and special pleading. They read what Washington newspapermen write. But they know nothing of what the farmer says to his neighbor. . . . I wish you would help us make these people's ideas heard" (3). Clearly, mainstream journalistic style of the Washington variety was inadequate for the task at hand, and Moley was calling for a journalism that more openly attempted to express or reflect the "farmer's" and the "neighbor's" subjectivities, something the distillation of objectified objective news could not do. Another revealing comment by Moley is that he praised Anderson as a journalist with "no axe to grind, no cause to promote" (3) The comment reflects the desire for a documentary reportage that was, in its intention, to be descriptive and not instrumental, whatever the problematic nature of subjectivity in an effort that poses as neutral.

In the same year Anderson's collection appeared in book form, Erskine Caldwell published his account of traveling across country, *Some American People.* In the volume he admonishes his readers to avoid the monuments, vistas, and other tourist sights. "What is worth traveling thousands of miles to see and know are people and their activity. . . . By visiting sections of the country . . . the stories of its people will be found in ever changing versions" (4). "To see and know . . . people and their activity" recalls efforts by earlier narrative literary journalists to narrow the gulf between subjectivity and the objectified brute. Moreover, Caldwell's "ever changing versions" reveal a form that has established for itself an impossible task: in the ever-changing versions lies an acknowledgment of an indeterminate world that resists critical closure. Stott adds that the "I've seen America" book became "the dominant nonfiction mode" by the end of the 1930s (251).

Despite such efforts at a descriptive literary journalism, neither Anderson nor Caldwell entirely escaped an open ideological stance in his writing. As Stott notes, Caldwell is guilty of offering "plumed panaceas" (242). Ironically, it was Caldwell who warned in *Some American People* against such panaceas (9). What does emerge in the reportage of both Anderson and Caldwell is that once they engaged their subjectivities they found themselves unable to avoid taking political stands. For example, Anderson says, "I cannot take the impersonal tone." Yet he also acknowledges the limitations of his subjectivity: "I blame myself that I do not get more of these stories, do not often enough get the real feeling of the people to whom I talk" (ix).

Anderson and Caldwell provide many clues that indicate how much their narrative ambition is to exchange subjectivities with their subjects—not objects. Forty years earlier Stephen Crane said in "An Experiment in Misery" that he wanted to write on what it was like to be homeless after seeing a homeless person—"Perhaps I could discover his point of view or something near it" (34). Anderson expressed a similar ambition when he noted in *Puzzled America*: "I have always, when broke, been more alive to others, more aware of others." In the first sketch in the collection Anderson provides what could be viewed as the sine qua

non of the narrative literary journalist's ambition: "There must be a
revolution in feeling before there can be a revolution in fact" (11).
In other words, facts can only be understood once there is a reflexive
understanding of feeling or subjectivity that determines which facts are
to be valued. To do that involves engagement, and Anderson confronts
a dilemma similar to that of Basil March, the fictional journalist in William Dean Howell's novel *A Hazard of New Fortunes*. March "devises concepts to remove himself from the immediacy of life. . . . This pose prevents March from finishing the sketches for which his trip around the
city has provided material" (Borus 180). Anderson opens his first
sketch, about life in a coal-mining town, facing a similar situation, and
in his reflexivity he attempts to overcome it: "The stories look at me
out of the eyes of men and women. They shout at me. I should not be
writing in this way. I should stay here in one of these shacks in this coal-
mining town. I should know for a long time these men, women, and
children. Why do I hurry from town to town?" (5) When one engages
in objective news, one can easily hurry from town to town, one's subjectivity disengaged.

Caldwell announces his attempt to narrow the gulf between an objectified world and his subjectivity when he says, "Travel should not be
confused with sight-seeing and touring, the latter two being pastimes
of idle wealth." To that might be added that they are pastimes of the
disengaged. He continues: "In its true meaning, a traveler is a stranger
who gains a sympathetic understanding with the people he encounters" (9). Similar is Trachtenberg's "exchange of subjectivities." In one
example, Caldwell describes an impoverished—and hungry—white
tenant family in the Deep South. Among the details, he describes two
hungry infants sucking at the teats of a female dog. Caldwell is perhaps
at his most compelling, however, when he describes a member of the
family, a young girl, not by the evidence of her hunger but by her
hopes, or rather the limited ambition of her announced hopes: "The
girl on the hearth, raising her corn-sack skirt to let the warmth of the
fire fall upon her body, said it ought to be easy to find something to
eat if you only knew where to look for it. Her sisters looked at her but
said nothing. The girl then asked herself a question. What wouldn't I do
for a heaping dish of hog sausage?" (235). But Caldwell's account suffers

perhaps the most from an open ideological frame, once again demonstrating that narrative journalism, even though it may attempt to resist closure, can nonetheless be entrapped, in his case by Caldwell's Communist sympathies. This is reflected, for example, in the last chapter when he calls for the collectivization of American farms on the Stalinist model, not understanding of course what a terror collectivization had become in the Soviet Union. And even the passage above, as descriptive as it is, is framed by a discursive challenge to conservatives who had called for the political disenfranchisement of the poor if they could not support their families. In other words, he fails in his "editorializing through . . . imagery," as his Communist colleague Joseph North had called for (121). This is not to suggest that such texts can ever fully escape ideology. They can, however, resist it, and in the resistance they can engage the reader imaginatively to draw his or her own conclusions.

Anderson does a better job of resisting such ideological temptations. Moreover, he seems to understand the ideological dangers of an objective journalism. In an indictment of mainstream objective journalistic practice, he confronts in one of his sketches the symbolic divorce of American mainstream journalism from the reality of the victims of the Depression. It is an example of narrative literary journalism challenging the influence of the objectivist paradigm on the subjectivity of a journalist. In a midwestern town a doctor who is sympathetic to the plight of the victims of the Depression and a newspaper editor who is not take Anderson out to a country bar that provides a gathering place for the unemployed and their spouses. Anderson contrasts it with the "old saloons I had known in my boyhood," characterizing it as a "new kind of meeting place" where there "was no heavy drinking," presumably because few could afford it (225–26). Throughout the evening the doctor and editor quarrel about the social significance of what they are observing, and it is during the argument that the alienation of the editor's subjectivity from what he is seeing—a world he objectifies professionally—emerges: "'But these farmers,' he said. 'The farmers,' he declared, 'had always been the champion belly-achers.' The newspaperman had got a good start and he kept going. . . . He said that it had been proposed in some of the States that people on relief be deprived of their vote. He was for that. 'A pauper is a pauper,' he said, winking at me. He began on the subject of man and his opportunities. 'I don't care what comes up, the man who has got the real stuff in him will survive'" (229).

Rather than attempting to understand the subjectivities of the un-employed, the unidentified editor separates himself from them and judges them by what he believes he is not, in effect the brutish Other. The divorce of his subjectivity from the world is most clearly expressed in the following passage, "'I'm an individualist,' he said. 'You must not listen to the doc here, he's a sentimentalist'" (227). What the editor implies then is that as an "individualist" he is separated from the experi-ence of others. The charge against the doctor is also revealing because it is reminiscent of the hopeful sentimentalism of Richard Harding Davis in longing for the hostages of Louvain not to be shot. The senti-ments may be sentimental, but they speak to the longing to understand other subjectivities.

The in-search-of-America theme prompted still other more strictly descriptive efforts of narrative literary journalism that went beyond the search via the automobile. In the late 1930s the publishing house of Farrar and Rinehart embarked on its Rivers of America series in which twenty-four volumes were planned that recorded the life and folklore along the country's major rivers. As Constance Lindsay Skinner, a Canadian-born novelist and the series' first editor, noted: "This is to be a literary and not an historical series. The authors of these books will be novelists and poets. On them, now in America, as in all lands and times, rests the real responsibility of interpretation" (n. pag.). For ex-ample, Cecile Hulse Matschat, a noted writer on flora and gardening, wrote *Suwannee River: Strange Green Land*. Writing in the third person as "the Plant Lady," Matschat records living among the inhabitants of the river and Okefenokee Swamp.

> One such spring morning two persons in a small, flat-bottomed skiff in the heart of the swamp did not hear the music of the wild, nor see the beauty of the gloomy water and the occasional ray of light that silvered the gray-tressed cypress and shimmered on the green bay leaves. Their attention was fixed on the big cottonmouth basking on a cypress root— knee, the swampers call it—which protruded above the water about the height of the Plant Woman's head. The bow of the boat, where she sat,

had brushed against the knee and stopped, fortunately without shaking
it. (12–13)

A drawback to such an "institutionalized" or "corporate" series was that
the writers were not always equal to the task. Matschat may have had a
creative eye for describing plant life, but at times her attempts at faith-
fully recording swamp dialogue among its human inhabitants is so styl-
ized as to sound more like parody, or like something from a "Snuffy
Smith" comic strip about hillbillies and country bumpkins. Regarding
the cottonmouth, her guide says: "'Lotsa varmints out this spring.' He
spat in the water. 'Purty, hain't he!'" (13).

What such institutionalized or corporate efforts do reflect is just how
much nonfiction focused on the theme of America. As Kazin notes,
"Whatever form this literature took—the WPA guides to the states and
roads; the reaction against the skepticism and now legendary 'frivolity'
of the twenties; the half-sentimental, half-commercial new folklore that
manufactured or inflated comic demigods out of the reclaimed past;
the endless documentation of the dispossessed in American life—it tes-
tified to so extraordinary a national self-scrutiny" (*On Native Grounds*
486). Indeed, Matschat's effort on the Suwannee River was probably
the kind of work Kazin had in mind when he took note of "the half-
sentimental, half commercial new folklore that manufactured or inflated comic demigods out of the reclaimed past." Clearly, not all was
worthy of literary merit. Nonetheless, as Kazin acknowledged in *On
Native Grounds*: "That literature has hardly run its course, and it may
even dominate the scene for many years to come; but for all its shapelessness and often mechanical impulse, it is a vast body of writing that
is perhaps the fullest expression of the experience of the American
consciousness after 1930, and one that illuminates the whole nature of
prose literature in those years as nothing else can" (485). If a narrative
literary journalism did not "dominate the scene for many years to
come," nonetheless it has proved durable, and would flourish once
again with the new journalism.

WHEN ANDERSON and Caldwell explored the lives of poor white
southern tenant farmers, among other marginalized groups, they an-

ticipated what is perhaps the most memorable of such accounts, James Agee's *Let Us Now Praise Famous Men*, published in 1941. The 1940s are important to narrative literary journalism because of two works. One is Agee's; the other is John Hersey's *Hiroshima*, the latter appearing first in the *New Yorker* in 1946 before it appeared in book form. Both occupy pivotal positions in the history of American narrative literary journalism. First, they derived respectively from the instrumental and descriptive strains of the form in the thirties, and second, they anticipate the new journalism of the 1960s. Ultimately, both represent the two poles of treatment that create a spectrum across which subjectivity appears to operate in the form in its attempt to narrow the gulf with an objectified world.

Agee, similar to Lafcadio Hearn when the latter arrived in Japan in 1890, was assigned in 1936 to write a story he found he could not treat in the manner in which his editors at *Fortune* magazine wanted. As Shelley Fisher Fishkin relates: "The tone of such pieces was one of 'breezy condescension'. . . ; the poor profiled were described in a manner designed to amuse or entertain *Fortune*'s affluent, powerful readers" (145). They were, in effect, reduced to sensational brutes. But as Agee became involved in the lives of three tenant families in Alabama he found himself unable to remove his subjectivity from the story. Instead, in his preface he acknowledged that he embarked on writing the book in order "to recognize the stature of a portion of unimagined existence, and to contrive techniques proper to its recording, communication, analysis and defense" (xiv). The result, he hoped, would be "an effort in human actuality, in which the reader is no less centrally involved than the authors and those of whom they tell" (xvi). Here, most clearly, is an announcement of the intention of the author, one in which "the reader is no less centrally involved than the authors and those of whom they tell." Again, the purpose of literary journalism is to share subjectivities between "teller, listener (spectator) and protagonist(s)" (Berger, "Stories" 286).

Let Us Now Praise Famous Men was published in 1941, and in it Agee makes clear his intentions: to acknowledge his own subjectivity in an effort to understand someone else's, such as that of tenant-farmer George Gudger: "George Gudger is a man, et cetera. But obviously, in the effort to tell of him (by example) as truthfully as I can, I am limited.

I know him only so far as I know him, and only in those terms in which I know him; and all of that depends as fully on who I am as on who he is" (239). In the reflexive acknowledgment of the role his subjectivity plays, Agee acknowledges his limitations, and thus the indeterminacy of a world whose conception resists critical closure when he concedes of Gudger, "I know him, and *only* in those terms in which I know him" (emphasis added). The question of course is what lies beyond the *only?* That is what remains indeterminate. Agee adds: "Of this ultimate intention [to provide a true account] the present volume is merely portent and fragment, experiment, dissonant prologue" (xv). As Fishkin notes of the passage, "Here we have a clue to the insight that enabled Agee to write at all: his awareness that his book would be 'true' only to the extent that it acknowledged its own incompleteness" (149).

Even as Agee's *Let Us Now Praise Famous Men* was one of the last of the "instrumental" examples of narrative literary journalism that had thrived in the early thirties, one designed to prompt social awareness, it was looking forward to the 1960s when it became a classic in some critical circles (Fishkin 147). Thus it fulfilled its intention across time as a work that, like Crane's "An Experiment in Misery," attempted to result in an exchange of subjectivities, or in shared subjectivities, not only by seeing from a distance how an objectified "other half" lived but also by attempting to experience it through Trachtenberg's "felt detail."

The first half of the 1940s was also, clearly, a time of notable war reportage. Liebling covered London and D-Day for the *New Yorker;* Ernie Pyle wrote about both the European and Pacific campaigns in such works as *Brave Men;* Robert J. Casey wrote about the war in the South Pacific, collecting and publishing his work in *Torpedo Junction,* among others; and Morris Markey, who had been writing for the *New Yorker* since the 1920s, covered the war from an aircraft carrier. On the home-front, John Dos Passos explored the country at war in a continuation of the in-search-of-America travelogue with his *State of the Union,* which appeared in 1944. But perhaps the most memorable effort was Hersey's *Hiroshima,* appearing a year after the war concluded. If James Agee's *Let Us Now Praise Famous Men* was instrumental narrative journalism, John Hersey's *Hiroshima* falls clearly into Stott's "descriptive" category. Its success at achieving the pose of a neutrality of tone—leaving it, as Asch said, "up to the reader to draw his own conclusions"—has prompted Phyllis Frus to cite such neutrality as a major flaw in the book, even though she acknowledges that it is "probably the best-known journalistic work of the post–World War II period" (*Politics and Poetics* 92). Almost entirely absent from *Hiroshima* is an acknowledgment of the author's subjectivity. It is, Frus adds, "an excellent example of the effect of taking aestheticized objective narration as a model" (92). It is also an example of what Dwight Macdonald called "denatured naturalism" common to the narrative literary journalism of the *New Yorker,* and it suffered from "moral deficiency" because of its "clinical" detachment ("Hersey's 'Hiroshima'" 308). As Frus observes, the result could "only objectify its subjects and provoke the reader's (as well as the writer's) condescension" (*Politics and Poetics* 93). For this reason, Frus dismisses *Hiroshima* as fundamentally sensational by suggesting it fits the definition of sensationalism offered by John Berger: "the reducing of the experience of the other into a pure framed spectacle from which the viewer, as a safe and separate spectator, obtains a thrill or a shock" ("Another Way" 63). Implicitly, in the distance created by the condescension, the Other could be kept at bay.

There is much to what Frus says, but she overlooks what could be characterized as a "reduced" subjectivity in the text, which exists on a spectrum between a hypothetical extreme subjectivity at one end and a hypothetical extreme objectification at the other. Subjectivity is reflected, for example, in the gorgeous metaphors reflecting value statements Hersey's subjectivity is forced to make—his "shaping consciousness"—in order to place the narrative in perspective. In one example, Hersey observes: "And now each knows that in the act of survival he *lived a dozen lives* and saw more death than he ever thought he would see" (2, emphasis added). Still later, Hersey's mere act of acknowledging that there are some things he cannot know as part of his reporting effort at what Frus calls "aestheticized objective narration" reflects in the aesthetics a subjectivity Hersey cannot deny: "It would be impossible to say what horrors were embedded in the minds of the children who lived through the day" (90). Hersey is acknowledging his own subjective limitations. The issue is not whether Hersey objectifies the experience of those who survived the bombing. Undoubtedly to some extent this is true, as it is to varying degrees in the accounts of other literary journalists. One example is the notorious lack of open emotion in Hemingway's spare style of his reportage, such as in "Italy, 1927."

Hiroshima exists instead somewhere on a spectrum between reflexive subjectivity and a "denatured" objectification. It may be situated more toward the objectified side of the spectrum, but its narrative ambition is still pointed toward narrowing the distance between the subject and the object because of the rhetorical choices made in selecting novel-writing techniques, as well as because of Hersey's acknowledging on rare occasions his subjectivity. This last moves to the foreground when, confronted by the inexplicable, he engages in metaphoric hyperbole, for example, by saying that someone has lived a dozen lives. In his own way, Hersey struggles in the direction of attempting to overcome the distance between subjectivity and objectification. Only, he has a longer distance to travel.

But by the mid-1940s the middle cycle of a narrative literary journalism had gone into decline, Connery suggests in his template. The reasons are not clear, but the triumph of science in World War II alone suggests that positivist assumptions had all but defeated subjectivity as a legitimate cognitive stance from which to interpret the world. Also, by the late 1940s and early 1950s the critical temper had all but solidified in the New Critical mold. Given that the New Criticism sought the meaning of a literary work in itself, that could not bode well for a discourse like narrative literary journalism, which openly acknowledged its phenomenological origins, or its means of production.

Nevertheless during this second lull in the fortunes of the form, the *New Yorker* continued publishing its descriptive pieces, such as Joseph Mitchell's accounts, not unlike Crane's, of pedestrian life in New York City. As Norman Sims notes, "Mitchell and several of his colleagues at the *New Yorker* were responsible for keeping literary journalism alive during the middle years of the twentieth century" ("Joseph Mitchell" 83). Although Mitchell's articles are informed by what Mitchell calls "graveyard humor" (author's note xiii), their personalities reflect once again the attempt to narrow the gulf between subjectivity and the objectified Other. In a piece about McSorley's saloon in Manhattan, for example, Mitchell's subjects are "a rapidly thinning group of crusty old men, predominantly Irish, who have been drinking there since they were youths and now have a proprietary feeling about the place" ("Old House" 3). Implicitly, Mitchell is posing the question, What are the subjectivities of elderly Irishmen who spend their days in a bar and who have a proprietary feeling about the place?

Other writers of the form in the aftermath of the war include Lillian Ross, A. J. Liebling, Mary McCarthy, Meyer Berger, and Ernest Hemingway.[2] Liebling and Ross were mainstays of the *New Yorker* during the postwar period. Liebling began with the *New Yorker* before World War II, writing sketches about New York City life, then covering the war for the publication. After the war the themes he examined became, if anything, more peripatetic, including examinations of Paiute Indians in Nevada and Gov. Earl Long of Louisiana. Lillian Ross demonstrated a similar versatility that included, in 1950, a searing portrait of Ernest Hemingway, which portrayed a painfully self-conscious man pretending not to be self-conscious while drinking conspicuously and frequently from a flask in public as he engaged in his trademark bravado. Like a number of lengthy *New Yorker* pieces, including Liebling's *Earl of Louisiana,* Ross's *Portrait of Hemingway* was subsequently issued in book form.

McCarthy and Hemingway are examined below in greater detail because McCarthy had difficulty having her narrative literary journalism taken seriously, and Hemingway ironically revealed his ambivalent attitude toward journalism in his narrative literary journalism. But first, it is worth noting that unlike a broadly engaged social portraiture—difficult to define topically—more clearly delineated topical genres such as sports and crime narratives continued to be popular. In a sense, they helped keep the model alive even if they were, as Kerrane and Yagoda have observed, "on the other side of the literary tracks" (97). Two prominent sports reporters writing narrative were Jimmy Cannon and W. C. Heinz (Kerrane and Yagoda 115, 461). Among notable crime reporting was the work of John Bartlow Martin who frequently contributed narratives to *True Detective* in the 1940s and 1950s. In 1950 he published *Butcher's Dozen,* a collection of narratives about crime, and in 1953 he published *Why Did They Kill?* an account of a murder committed by three juveniles, which has been characterized as a forerunner of Capote's *In Cold Blood* (Applegate 165).

---

2. See Applegate on Berger; Mansell on McCarthy.

Mary McCarthy had difficulty having her reportage taken seriously
as narrative literary journalism in the face of aesthetic essentializing.
In a 1953 article in *Harper's*, "Artists in Uniform," she recalls confronting an army colonel's anti-Semitism. Through her own openly acknowledged subjectivity, McCarthy attempts to transform readers from passive spectators to political participants by means of her own subjective
understanding of the issue and through techniques associated with
novel-writing. For example, in the story the colonel attempts to account for McCarthy's progressive views by taking note of her bright
green dress of raw silk, her sandals, and her hair in a bun that could
suggest she is bohemian: "Refracted from [his] eyes was a strange vision
of myself as an artist, through and through, stained with my occupation
like the dyer's hand" (233). Thus she has to defend herself from the
conception "others" have of *her* as Other and in her doing so readers
see from her perspective what it is like to be placed in a marginalizing frame.

Equally important, however, the story prompted a response from
readers that reveals just how much narrative literary journalism was
marginalized by the oppressive weight of the New Criticism and literary
formalism. McCarthy responded with an article in the February 1954
Harper's defending her first piece as a true story. Her response came
about in part because one college English teacher wrote her, asking:
"How closely do you want the symbols labeled?" such as in the "two
shades of green with pink accents" ("Unsettling" 250). In "Unsettling
the Colonel's Hash" she insists that the story was not fiction and that
whatever symbolism was contained in the story was incidental to its being true. Nonetheless, that she found herself defending the story as a
true one reflects the near totalizing sway in the English academy of the
focus in literary criticism on the assorted accouterments of formalism
and the New Criticism.

Among examples of Hemingway's literary journalism during the fifties is an article that reveals his ambivalent attitude toward the form.
Also, among the writers discussed here, he is in many ways the most
problematic because of his reticence in revealing his own subjectivity.
What he does reveal about himself is through indirection. In 1956 *Look*
magazine ran what he called "a situation report of how things go until
we go back to work tomorrow on the long book" ("A Situation Report"

472). In the article he notes, "As for journalism, that writing of something that happens day by day, in which I was trained when young, and which is not whoring when done honestly with exact reporting; there is no more of that until this book is finished."

His ambivalence is reflected in the nature of the article he is writing for *Look*: an account of what "happens day by day" in the intervening time when he is not working on "the big book." Among other things that happen day by day is that "Miss Mary [his fourth wife] was away and I was lonesome as a goat and felt like going on the town" with a group of navy officers. He did, and committed to paper that account, so that when he says there is no more journalism "until this book is finished" he seems to have forgotten the practice he is engaged in: journalism. Whether he is aware of the irony is unclear. But evidently journalism, or the literary version under discussion here, got the better of him. He could not help but attempt, once again, to narrow the gulf between a subjectivity that rarely reveals itself and an objectified world.

Perhaps it is fitting that one of Hemingway's last published works, *A Moveable Feast,* was also a kind of narrative literary journalism. Properly, it is a memoir of his Paris years. But its sketches of other people such as his vengeful portrait of Gertrude Stein also places it as a narrative literary journalism because it is outward-directed toward the social milieu, as opposed to inward-directed toward the self of memoir. That so much of it was about other people was something Mary Hemingway noticed. "Mary, who typed the sketches as he finished them, recalled that she found them disappointing. 'It's not much about you,' she objected. 'I thought it was going to be autobiography.'" Mary concluded "that he was trying to create a portrait of himself by reflection; his life seen in light of others" (Weber, "Hemingway's Permanent Records" 44). In doing so, of course, Hemingway could avoid directly confronting his subjectivity and approach it by means of indirection, a point that ultimately raises questions about just how successful the book can be as narrative literary journalism. In any event, given Hemingway's ambivalence about journalism, it is again a curious irony that one of his last published books (it appeared in 1964 after his 1961 suicide) was journalism. Within his conflict is mirrored the problematic relationship between literature and journalism. That problematic relationship continues to historicize the form, defining narrative literary journalism by what it was not permitted to be.

One work that looks back to earlier examples while anticipating attempts by the new journalism to explore the other is John Howard Griffin's *Black Like Me,* published in 1961. Medically changing the color of his skin, Griffin, a white journalist, traveled across the segregated South passing himself off as a black during a month's period in late 1959. He would later be hung in effigy for his efforts. In undertaking his trip he recalls once again Stephen Crane's effort in "An Experiment in Misery"—to try to understand the subjectivity of someone else's travail. But clearly Griffin was more ambitious: "How else except by becoming a Negro could a white man hope to learn the truth? . . . The only way I could see to bridge the gap between us was to become a Negro" (1–2). Here is one of the clearest statements yet of what narrative literary journalism attempts to do, narrow the gulf, in this case between racial subjectivities. Indeed, *Black Like Me,* even though it clearly engages in social portraiture, may offer the most compelling example of where narrative literary journalism and autobiography so completely merge.

GIVEN THE long if rarely acknowledged shadow cast by narrative literary journalism earlier in the century, the appearance of the "new journalism" in the 1960s, the third major period of narrative literary journalism according to Connery, was hardly "new." Perhaps because the new journalism is within living memory of the generation that grew up at that time and many of its writers are still alive, it would be easy in the hubris of that generation to examine the form as having a larger claim to our attention and being distinctive in its own right. But it is really part of a long history. What does make it different from what preceded is that it achieved considerable critical recognition. To be sure, there had been critical recognition at the turn of the century in the debates about the relationship between journalism and literature. But by the 1960s that memory was all but lost, as reflected in the perception that a "new" journalism had appeared. In reality the form was part of an evolution sharing much in common with what had preceded. What the new journalism shared with the 1930s and 1890s versions was that it developed in response to significant social and cultural transformation and crisis. These were reflected in the civil rights movement, assassinations, disruptions in prevailing middle-class culture, the drug culture, growing environmental awareness, and of course the Vietnam War.

Narrative literary journalism examining these issues found expression in publications such as *Esquire* under the editorship of Harold Hayes, the *Village Voice,* and *Rolling Stone,* among some of the more prominent. They would also be examined in the narrative literary journalism of the dying *New York Herald Tribune* and in that newspaper's resurrected Sunday supplement, *New York Magazine,* in 1968 under the editorship of Clay Felker.[3] The *New Yorker* found it had competition. This said, it should be emphasized that *Esquire* had published narrative literary journalism in the late 1950s as well (Wakefield, "Harold Hayes," 32). As for book-length efforts, in 1965 would come Truman Capote's *In Cold Blood* and in 1968 Tom Wolfe's *Electric Kool-Aid Acid Test,* among others.

The origin of the term "new journalist" as applied to this period is not entirely clear. It has been attributed to Pete Hammill, a sometime new journalist, who attempted in the mid-1960s to characterize the new journalistic trends (Zavarzadeh 63). As scholar John J. Pauly notes, "the New Journalism persistently disrupted taken-for-granted relationships" ("Politics" 111–12). Those relationships were reflected in how Americans negotiated just such contentious issues as the Vietnam War, the drug culture, and middle-class values. For example, Capote engaged in his assault on the totalization of the American dream in *In Cold Blood.* Wolfe portrayed Ken Kesey and the latter's companions, dubbed the Merry Pranksters, traveling across country while they were on drugs. Other authors from the period engaged in similar challenges to critical and cultural paradigms include Gay Talese, who wrote about personalities and New York before taking on larger, book-length themes in works such as his 1969 best-seller *The Kingdom and the Power.* Norman Mailer wrote about U.S. opposition to the Vietnam War in the

---

3. See Hellmann 6, 7, 72, 101, 126, 142; Weber, *Literature of Fact* 9, 18, 24; Frus, *Politics and Poetics* 134; Mills iv–vii, xv; Wakefield, "Harold Hayes" 32–35; and Harvey 40–45.

1968 *Armies of the Night*. Sara Davidson along with her friend Joan Didion wrote about social crisis and alternative lifestyles in the late 1960s
and 1970s. Richard Rhodes wrote about the Midwest in the 1960s, and
Michael Herr was just one of a number of narrative literary journalists
who wrote compellingly about life on the battlefront in South Vietnam.
Meanwhile, John McPhee, after achieving recognition with a profile on
basketball star and political aspirant Bill Bradley, began writing about
the relationship between man and nature. Then there is the "gonzo"
journalism of Hunter Thompson in which Thompson does Wolfe one
better by reporting on the world *while on* drugs.

At the same time, newspaper columnists continued their long tradition of writing narrative literary journalism, oblivious to the idea that
they were doing anything "new" because they were doing what they had
always done. One example, discussed earlier as part of the Chicago
tradition of narrative literary journalism that reaches back to the
1890s, is that of Mike Royko who like his predecessor Ben Hecht some
forty years earlier wrote tales of everyday Chicago life that reflect,
among other things, working men's and women's lives (*Slats Grobnik*).

At the heart of the negotiations over contentious issues that new
journalists took up was the same problem advocates of a narrative literary journalism had detected in the 1890s: mainstream journalism, objectifying in nature, failed to adequately account for and make meaning out of the transformations and crises. This is an oft-announced
theme during the period by practitioners of the new journalism and it
was not uncommon for them to try to publicly distance themselves
from the mainstream press. For example, when many of his short
pieces from the 1960s were collected and published as *Fame and Obscurity* in 1970, Talese, one of the earliest of those recognized as a new
journalist, observed: "The New Journalism, though often reading like
fiction, is not fiction. It is, or should be, as reliable as the most reliable
reportage although it seeks a larger truth than is possible through the
mere compilation of verifiable facts" (vii). Talese is one in a long line
echoing Stephen Crane's observation during the Spanish American
War that casualty figures in newspapers, "facts" with a phenomenalist
status, failed to do justice to the singular subject of a dead enlistee.
Instead, such a fact was only "a unit in the interesting sum of men slain"
("Regulars Get No Glory" 171). Moreover, as John Hellmann observes,

Talese's "larger truth" is "a key statement of the need that caused new journalists to abandon the limitations of conventional journalism. The contemporary individual was in less need of facts than of an understanding of the facts already available" (3).

Other practitioners of the form to detect the problem include Norman Mailer. Mailer took contemptuous aim at the mainstream press when he wrote in *Armies of the Night,* "Now we may leave *Time* [magazine] in order to find out what happened" (12). He maintains his assault elsewhere when he remarks, "The mass media which surrounded the March on the Pentagon created a forest of inaccuracy which would blind the efforts of an historian" (243). Michael Herr, as a correspondent in Vietnam, quickly realized an epistemological futility to reporting on the war utilizing the formulas of conventional mainstream journalism. Herr echoes Crane: "The press got all the facts (more or less); it got too many of them. But it never found a way to report meaningfully about death, which of course was really what it was all about" (214–15). And still later: "Conventional journalism could no more reveal this war than conventional firepower could win it, all it could do was take the most profound event of the American decade and turn it into a communications pudding" (218).

The year 1965 is often viewed as the decisive moment when the new journalism emerged as a response to the perception of a failed journalistic rhetoric. We see that year the publication of such works as Truman Capote's *In Cold Blood,* as well as Tom Wolfe's *Kandy-Kolored Tangerine-Flake Streamline Baby.* As Hellmann observes, "It must be considered more than a coincidence that Wolfe and Capote developed the forms simultaneously, for they were only the most visible experiments in a genre responding to a unique shift in American culture," a shift reflective of cultural transformation and crisis (1–2). That same year, for example, saw Joan Didion engaged in her own form of new journalism in California, independent of what was taking place in New York, when she published new journalistic articles in the *Saturday Evening Post* and *Holiday* on such themes as John Wayne, the California lifestyle, and Guaymas, Mexico (*Slouching* ix, 41, 186, 216). Meanwhile, in January of that year John McPhee published his profile of Bradley in the *New Yorker* before it appeared later in the year in book form (preface).

But it would be a mistake to suggest that 1965 was the year the new journalism appeared. As Wolfe acknowledges, he was inspired by

Talese, who had been writing for *Esquire* since 1960 after working as a conventional reporter for the *New York Times*. In particular, Wolfe credits a sketch Talese published in 1962 for *Esquire* on the heavyweight boxer Joe Lewis as his inspiration for developing a new journalistic style (Wolfe, "New Journalism" 10–36; Talese, *Fame and Obscurity* viii). Moreover, by his own account Talese was self-consciously literary in his journalism. As he recalls, "I wanted to be a writer more than a news reporter. I loved short stories, especially DeMaupassant. I wanted to write about real people the way a short story writer did, showing the person's character. . . . I wanted to write in the style of fiction but I didn't want to change the names. I wanted to write 'short stories for newspapers'" (Wakefield, "Harold Hayes" 34).

One reason 1965 is often viewed as the year the new journalism came of age is that when *In Cold Blood* appeared, Capote proclaimed in an interview with George Plimpton (also a sometime new journalist) that he had invented a new form, the "nonfiction novel" (Plimpton, "The Story"). What *In Cold Blood* did was ignite critical debate about the drafting of techniques associated with the realistic novel and applied to journalistic accounts (Hellmann ix), or accounts making a claim to reflecting a phenomenalistic status.

Capote's claim as inventor of the new form is further compromised because that same year Wolfe's "Kandy-Kolored Tangerine-Flake Streamline Baby" appeared in *Esquire* and was later included as the title piece in a collection of his new journalism. In the 1960s Wolfe worked for the *New York Herald Tribune* as a feature writer where he was already pushing the boundaries of that form. His freelance foray with *Esquire* turned into a creative breakthrough when he found he could not complete an assignment for the publication about a hot rod and custom car show. Finally, out of frustration, he sent his notes on the story to his *Esquire* editor in the form of a personal letter. The editor liked the letter so much that he ran it as the article (*Kandy-Kolored* xi–xiii). Since then, as John Hellmann notes, "Tom Wolfe has been the writer most completely identified with new journalism, both as practitioner and as spokesman" (101).

Perhaps what most attracted readers to Wolfe and created a critical furor around him were his linguistic pyrotechnics that seemed to pose a taunt to advocates of standard English usage. In a story he wrote about 1960s stock car racer Junior Johnson, he demonstrated just how flexible the English language could prove, writing as if he were out of breath and grammar as he described efforts by revenue agents to catch Johnson bootlegging moonshine:

> Finally, one night they had Junior trapped on the road up toward the bridge around Millersville, there's no way out of there, they had the barricades up and they could hear this souped-up car roaring around the bend, and here it comes—but suddenly they can hear a siren and see a red light flashing in the grille, so they think it's another agent, and boy, they run out like ants and pull those barrels and boards and sawhorses out of the way, and then—Ggghhzzzzzzzhhhhhhggggggzzzzzzzeeeeeong!— gawdam! there he goes again, it was him, Junior Johnson! with a gawdam agent's si-reen and a red light in his grille! ("Last American Hero" 129)

What also attracted attention to Wolfe was his eye for phenomena that reflected and marked the tensions, ironies, and existence of subcultures (and that would generally be ignored in belletristic circles), or what elsewhere he characterizes as "status" or "symbolic details" such as gestures and styles of furniture and clothing ("New Journalism" 31–32). For example, in "The Kandy-Kolored Tangerine-Flake Streamline Baby," Wolfe describes the "symbolic details" that characterize young custom car aficionados. Among such sections: "Don Beebe is saying, over a loudspeaker, 'I hate to break up that dancing, but let's have a little drag racing.' He has a phonograph hooked up to the loudspeaker, and he puts on a record, produced by Riverside Records, of Drag-strip sounds, mainly dragsters blasting off and squealing from the starting line. Well, he really doesn't break up the dancing, but a hundred kids come over, when they hear the drag-strip sounds" (80–81). The subculture has revealed the siren call of its anthem.

While Capote's claim may have proved dubious, there is no doubt he achieved a literary and even philosophical depth in *In Cold Blood* that could rival canonical writers. For example, *In Cold Blood* echoes Dostoyevsky's *Crime and Punishment*. At the moment when Perry Smith is prepared to cut Herb Clutter's throat with a knife and embark on a murderous rampage, we see in Perry the image of Rodion Raskolnikov. As Smith recalls to Capote the shaping consciousness:

> After, see, after we'd taped them [the Clutter family], Dick and I went off in a corner. To talk it over. Remember, now, there were hard feelings

between us. Just then it made my stomach turn to think I'd ever admired
him, lapped up all that brag. I said, "Well, Dick. Any qualms?" He didn't
answer me. I said, "Leave them alive, and this won't be any small rap.
Ten years the very least." He still didn't say anything. He was holding the
knife. I asked him for it, and he gave it to me, and I said, "All right, Dick.
Here goes." But I didn't mean it. I meant to call his bluff, make him
argue me out of it, make him admit he was a phony and a coward. See,
it was something between me and Dick. I knelt down beside Mr. Clutter,
and the pain of kneeling—I thought of that goddam dollar. Silver dollar
[Smith and Richard Hickock planned to rob the Clutters but found little
money in the house. Instead, Smith found a silver dollar under a bed].
The shame. Disgust. . . . But I didn't realize what I'd done till I heard the
sound. Like somebody drowning. Screaming under water. I handed the
knife to Dick. I said, "Finish him. You'll feel better." (276)

What William Barrett says of Raskolnikov can also be said of Smith:
"Thus Rakolnikov kills out of insecurity and weakness, not out of an
excess of strength; he kills because he is desperately afraid that he is
nobody" (137). In Smith's case, Richard Hickock serves as his goad,
his reminder at some level of consciousness that in reality he is desperately afraid that he is indeed a "nobody." Smith's "bluff" then is fundamentally an existential problem, a desperate attempt to realize meaning. The investigating detective, Alvin Dewey, seems to intuit this when
he observes after hearing Smith's confession, "The crime was a psychological accident, virtually an impersonal act" (277). Only, the Clutter
family had to pay the price because of the face-off between Dick Hickock and a Perry Smith internally confronting his own existential dilemma. However, in the Russian *Crime and Punishment* there is redemption in the end; the same cannot be said of its American counterpart.
Ultimately, what one detects in *In Cold Blood* is the death of the smug
reification known as the American dream.

But if Capote was capable of such profundity, *In Cold Blood* was not
without its flaws, flaws that traditional mainstream journalists often
used in dismissing the new journalism. This was that new journalists
had too much freedom. Since shortly after *In Cold Blood* appeared, Capote has been accused of inventing scenes. Assuming this is true, there
is still little doubt that the book by and large is true to life. Nonetheless,
the charges remain troubling given that Capote insists in his acknowledgments that "all the material in this book not derived from my own

observation is either taken from official records or is the result of interviews conducted over a considerable period of time" (6). To the contrary, however, participants in the events have challenged his observations and interviews. For example, while Capote describes in detail the execution of both Richard Hickock and Perry Smith, Capote only observed Hickock's; he fled when Smith was brought in for execution, according to one observer present (Plimpton, "Capote's Long Ride" 70). Such are the temptations of a gorgeously affirmed subjectivity that slips into its own invention, and undoubtedly this will continue to be a problem that periodically surfaces in narrative literary journalism.

Nonetheless, the common thread that connected earlier practitioners with the new journalists remained the writers' subjectivity and the motivation to narrow the distance between subject and object. To varying degrees they were willing to grant their subjectivities greater play in their work instead of maintaining the pretense of a mainstream practice that denied subjectivity. The work of Mailer and Didion illustrate this increased respectability for a heightened subjectivity during this period. In Mailer's 1968 *Armies of the Night,* the role of his subjectivity is reflexively acknowledged. When he says, "Now we may leave *Time* [magazine] in order to find out what happened" (12), the alternative he offers for finding out what happened at the march on the Pentagon is himself. His subjectivity is acknowledged again in his 1979 account of murderer Gary Gilmore in *The Executioner's Song.* As Phyllis Frus notes, Mailer's reflexivity—his acknowledgment of his subjectivity in attempting to write about the phenomenal—helps him overcome the kind of objectification of the world that marginalizes other classes as the inaccessible Other (*Politics and Poetics* 183). Similarly, in her 1968 collection of periodical articles, *Slouching towards Bethlehem,* Didion acknowledges that in her stories she was attempting to "remember what it was to be me" (136). As Sandra Braman notes, "Didion rejects the canon of objectivity that still, at least rhetorically, drives conventional journalism. . . . Her subjectivity is a deliberate stance understood *to be a position of strength,* the source of her credibility" (355, emphasis added). Ultimately, in their efforts to understand the subjectivities of others by acknowledging their own, Mailer and Didion conclude with the inconclusive present and the inability to come to critical closure. Mailer does so in *Armies of the Night* when he attempts to divine America's future:

"Deliver us from our curse. For we must end on the road to that mystery where courage, death, and the dream of love give promise of sleep" (317). It is, in the end, an ambiguous sleep at best, one conspicuously similar to the one attributed to Albert Jones by Lafcadio Hearn nearly a hundred years earlier.

Didion also ends in inconclusion in the title piece of her collection *Slouching towards Bethlehem*. In it, she explores the drug culture in San Francisco's Haight-Ashbury section in the 1960s. At a commune, a three-year-old by the name of Michael starts a fire that is quickly extinguished. Later, Michael chews on an electric chord, only for his mother to warn: "'You'll fry like rice,' she screamed." It is then Didion concludes the piece by surveying the other members of the commune who are present: "And they didn't notice Sue Ann screaming at Michael because they were in the kitchen trying to retrieve some very good Moroccan hash which had dropped down through a floorboard damaged in the fire" (128). Didion cultivates such incongruities in her writing precisely because they demonstrate how impossible it is to reduce phenomenal experience into a tidy package or, in other words, to critical closure. In the face of such evidence she records, she is reflecting how she feels, or "what it was to be me" when she confronted the evidence, in this case a kind of disbelief about the circumstances she found.

In "Some Dreamers of the Golden Dream," originally published in the *Saturday Evening Post,* Didion sets her sights on the shallow promise and Gothic nature of the California dream. Didion covers the trial of Lucille Miller, who is accused of killing her dentist husband by burning him to death, this for the sake of an attorney with whom she was having an affair. But her plans go awry; she is charged, tried, found guilty and pregnant (the father is not identified), and sentenced to prison. Meanwhile, the attorney, whose own wife had died earlier under unclear circumstances, marries his twenty-seven-year-old Norwegian governess. On that note, Didion, having left Lucille in prison after giving birth, concludes with her characteristic understatement that has the effect of satirizing formal wedding announcements in newspapers (in still another attack on journalistic "business as usual") when Lucille's former lover marries the young governess: "The bride wore a long white *peau de soie* dress and carried a shower bouquet of sweetheart roses with

stephanotis streamers. A coronet of seed pearls held her illusion veil"
(*Slouching* 28). Thus Didion seems to intimate, we detect another
young and pretty dreamer of the golden dream, behind her "illusion
veil." Beyond the phenomenal evidence of such an inconclusive present, the dream hardly seems golden.

Although Hunter Thompson is often characterized as a new journalist,[4] his "gonzo" journalism, as it has been described, occupies an
anomalous position in relation to narrative literary journalism. Part of
the difficulty is that while his work is often narrative, it also engages in
outrageous satire and the boundary between fiction and nonfiction is
unclear. Hence, so the story goes, his work was described as "real
gonzo" by Bill Cardoso, a reporter for the *National Observer* whom
Thompson met while covering the 1968 Nixon presidential campaign
(Anson 24). The term stuck to Thompson's variety of new journalism.
In some ways, Thompson is a latter-day Ned Ward (including the vulgarisms). In the case of the 1971 *Fear and Loathing in Las Vegas,* Thompson ostensibly goes in search of the American dream in the heart of
America's gambling mecca. But satire raises questions about whether
the real intent is to narrow the gulf between subjectivities or to widen
it with sensational outrage. That may well be part of the answer regarding the relationship of "gonzo" journalism to a narrative literary journalism. Because another aspect to that relationship is that if the ideological purpose of narrative literary journalism is to narrow the gulf
between subjectivities, or between Others, Thompson's gonzo journalism represents, to borrow from postcolonial criticism, the colonial
Other writing back to the empire. In the satire, the "empire" (or the
American dream as the case may be) is forced to see a side of itself that
only the marginalized Other can provide.

Such overt reflections of subjectivity in Thompson, Mailer, and Didion should not obscure the fact that other narrative literary journalists
were also indulging their subjectivities, if conservatively so. Frus attacks
Capote for not indulging the first person in *In Cold Blood.* But as Talese
observed of the new journalism, the degree of involvement by the author is relative: "It permits the writer to inject himself into the narrative

---

4. See Kerrane and Yagoda; Kaul; Applegate; and Connery (*Sourcebook*).

if he wishes, as many writers do, or to assume the role of a detached observer, as other writers do, including myself" (vii). That said, it should be recalled that in the contrast between narrative literary journalism and mainstream objectified journalism, writers such as Talese, Capote, and McPhee, whose subjectivities are relatively more covert compared to Mailer, Didion, and Thompson, still reflect in the comparison a more flagrant shaping consciousness.

One consequence of these efforts to close the distance between subject and object is that once again many of the new journalists would be politicized as they became familiar with the subjectivities of the Other. Mailer's *Armies of the Night* hardened his already public opposition to the Vietnam War. Didion, in her book *Salvador,* opposes American support for the right-wing government in El Salvador precisely because her subjectivity experienced to some degree what she perceived as the subjective terror of an entire society by that government's shadowy death squads. The issue is not whether she feels it completely but whether as part of her narrative ambition she can narrow the gulf to feel what a distanced object could not provide. What she feels, however, must ultimately remain imprecise as she confronts the inconclusive present. For example, when she leaves El Salvador, terrified by an experience she can never neatly sum up, she writes: "I boarded without looking back, and sat rigid until the plane left the ground. I did not fasten my seat belt. I did not lean back" (106).

In his postimperial satire, Thompson remains America's bad boy, not only symbolically defecating on traditional American values but also, in his drug-induced narratives, challenging the very notion of what qualifies as the correct state of consciousness (sobriety) in reporting on the world. As with Didion, the center cannot hold. Meanwhile, Capote could not escape the consequences of his subjectivity's engagement with the killers Para Smith and Dick Hickock. Frus compellingly argues, as she did with Hersey, that Capote reinforces the stereotype of the two as drifters on the margin, or as social Other, because he denies his subjectivity. Nonetheless, on the narrative spectrum between objectified mainstream news style on the one side and an overt or reflexive subjectivity such as Mailer's on the other, Capote's very choice of the gorgeous metaphors of novelistic technique (given that all language is metaphor) reflects a more open subjectivity engaged with the object. So much was this the case that Capote became an opponent of the death penalty after the execution of Smith and Hickock. Mailer, Didion, and Capote, then, were all in search of the symbolic brute, and they sought in their own way and according to their abilities to make peace with him (or her).

INSTEAD OF a beginning, then, the new journalism was part of a form long practiced. What would be different with the new journalism is that scholars would begin to take it seriously when Gay Talese, Truman Capote, Joan Didion, and a host of others appeared in the 1960s. Yet despite that seriousness of scholarly effort, the form's history has still managed—even at the beginning of the twenty-first century—to remain largely unnoticed by most of the academy. In reality, Talese, Capote, Didion, and others are part of a long and distinguished tradition traceable in various forms and fragments at least as far back in the Western tradition as Plato. The narratives they and other literary journalists before them wrote were done so over the course of this period in order to humanize by introducing what makes us human, the "I," whether it is Capote's submerged "I," or one like Mailer's that outrageously exposes itself to the reader's scrutiny. Indeed, on the spectrum between objectified style and a reflexively subjective style, the issue is not where the divide exists between the two, given that subjectivity is present in all objectification. Moreover, objectification is present in all discourse, no matter how subjective. Otherwise, the latter would not be discourse, but only solipsism of the most extreme kind, disconnected and once again alienated.

To be sure, debatable exceptions arise, such as Lowell Thomas's *With Lawrence in Arabia,* which engages in a kind of pseudoliterary journalism trapped within the distanced image of the absolute past. In Thomas's pose as a latter-day chronicler of historical romance, there is no confrontation with the inconclusive present.

In any event, modern American literary journalism, of the kind defined and delineated here, fundamentally has been a reaction in this century against the alienating gulf created by the objectification of news in the American mainstream press. That kind of objectification is, like the emperor's invisible clothes, a pose or a conceit that makes a claim to critical closure. Subjectivity alone undoes the lie, and in undoing it literary journalists resist coming to critical closure. That opens the way for attempting to engage in an exchange of subjectivities with the Other.

But while this accounts for a history of the form, it does not account for why the form was for so long marginalized as a literature and a journalism. This is also important to examine; in doing so we deepen our understanding of narrative literary journalism by the history it was not permitted to have. Such an understanding can only critically situate the form further.

6 The Critical

Marginalization of

American Literary

Journalism

IN 1975, as the new journalism began to settle into middle age and an American public found itself wearied of what was so
closely identified with the cultural upheavals of the 1960s and defeat in
Vietnam, critic Thomas Powers, in an article that reflected the cultural
fatigue, assaulted that variety of narrative literary journalism. Specifically, Powers took to task Tom Wolfe: "So, the novel is alive and well,
the sweetheart of writers everywhere, which is okay with me, and journalism, from which Wolfe hoped to see such great things, trapped for
so long in leaden boots—well, journalism, alas . . . is still journalism"
(499). Smugly, he asked, "Whatever happened to the New Journalism?" (497).

Critical condescension toward a narrative literary journalism is
hardly new, and in privileging the traditional fictional novel over the
new journalism, Powers reflects what has been, largely, the response of
criticism to literary journalism in the twentieth century despite its widespread practice. At best, the critical attitude up to the new journalism has been ambivalent. Often, however, it has been outright hostile.
Moreover, not only has the literary establishment been ambivalent or
hostile toward the form, but so also has the journalism world, practitioners and academicians alike. Not until the 1960s would critics from
that sector begin to appraise the form seriously. Paradoxically, the hos-

tility and ambivalence of the journalism community—among its practitioners and academicians—derived from much the same reasons, I
propose, as that of the literary establishment. Despite their seemingly
different emphases, both had similar aims: to construct a critical hegemony that had the indirect effect of excluding a narrative literary journalism as a discourse to be taken seriously. Ultimately, the form would
prove to be a narrative cripple, a narrative imperfection for both, and
ultimately too a reminder of what both those sectors of the academy
sought so diligently to avoid in their own critical essentializing. Such
marginalizing politics, however, tend to come a little later to journalism
when the practice was theorized in the 1920s and when mass communication studies emerged in the 1940s, a study that quickly claimed journalism, broadly conceived, for its own.

In this chapter I trace historical evidence of the critical ambivalence
and hostility, first toward journalism broadly conceived as including
both the discursive, or information, model, and the narrative, or story,
model. In a sense, what emerges is that narrative literary journalism
suffers from guilt by association with that broad conception. Specifically, I explore some of the complex factors that account for journalism's fall from literary grace since the eighteenth century—if, indeed,
it can be considered to have "fallen." I then explore the dominant critical stance of the literature community in this century, which grew out
of earlier attitudes about what constituted literature. Next I explore the
dominant critical stance of the journalism and mass communication
communities. Finally, I examine those few critical voices that rose in support of a narrative literary journalism from the end of World War I to
the beginning of the 1960s and the advent of the new journalism. It is
important to establish the dialectic between those who were hostile to
the form and those few who defended it. In that dialogue the form can
be further situated.

Such an examination is necessary if we are to understand why a
modern form that has proved as durable as it has since at least Lafcadio
Hearn's sketches of African American life in the 1870s and Stephen
Crane's city sketches of the 1890s has received relatively little acknowledgment by the academy. Such an examination also helps delineate
and thus define the form further by the presence, historically, it was

not permitted to have and, in the end, of what epistemologically it had no intention of having any part.

IN HIS 1915 history of American literature, Fred Lewis Pattee characterized the journalist and writer Charles Dudley Warner as "the transition figure in the history of the American essay" (418). On the one hand, Pattee describes Warner, who is perhaps best remembered now as the coauthor with Mark Twain of the novel *The Gilded Age,* as "the last of the contemplative *Sketch Book* essayists" epitomized by Washington Irving. On the other, he is described as "a leading influence in the bringing in of the new freshness and naturalness and journalistic abandon" in late nineteenth-century prose (418). Pattee's comments about Warner reflect an awareness that some kind of change was taking place in nonfiction forms in the nineteenth century. Moreover, they conceal a divide that had nonetheless appeared and that separated literature from journalism, a divide that would only widen in the twentieth century. Pattee, then, is a good point of departure for exploring the nature of the changes and the divide.

What remains curious is that some American journalism, broadly conceived, from the eighteenth century is still considered literature. One revealing measure of this is reflected in that arbiter of undergraduate literature *The Norton Anthology of American Literature.* For the period 1620 to 1820, the second edition (1986) anthologizes twenty-four authors of whom eighteen wrote some form of nonfiction (Baym et al. 1:vii–xii). Included among the works are the *Federalist* papers, which attempted to persuade readers to adopt the proposed Constitution. While we may now consider them essays, they appeared first in New York newspapers and thus can make an equal claim to being journalism. Nor is this an idle claim given that this period from the perspective of journalism history is widely characterized as the era of partisan journalism.[1] From a late twentieth-century perspective then, partisanship appears to be one denominator of what was both literature and journalism during that earlier period.

Still other texts included in the anthology that today could be viewed as forerunners of a modern narrative literary journalism be-

---

1. See Mott 113; Folkerts and Teeter 104; F. Hudson 142; and Sloan 69.

cause they make a claim to being true-life narratives are excerpts from William Bradford's journal of the history of Plymouth Plantation, Mary Rowlandson's account of her Indian captivity, Sarah Kemble Knight's account of her 1704–5 journey, and Hector St. John de Crèvecoeur's *Letters from an American Farmer.* Indeed, of the twenty-four authors in the section, the texts of at least twelve could qualify, in whole or in part, as an early form of a narrative literary journalism because they go beyond the inward-directed examinations of autobiography, such as Jonathan Edward's spiritual struggles, to provide discussions and sketches of contemporary colonial society, sketches that are fundamentally outward-directed in their social and cultural portraiture.

As a consequence, in the latter part of the twentieth century, eighteenth-century nonfiction journalistic texts have been elevated as elite literature in the *Norton Anthology.* What remains striking is that the same cannot be said of texts broadly labeled "journalism" throughout much of the twentieth century because they have been excluded from the traditional literary canon as reflected in the *Norton Anthology.* Missing are such notable writers as James Agee, John Hersey, Tom Wolfe, Joan Didion, and Truman Capote. The one exception is Norman Mailer, whose *Armies of the Night* is excerpted (Baym et al. 2:2091). But *Armies of the Night* could also serve as memoir, thus sidestepping the issue and proving more politically palatable to the litterateur.

Several related factors can help account for this shift in critical perspective from the eighteenth through the nineteenth centuries. The first was the invention of the idea of a high and transcendent "literature." The second was the stranglehold neoclassical rhetoric maintained as the basis for a "polite" literature until it was usurped by the idea of a "high" literature. The third was the emergence of the penny press in the 1830s. A fourth was a detectable shift in consciousness as to what was appropriate as "literary" subject matter. A fifth was the emergence of positivist assumptions in the nineteenth century as a critical frame or paradigm from which to interpret phenomenal experience. A sixth was a new consciousness after the Civil War as to what could be considered "literature." The combined results of these would be that "journalism" broadly conceived, whether it was an objectified version or the narrative literary version, would be increasingly marginalized.

The concept of a high and transcendent literature reflecting the claim of "universal" values is largely a nineteenth-century invention with roots in the eighteenth century. Indeed, throughout most of the eighteenth century literature remained pretty much what it had always been, humane or polite letters. This can be detected in the title of one of the most widely studied treatises on neoclassical rhetoric, Hugh Blair's 1783 *Lectures on Rhetoric and Belles-Lettres*.[2] Moreover, polite or fine letters clearly included the journalism of the time, as Blair's rhetoric reveals in an admiring analysis of the journalism of Joseph Addison (28). A slight shift can be detected with Samuel Johnson who, in his *Lives of the Poets,* characterizes Thomas Sprat, the seventeenth-century bishop, biographer, and historian of the Royal Society, as "an author whose pregnancy of imagination and elegance of language have deservedly set him high in the ranks of literature" ("Abraham Cowley" 323). Thus can be detected an early example of the elevation into divine ether of the idea of "literature." But even here, as Sprat's wide-ranging writing interests illustrate—religion, science, history, biography—literature is still "the activity or profession of a man of letters, the realm of letters," to cite the *Oxford English Dictionary* (*Compact Edition* 1:1638).

Still another measure of the nonexistence of a high "literature" in the eighteenth century is to be found in *Hall's Encyclopaedia,* also known as the *Royal Encyclopaedia,* compiled by William Henry Hall in the mid- to late 1790s.[3] Hall's effort is largely forgotten today, but in the hubris of his time, in the waning days of the Age of Reason that was being eclipsed by the preromantics and early romantics, Hall made claim to providing "the most comprehensive library of universal knowledge that was ever published in the English language" (front matter) by including the material contained in Chamber's *Cyclopaedia* of 1728, the *Encyclopaedia Britannica* (volumes first issued in 1768), and *L'Encyclopédie* of Diderot and the French philosophes (volumes first issued in 1751). Hall's enterprise was ambitious and provides a cultural window on what was considered "knowledge" at the time. Characterized as the "new royal encyclopedia," it also had the sanction of royal patron-

---

2. See the discussion by Connors; Golden and Corbett.

3. *Hall's Encyclopaedia* does not contain a publication date, but bibliographers assign it to the 1790s, which is borne out by engravings dated as late as 1795.

age: it was, in a sense, "official" knowledge. Conspicuous by its absence is the lack of a listing for "literature." What the encyclopedia does discuss at length is neoclassical rhetoric.

"Literature" as an enterprise conflated with a "high art" and reflecting eternal and universal values begins to appear more commonly in the early decades of the nineteenth century according to the *OED*. In 1812, for example, Sir Humphrey Davy, natural philosopher, chemist, inventor of the miner's lamp, and author of literary essays on angling in the tradition of Isaak Walton, wrote, "Their literature, their works of art offer models that have never been excelled." The *OED* cites this as one of the earliest usages of a "literature" that has "a claim to consideration on the ground of beauty of form or emotional effect" (*Compact Edition* 1:1638). Davy, of course, was writing at a time of the transcendent ambitions of the British romantic movement, when Wordsworth sought through the claims of emotion and "imagination" to fathom the transcendent in such poems as "Intimations on Immortality." In its aspiration, literature was taking on New Age–like spiritual connotations that would be reflected in attitudes toward it by the American transcendentalists. For example, Ralph Waldo Emerson in his essay "The American Scholar," delivered before the Phi Beta Kappa Society and published in 1837, calls for an ennobled "literary" undertaking: "To create,—to create,—is proof of the divine presence" (863). It is also true that Emerson calls for the examination of phenomenal "nature." But in doing so it must be examined for the ultimate purpose of arriving at eternal, timeless truths:

> I embrace the common, I explore and sit at the feet of the familiar, the low. Give me insight into to-day, and you may have the antique and future worlds. What would we really know the meaning of? The meal in the firkin; the milk in the pan; the ballad in the street; the news of the boat; the glance of the eye; the form and the gait of the body;—show me the ultimate reason of these matters;—show me the sublime presence of the highest spiritual cause lurking, as always it does lurk, in these suburbs and extremities of nature; let me see every trifle bristling with the polarity that rangers it instantly on an eternal law;—and the shop, the plow, and the ledger, referred to the like cause by which light undulates and poets sing;—and the world lies no longer a dull miscellany and lumber room, but has form and order; there is no trifle; there is no puzzle; but one design unites and animates the farthest pinnacle and the lowest trench. (68)

To such an "eternal law," then, literature must aspire even if its material is profane. Still elsewhere, in a discussion of memory that has consequences for any account making claims to a phenomenalist status, he notes that "the corruptible has put on incorruption. Always now it is an object of beauty, however base its origin and neighborhood. . . . In its grub state, it cannot fly, it cannot shine,—it is a dull grub. But suddenly, without observation, the selfsame thing unfurls beautiful wings, and is an angel of wisdom" (60).

What remains curious about Emerson is that he offers his views—by calling for the examination of the profane—as a contrast to those of the neoclassicist Samuel Johnson whom he characterizes as "cold and pedantic" (68). Yet at the same time Emerson reinscribes his own views into the same kind of totalization as Johnson, thus helping to nurture the concept of a reified literature, which Johnson hints at in his discussion of Sprat. Such a theme is ultimately traceable up through the New Criticism of the twentieth century. Moreover, it is one, to recall Bakhtin, that ultimately is "structured . . . in the distanced image of the absolute" divine or critical past, or in a "zone outside any possible contact with the present in all its open-endedness." What we begin to see is a philological elasticity to "literature" at this time, but one whose profane "suburbs" and "extremities" must nonetheless aspire to essentialized "eternal law." As a cultural document, "The American Scholar" reflects the critical challenges posed to men of letters and emerging litterateurs by the increasing focus in the nineteenth century on the materiality of experience, a focus driven in part by the emergence of the positivist paradigm as the critical paradigm from which to view the universe.

So it would be that in 1854 Emerson's friend and pupil Henry David Thoreau, a sometime narrative literary journalist, would also inscribe a high literature when he noted that "we should read the best that is literature" (*Walden* 86). Elsewhere, he attacks his fellow Concordians for not being sufficiently literary: "Even the college-bred and so called liberally educated men here and elsewhere have really little or no acquaintance with the English classics" (87). Thoreau elevates English literature to the level of the classics, or what was perceived as timeless. In contrast to such worthy aspirations, he points an accusing finger at contemporary newspapers (and the popular novel elsewhere) when he notes: "We are a race of tit-men, and soar but little higher in our intellectual flights than the columns of the daily paper" (88). The contempt

that Thoreau had for contemporary journalism is reflected in the de-
rogatory meaning of the epithet "tit-men," which is both a dwarf and a
regionalism for the smallest pig in a litter (Sayre 287). In such dimin-
ishment, journalism can only ignominiously descend when placed beside an ascending literary grace. Thoreau's sneering at contemporary
journalism as reflected in newspapers intensifies still later when, drawing on the metaphor that most readers are suckling "tit-men," he observes: "If we will read newspapers, why not skip the gossip of Boston
and take the best newspaper in the world at once?—not by sucking the
pap of 'neutral family' papers" (90, emphasis added). In the extended
metaphor, Thoreau hints mischievously at the consequences of the rise
of the independent and family-owned press, that it is in effect like a
sow nursing its runtish readers with pap of little nutritional value. It is
small wonder that there has been such animosity between literature
and journalism.

As a result, by midcentury the idea of a high literature was one that
included both the older meaning of polite and humane letters, as well
as a newer one that aspired to the exalted status of art and truth to
which journalism would eventually be excluded. Evidence for this is to
be found in the Duyckinck brothers' 1855 *Cyclopaedia of American Literature,* which was the most comprehensive work on the subject at the
time, even if the subject of "literature" was not defined as it would be,
say, by the mid-twentieth century. Taking up in one section literary history from 1800 to the Duyckinck brothers' own present, and characterized as the "present century" (vi), their conception of literature continues to include the subjects and genres considered polite and humane
letters in the eighteenth century, such as "divinity and moral science,"
"political science," "law," "oratory," "history," and poetry. But signifi-
cantly, they add the "fiction and polite *literature*" of "Paulding, Irving,
Cooper, Simms, Emerson" (vii, emphasis added). Thus in the case of
Emerson, for example, what once would have been polite *letters* has
metamorphosed into polite *literature.* Moreover, fiction, which in the
early eighteenth century had been a lowbrow form and treated with
some suspicion by no less than a moralizing Johnson, was now included.[4] In a telling indication of the decline in the fortunes of journalism, this discourse is conspicuously absent although some of the writers

---

4. See Johnson, "Contemporary Novels."

the Duyckincks include could be considered literary journalists in the broadest sense of the term, either as discursive or narrative: Emerson, Thoreau, Augustus Baldwin Longstreet, and Thomas Bangs Thorpe. All published in popular journals and were anthologized in the twentieth century in the *Norton Anthology of American Literature*. The early evidence of the divide between literature and journalism has emerged. Clearly, what was taking place was a struggle for the soul of what would be considered high literature, and journalism broadly conceived, whether of the daily newspaper type or of the literary type, would prove the loser.

As the concept of a high literature emerged in the nineteenth century, it did so against the dominance of a neoclassical rhetoric as the correct rhetoric for "politely" examining phenomenal experience. One measure of this is to be found in *Hall's Encyclopaedia*. If a discussion of literature is absent, the tome does explore at length "rhetoric" as a subgenus of "oratory" in "Treatise on Oratory; Or, The Art of Speaking well upon any Subject, in order to persuade" (3:no. 121 [Y1r]). Instruction in oratory is clearly in the neoclassical tradition, given the ample references particularly to Cicero and Quintilian, but also to Seneca, Hermogenes, Longinus, and Aristotle. Indeed, the discussion on oratory frames the plain style (which had been called for in the previous century by no less a personage than Bishop Sprat on the founding of the Royal Society) as the same as a neoclassical "low" style.[5] Thus rhetoricians attempted to shoehorn changes in writing style into neoclassical models. Nor, on the issue of modern languages, does English fare well. The treatise notes of Chaucer that "whoever looks into him, will perceive the difference to be so great from what it is at present, that it scarce appears to be the same language" (3:no. 122 [Bb2r]). By example, then, what Chaucer lacked was the ostensible timelessness of classical rhetoric, a stance that could not bode well for the timeliness of journalism.

As eighteenth-century scholar Alan McKillop has noted of that era, "The precepts of neo-classicism go back to the doctrines of Aristotle,

---

5. See Kenner's discussion on the "plain style." But indeed the plain style's origins can be traced back to the sectarians, as William Bradford's introduction for his journal on the Plymouth Colony reveals.

Longinus, Horace, and Quintilian as interpreted by the critics of the
Italian Renaissance. Rules supposedly derived from the ancients, such
as the unities of time, place and action in drama, were used as yard-
sticks to measure the practice of the moderns. . . . Grammar-school and
university curricula, with their exclusive emphasis on Latin and Greek
and their endless exercises in Latin prose and verse, made it inevitable
that educated men should accept ancient authors as models of imitation" (xix). As a consequence, despite the increasing calls for a plain
style, that plain style was still being shaped by the rhetorical decorum
of neoclassicism with its appeal to imitation of the deified ancients.

This was the situation reflected in the American colonies and continued in the subsequent United States, which accounts for the survival
of polite letters or literature. As McKillop notes, "There was no sudden
shattering of the forms, and the partly spurious stateliness of late
eighteenth-century worthies stalked on into the nineteenth. American
students will find it in the accepted language of politics and patriot-
ism in their own country from the Revolution to the Civil War" (xxii)
And then some, one might add. Emerson and Thoreau are indeed
transitional because they would attempt to break with stylistic form,
while at the same time they would continue to "conform" or reinscribe
their beliefs in neo-Platonic forms or totalizations. Indeed, Thoreau
graduated from Harvard in 1837 as a Greek and Latin scholar. It is no
wonder then that in *Walden,* even as he pushes to examine the "open-
ended present" of the phenomenal particular, he invokes at the same
time the ancients for their profundity. For example: "No wonder that
Alexander carried the Iliad with him on his expeditions. A written word
is the choicest of relics. It is something at once more intimate with us
and more universal than another work of art. It is the work of art nearest to life itself. . . . The symbol of an ancient man's thought becomes
modern man's speech" (84).

Thus if one were college-educated before the Civil War, one studied
classical rhetoric and not literature because literature had not yet fully
attained scholarly respectability. For example, in the pioneering program in English literature begun at Lafayette College in 1855, students
were required to finish their Latin, Greek, French, and German studies
before they could take two terms of Anglo-Saxon and Modern English
(Graff 37).

At the same time that a high literature was emerging, drawing from while rising in resistance to a neoclassical rhetoric, changes in technology were taking place that helped to separate literature from journalism as a "fallen" and lowbrow form, a separation ultimately based on class differences. The economics wrought by the technological changes reveal that difference. By 1800 the average price of a daily newspaper was $8.00 a year, while the standard *weekly* wage for a journeyman printer was the same (Mott 162, 159). Newspapers were largely affordable only to a monied or propertied class. Because of mass production a newspaper of a medium-size daily today is available for roughly a tenth of what it would have cost in 1800. Clearly, such early papers were for the wealthy. "This definitely was class journalism; indeed the price of six cents a copy . . . put these papers beyond the reach of the popular audience" (Mott 118).

Hence, in post-Revolutionary America such papers were not only partisan but also elitist, directed toward a propertied and presumably more-educated class. This was reflected in the *Federalist* papers. They were framed in an Augustan or neoclassical rhetoric for a propertied class. Among the many indicators of that rhetoric is the nature in which the essays were signed in neoclassical homage to that past, by "Publius," a reference to "Publicola," one of the founders of the Roman Republic. Moreover, the authors of the *Federalist* papers, in choosing their moniker, were responding to the anti-Federalist essays signed with the monikers of "Caesar," "Brutus," and "Cato" (Furtwangler 51). Finally, Joseph Addison's journalism in the *Spectator* and other publications was written in neoclassical form and proved ubiquitous as a source of instruction in rhetorical style among men of learning and means, such as James Madison who acknowledges as much and who was one of the authors of the *Federalist* papers (Furtwangler 89–91). A proper neoclassical rhetoric, one that reflected genteel class values, dominated the public discussions.

Technological advances in printing processes, however, made newspapers available for a penny a copy—hence the "penny press"—and the "addition of a new economic level of the population to the newspaper audience" (Mott 215). The result was the rise of an independent press that was not reliant on party allegiances and subscriptions, and that catered to a broader economic level of the population, or what conventionally might be called the nonpropertied lower classes. As a consequence, the rhetoric ceased to be Augustan and genteel. When Benjamin Day founded the first successful penny newspaper in New York in 1833, he filled it with snippets of police news precisely about those lower classes because he understood his market. The result was that the arbiters of literary taste found themselves confronted by the "rabble" in short sketches like these from Day's *Sun*:

> Catharine McBride was brought in for stealing a frock. Catharine said she had just served out 6 months on Blackwell's Island, and she wouldn't be sent back again for the best glass of punch that ever was made. Her husband, when she last left the penitentiary, took her to a boarding house in Essex st., but the rascal got mad at her, pulled her hair, pinched her arm, and kicked her out of bed. She was determined not to bear such treatment as this, and so got drunk and stole the frock out of pure spite. Committed.
>
> Bill Doty got drunk because he had the horrors so bad he couldn't keep sober. Committed. ("Police Office")

Gone, clearly, from the class-based public discussion is the neoclassical, genteel elegance of the *Federalist* papers.

That class played a large part in determining what would be accepted into the ranks of high literature is reflected in the *Spirit of the Times: A Chronicle of the Turf, Agriculture, Field Sports, Literature, and the Stage*. In his 1873 journalism history, Frederic Hudson characterizes it as "the first weekly sporting paper published in the United States" (341). He does so despite the subtitle. Among articles printed in it were Thomas Bangs Thorpe's tall-tale yarn "The Big Bear of Arkansas," as well as true-life sketches of hunting experiences. Indeed, "The Big Bear of Arkansas" can be considered a true-life sketch because its narrator is only relating the yarn he has been told by an Arkansas backwoodsman while the two travel together on a steamboat. Today "The Big Bear of Arkansas" can be found in *The Norton Anthology of American Literature* and thus has been elevated to literary status by one measure (Baym et al. 1:1534–45). On first examination that might suggest that literary arbiters then and now have been open to popular journalism qualifying as a high literature. But such a position would fail to acknowledge the nature of the newspaper Thorpe's sketches appeared in, a nature that is partly masked by Hudson's characterization that the paper was a "sporting" weekly. Indeed, given the *Spirit*'s subtitle, the paper might appear to possess an admirable breadth of vision in its scrutiny of the world: *Turf, Agriculture, Field Sports, Literature, and the Stage.* But the question arises as to who in the 1840s was capable of affording to indulge all five categories of leisure? Hudson characterizes the *Spirit* as one of several "class papers" (343). That class connection was more forthrightly acknowledged when the paper changed hands in the 1850s (Thorpe became one of the owners) and the subtitle was changed to the *American Gentleman's Newspaper.* Thus Thorpe's sketches had a class pedigree that made it possible to enter the respectable parlors of genteel society even if the subject matter might prove, by those genteel values, "uncouth."

The concern over whether journalism was appropriate for such a class is reflected in the sketches of Augustus Baldwin Longstreet. A Georgia patrician, as well as the founding president of Emory University, he took for study the common people of Georgia in his *Georgia Scenes,* the sketches of which were first published in Georgia newspapers in the 1830s and are predecessors of modern American literary journalism. In his preface to the collection, Longstreet acknowledges that his subject matter may be distasteful to a more genteel class: "I cannot conclude these introductory remarks without reminding those who have taken exceptions to the coarse, inelegant, and sometimes ungrammatical language which the writer represents himself as occasionally using, *that it is the language accommodated to the capacity of the person to whom he represents himself as speaking*" (iv, Longstreet's emphasis). Even as Longstreet acknowledges that he is violating the conventions of a more genteel society, he also points the direction to literary realism and literary journalism later in the century—with emphasis. In other words, class strictures on what is publicly printable have been set aside. When he writes that his sketches are composed in "the language accommodated to the capacity of the person to whom he represents himself as speaking," Longstreet acknowledges that his texts will not be framed by a privileging rhetoric but rather by the phenomenon of utterance outside such a rhetorical frame, or outside what he has control over, Bakhtin's inconclusive present reflected in the stray spoken utterance of the common people. In his willingness to observe external phe-

nomena, seemingly unencumbered by class rhetoric, Longstreet's colloquial rhetoric reflects the emerging positivist paradigm with its emphasis on drawing conclusions from external observation. Thus another reason for the eventual exclusion of journalism as literature was
a changing understanding of what and how to report on the world.

But the Longstreet passage is suggestive of still another factor that
accounts for journalism's decline from literary grace. Even as Longstreet pursues the inconclusive present, he offers, in his own way, a
discrete apology to his genteel readers, because as he acknowledges,
he "cannot conclude" until he explains himself, or why he has engaged
in his public indiscretion. Thus class consciousness determined what if
any of those reports would or could be considered admissible to genteel parlors. One could engage in such "rabble rousing" as long as one
apologized in advance for the offense to one's class. If one did not,
then he or she could expect to be excluded from consideration as a litterateur.

After the Civil War, we see the rise of literary realism and naturalism.
But it was also after the Civil War that modern literary studies began to
emerge (although not without resistance from the rhetoricians).[6] That
emergence could only further marginalize journalism as a potential
literature. For example, Theodore W. Hunt, first chairman of the English Department at Princeton, observed in the 1884–85 issue of the
PMLA, that one of the benefits of studying vernacular literature would
be the "*marked increase of English Literary Culture in our colleges and in the
country*" (46, Hunt's emphasis). While the study of vernacular literature
may well have been laudable in its time, what can also be detected in
the uppercasing of "Literary Culture" is a literary elitism. Hiram Corson, a founding faculty member of English studies at Cornell in 1870,
noted in his *Aims of Literary Study:* "We must long inhale the choral
atmosphere of a work of genius before we attempt, if we attempt at all,
any intellectual formulation of it; which formulation must necessarily be comparatively limited, because genius, as genius, is *transcendental,* and therefore outside the domain of the intellect" (93, emphasis
added). Thus literature had taken on a cryptotheological aura. Indeed,

---

6. For a fuller examination, see Graff, *Professing Literature* chaps. 1 and 2.

Corson became a spiritualist who believed he could commune with the spirits of dead authors (90 editor's note). The concept, then, of a transcendental literature largely derives from the nineteenth century, with roots in neoclassical rhetoric and oratory that provided universal forms even as such a literature was reacting against neoclassical rhetoric. Journalism never made a claim to such a transcendent universality.

By the time of Pattee's 1915 American literary history, exclusionary literary politics are reflected in his discussions of naturalism and the essay. Such discussions are important because they appeared in the immediate aftermath of the first major period of modern American narrative literary journalism. Thus they reflect a critical perspective on what had immediately preceded, which in Pattee's case would *appear* to be nothing (preface xii–xiii). Vocal advocates of a narrative literary journalism such as Lincoln Steffens and Hutchins Hapgood are never mentioned in Pattee's influential history. What discussion journalism does receive is by association with literary naturalism and some writers who openly accepted if not practiced narrative literary journalism, or by reference to journalists who legitimately could be considered literary journalists but who preceded the 1890s and that era's critical climate that took recognition of it as a form.

Regarding the conflation of naturalism and journalism, Pattee says: "During the closing years of the century there came into American literature, suddenly and unheralded, a group of young men, journalists for the most part, who for a time seemed to promise revolution" (*History* 396). Among them he includes Garland, Crane, Frank Norris, and Richard Harding Davis, but not Steffens, Hapgood, or Dreiser. Pattee continues:

> They would produce a new American literature, one stripped of prudishness and convention; they would go down among the People and tell them the plain God's Truth as Zola defined Truth, for the People were hungry for it. "In the larger view ... the People, despised of the artist, hooted, caricatured, and vilified, are, after all, and in the main, the real seekers after Truth." The group was a passing phenomenon. Many of its members were dead ... and the others, like R. H. Davis, for instance, turned at length to historical romance and other conventional fields. (396–97)

Clearly, Pattee is responding to the earlier attacks on historical romance by Howells and Garland in a battle for the soul of literature. It was a battle that had been going on at least since Longstreet apologized for indulging the common and profane. In Pattee's critical condescension can be detected the reduction of the literary naturalist—and those like Crane, Norris, Garland, and Davis who in one way or another had been narrative literary journalists—as Other because they dared to "go down among the People." It is still another elitist stance that makes of "the People" the brutish Other. The dismissal especially of Crane as a passing phenomenon would of course amuse those engaged in the extensive Crane scholarship that has since emerged in the academy. And the comment about Davis is equally revealing of the shifting critical currents. Davis's fiction is largely forgotten today although he was one of the most popular writers of his time.

The remark about Davis taking up historical romance also opens on to larger related issues, not the least of which is how different Pattee's critical perspective is on American literature of the period and just how much his dismissal of Crane and Norris, and his ignoring of literary journalism, is and has been coming full circle. According to Pattee, "The new realism was short lived. Even while its propaganda . . . were spreading the news that Walter Scott was dead and that the god of things as they are had come in his power, a new romantic period already had begun" (*History* 401). That "new romantic period" was one in which the historical romance attributed to Scott was taken up by writers such as Richard Harding Davis. The ascendancy of historical romance practiced by Davis was the result, according to one prominent literary critic of the time, of a need to interpret history as part of the progress of "great world changes." The quote is Maurice Thompson's and deserves to be quoted in full.

> Many facts . . . point to a veering of popular interest from the fiction of character analysis and social problems to the historical novel and the romance of heroic adventure. We have had a period of intense, not to say, morbid, introversion directed mainly upon diseases of the social, domestic, political and religious life of the world. It may be that, like all other currents of interest when turned upon insoluble problems, this rush of inquiry, this strain of exploitation, has about run its course. . . . Great commercial interest seems to be turned or turning from the world

of commonplace life and the story of the analysis of crime and filth to
the historical romance, the story of heroism, and the tale of adventure.
People seem to be interested as never before in the interpretation of
history. It may be that signs in the air of great world changes have set all
minds more or less to feeling out for precedents and examples by which
to measure the future's probabilities. (1182)

It may also be that minds turning to "historical romance, the story of
heroism, and the tale of adventure" are engaging in little more than
sentimental escapism into the safety of what Bakhtin calls "the distanced image of the absolute past." The passage is noteworthy for additional reasons. First, "morbid . . . filth" as conceived by Thompson is
the stuff of literary and muckraking journalism. Second, the "insoluble
problems" reflect an indeterminate world that resists critical closure.
Third, the interest in the "interpretation of history" determined by
"precedents" in order to predict and thus dictate "the future's probabilities" reflects an escapism to a terrain of history as the ground against
which human activity *must* be enacted much like the hegemonic pose
of Hegelian history that claims critical closure. The concept of Hegelian history and its variations such as Marxist had, of course, widespread critical currency at the time.

Finally, in turning to that kind of reified history, where the probabilities can be safely forecast from an objectified distance based on the
past of Walter Scott–like historical romance, one need not engage in
the morbid and filthy exchange of subjectivities, or at least a narrowing
of the gulf between subjectivity and what has been objectified, much
less trying to figure out insoluble problems. By implication, such efforts
were not necessary. All that was necessary was to continue playing the
believing game. What Thompson is suggesting is an escapism not unlike that practiced by the character Hurstwood in Theodore Dreiser's
Sister Carrie. Hurstwood immerses himself in objectified news that, because it makes a distant object of the world, keeps the "filth" of that
world at a safe distance. Nor is it unlike the escapism of reading historical romances such as *Lorna Doone,* which kept the brutish filth of the
world at a safe, sublimated distance. To put it in a more colloquial vein,
out of sight, out of mind.

Indeed, Pattee cites Richard D. Blackmore's *Lorna Doone,* published
in 1869, as establishing the modern tradition of historical romance

(*History* 402), thus implicitly suggesting that it had the potential for lasting literary value. The timing of Pattee's aesthetic judgments— he endorses Thompson's position that the world was turning "to the historical romance, the story of heroism, and the tale of adventure. People seem to be interested as never before in the interpretation of history" (401–2)—is of course highly ironic, coming as it does when similar romantic reifications such as the élan of the *poilus* and the *schlag* of the Hapsburg Empire were then confronting their Waterloo at the Marne and Lvov. Pattee, like many generals, was dreaming his own history in one last nineteenth-century dream-escape.

The privileging and privileged aesthetics of the academy are reflected still further when Pattee takes up the essay.

> Instead of the Irving sketch there has been the vivid, sharply cut short story; instead of the contemplative, dreamy study of personalities and institutions—Irving's "The Broken Heart," Longfellow's "Pere la Chaise"—there have been incisive, analytical, clearly cut special studies, like Woodrow Wilson's *Mere Literature and Other Essays;* instead of the delightful, discursive personal tattle of a Charles Lamb and a Dr. Holmes there has been the colorless editorial essay, all force and facts, or the undistinctive, business-like special article, prosiest of all prose. (*History* 417–18)

Except perhaps for the ambiguous "sharply cut short story," which Pattee does not explain, nowhere in his consideration of the essay does he reflect an awareness of a journalism style that adopts the techniques of novel-writing. Yet curiously he does discuss as among the leading essayists during his survey period Charles Dudley Warner and Lafcadio Hearn. Hearn's treatment by Pattee is problematic because he was a fan of Hearn's; yet Pattee ignores Hearn's earlier sketches from the Cincinnati of the 1870s, though they probably would have belonged more in the mainstream of what would have been considered narrative literary journalism two decades later in the New York press. Notwithstanding his high praise for Hearn, who indulged subjectivity to a degree that would anticipate James Agee, Joan Didion, and Norman Mailer, Pattee longs for an older essay form when he notes: "Never before such eagerness to uncover new facts, to present documents, to be realistically true, but it has been at the expense of literary style" (416). In the "literary style" can be detected a coded language for a privileged rhetoric. As a consequence, although many of Pattee's comments indirectly acknowledge the methods and concerns raised by narrative literary journalism, the critical stance is incapable of conceiving journalism and literature making common cause.

There were other signs of opposition to a narrative literary journalism during the first decade of the twentieth century, even though there had been a critical spirit at the time that warmed to the possibilities of the form. The opposition was stated forthrightly in Julian Hawthorne's comments about "journalism the destroyer of literature" in a 1906 article of the same name. What emerges is an opposition driven critically by the belief in literature—derived of class difference from the previous century—having eternal, transcendent value, and if transcendent, then all-embracing in a closed critical system. Clearly, Hawthorne, only son of Nathaniel, but now recalled, if recalled at all, as a writer of historical romance, was himself objectifying journalism. His was a journalism broadly conceived, incapable of being distinguished between the objectified and literary versions, and implicitly demonized as the Other, or the brute, when Hawthorne charges that its concerns are only "material" while those of literature are characterized as "spiritual" (166). Hawthorne was sounding an alarm in response to an ascendant journalism and what was perceived as a declining literature:

> But, owing to our unspirituality, literature for the time being languishes. Journalism, the lower voice, attempts to counterfeit the tones of the higher, but the result is a counterfeit. So long as journalism attend to its own (material) business, it is not only harmless, but useful; but as soon as it would usurp what is organically above it, it becomes hurtful; not only because it does not give us what it pretends to give, but because the plausibility of that pretence may lead us to accept it as genuine, and thus atrophy the faculties whereby literature, the true voice of the spiritual, is apprehended. (166–67)

The privileging of a high literature is self-evident and anticipates literary modernism's and the New Criticism's critical stances that literature exists unto itself as some kind of aesthetic and transcendent essence. Journalism was capable then only of utility because it was broadly conceived as the brute "organically" beneath literature with little if any distinction made between mainstream objectified practice and the more openly subjective literary version. This was the case despite the attempts of advocates of the form such as Lincoln Steffens, Hutchins Hapgood, and Stephen Crane to narrow the gulf between subjectivity and the object. Indeed, the suspicion lingers that this is precisely what Hawthorne is advocating avoiding, the attempt to close the distance between subject and object. Hawthorne's stance is anticipated in a sense in Gerald Stanley Lee's 1900 *Atlantic* article "Journalism as a Basis for Literature" when he notes: "That no good can come out of it [journalism as a basis for literature] is one of the settled convictions of what might be called the gentlemanly literary life" (231). Clearly, Lee has taken aim at the class-based genteel aesthetics of Hawthorne.

The disrepute into which journalism was descending is reflected perhaps most forcefully in Pattee's attitude toward what can only be characterized as the fall from literary grace of Julian Hawthorne, who feared the "destroyers of literature" only to become one. As Pattee notes: "Of the romancers of the period the leader for a time unquestionably was Julian Hawthorne, only son of the greatest of American romancers. In his earlier days he devoted himself to themes worthy of the Hawthorne name. . . . But the man lacked seriousness, conscience, depth of life, knowledge of the human heart. After a short period of worthy endeavor he turned to the sensational and the trivial, and became a yellow journalist" (408). In becoming a debased "yellow journalist" the younger Hawthorne had rejected his literary patrimony.

Pattee was writing at a time when the old order of totalized ideas, of "man's" place in a romanticized history, whether reflected in the republican élan of the *poilus* or the *schlag* of the Hapsburg Empire, was breaking down under the pressure of the conflagration in Europe. One consequence after the war was a modesty of critical outlook, reflected in existentialism, studies of the power and influence of human subjectivity, and in a later epistemological parallel to existentialism's ontological concerns, deconstruction. Paradoxically, however, the conflagration resulted not only in such a modesty of critical outlook but also in the reinscription of totalized critical conceptions as the ground against which human activity must be enacted, and in some instances their phenomenological application in totalitarianism. Witness the replacement of Hegelian history with Marxist history in Russia and National Socialism in Germany. Such a replacement was part of the continuing effort to remove contingency in order to conclude with probabilities: world revolution, for example, or a thousand-year Reich.

A "frustrated, defeated consciousness" attempting "to cover up its own negativity," to borrow a phrase from Paul de Man (12), in the aftermath of World War I expressed the desperation wrought of its defeat by the reinscription of faith in a hope reified as tangible while abandoning the trappings of the pre–World War I rhetoric for doing so. Such was the position of the "Self-Taught Man" in Jean Paul Sartre's seminal novel *Nausea* who has faith in the hope that by pursuing learning he can find the reified answer. This is reflected in one comment when he tells Roquentin, who is suffering from an existential nausea or is sickened by such existential self-delusion, that "no one was better qualified than Noucapie to attempt this vast synthesis. Isn't that true?" (75). In the vast synthesis lies the formal truth of a closed critical system. The "Self-Taught Man's" conclusion, as a result of his faith in the hope that by pursuing learning he could find the reified answer, was that the brotherhood of mankind could be realized on earth, or as he says: "There is a goal, Monsieur, there is a goal . . . there is humanity" (112). Committed to the ideal of the goal, he becomes a card-carrying Socialist, as if the physicality of the card were a certifiable confirmation of the ideal.

Similar are the considerations of aesthetic and journalistic discourse. Poets and writers reinscribed their hopes in aesthetic modernism, while journalists did the same in a journalistic modernism. The academy took the assumptions of those hopes for granted, resulting in the critical hegemony of New Criticism and the critical hegemony of the concept of "objectivity" and journalism as a "science." For any discourse such as narrative literary journalism, which is committed to individual subjectivity whose perspective reveals an indeterminate rather than closed critical view, the consequences could not be "hopeful."

The year 1915 is pivotal too because even as Pattee was longing for a "new romantic period," T. S. Eliot published "The Love Song of J. Alfred Prufrock," which has been characterized as "the exemplary modern poem" (Ruland and Bradbury 257). It is a year, then, when aesthetic modernism was ascendant. The modernist spirit and the essentializing search for transcendent artistic truth would be articulated by Eliot, among others, in "The Perfect Critic" in 1920, and such views would influence the rise of the New Criticism, which has been described as "arguably, the most influential literary theory of the twentieth century" (Childers and Hentzi 205). Art, Eliot said in a statement that became gospel, should "result in the production of a new object which is no longer purely personal, because it is a work of art itself" ("Perfect Critic" 53). In the expulsion of the "purely personal," Eliot sought to separate subjectivity from the "new" object. Thus a text that acknowledges its origins of production cannot be art, according to Eliot's prescription.

Journalism could only lose out because the claim of reporting acknowledges, at the least, phenomenological origins. But to deny phenomenological origins raises profound moral questions regarding the value of bearing witness. That would mean denying, for example, that in Garden City, Kansas, are graves that contain the mutilated remains of the Clutter family, whose murder was examined by Truman Capote in *In Cold Blood*. The same could be said of the events portrayed in Thomas Keneally's book *Schindler's List,* which is more widely known as a film. Those moral issues can be conveniently sidestepped, or at the least distanced, by denying the phenomenological origins of those texts and concluding that they are merely fictions. In sidestepping those issues, or in distancing oneself from them, one's subjectivity can remain alienated and disengaged—from murder and the Holocaust.

The critic Edmund Wilson takes up a similar point in his 1931 *Axel's Castle.* He chastised Eliot, among other aesthetic modernists, for promoting "a conception of poetry as some sort of pure and rare aesthetic essence with no relation to any of the practical human uses for which, for some reason never explained, only the technique of prose is appropriate" (119). Wilson's challenge to a conception of prose as only useful in "relation to any of the practical human uses" is becoming by this point a recurring theme in the marginalization of journalistic prose by the literary establishment. As a challenge it can be directed with equal effect against Pattee's 1915 comment about the decline of the essay into business articles, the "prosiest of all prose," and Hawthorne's 1906 remark that "so long as journalism attend to its own (material) business, it is not only harmless, but useful."

The New Criticism of the English academy would prove to be a legacy of Eliot's modernism. The critical movement "concerned itself with treating works of literature 'objectively,' viewing them as self-contained, autonomous, and existing for their own sake" (Childers and Hentzi 205). In the autonomy of art for its own sake, the acknowledgment of phenomenological origins in a discourse could only doom it as literature. This circumstance would be reflected in the attitude of the English academy toward journalism still broadly conceived and indistinguishable between objectified and literary versions. As Gerald Graff has noted in his institutional study of English studies, by the 1930s "scholars" had assumed leadership of English departments at the expense of "generalists" (146). As a consequence, "many of the younger critics with generalist inclinations gravitated toward journalism and bohemia—options still open in an economy that permitted a living to be eked out on book reviewing, translating, and occasional editorial work. A distinctly antiacademic class of literary journalists took shape in the twenties, enlisting figures such as Van Wyck Brooks, H. L. Mencken, Edmund Wilson, and Malcolm Cowley" (147). Clearly, gravitating toward "journalism and bohemia" was viewed as a step down in the world from the perspective of the English academy. Those generalists who did remain in the academy "began to fit their generalist interests into the methodological mold of the New Critics" (147), in other words, to succumb to the coming critical hegemony of the New Criticism.

Two tangential issues having a bearing on literary journalism also arise from Graff's observations. First, his "literary journalist" is a problematic terminology. To be sure not all were engaged in the kind of literary journalism we now attribute to Joan Didion or Truman Capote. It is an ambiguous terminology, a kind of catchall in the past that has also meant "literary critic." Second, Wilson, among others, partakes of both kinds of literary journalism. He not only was a literary critic but also engaged in 1930s-style "documentary reportage" for the *New Republic* in his story about the Communist-sponsored labor march in Manhattan.

The marginalization of the journalistic enterprise by an elitist English academy is reflected in the 1929 remarks of William A. Nitze when, in his MLA presidential address, he noted, "As it is, our literary critics are a cheerless lot. Either, in this 'devaluated world,' they are still groping for a principle of order, or they have an axe to grind that is sociological or journalese rather than literary" (v). Clearly, in a "devaluated world," those who engage in "journalese" had no business being "literary." Moreover, "journalese" clearly lacked "value" as reflected in the Latin prefix "de." This consideration of journalism incapable of being transcendent art may help to account for why Hemingway the sometime aesthetic modernist and sometime literary journalist decided, with aesthetic modernism ascendant, to rename "Italy, 1927," narrative literary journalism he did for the *New Republic,* and include it in his collected short stories as "Che Ti Dice La Patria?" Except for the change in title, the texts are identical. Nonetheless, by sleight of hand his literary journalism had ascended to literary heaven. Phyllis Frus goes so far as to accuse Hemingway of "ensuring that journalism and fiction would split along hierarchical lines" (*Politics and Poetics* 91).

As a result, by the late 1940s and early 1950s the critical temper had all but solidified in the New Critical mold to which Graff refers. The ambivalence of the English academy toward any kind of nonfiction was clearly expressed by William Van O'Connor and Frederick J. Hoffman in the preface to their 1952 *American Non-Fiction, 1900–1950.* They spoke to the difficulty of examining nonfiction as literature in what is reminiscent of the same difficulties scholars have today: "Despite difficulties of definition, poetry, fiction, criticism, and drama can be analyzed as literary forms or at least discussed in literary terms. Nonfiction, especially in our time, is another matter" (v). They suggest that future generations of scholars may be more successful in accounting for "nonfiction" broadly conceived. "Perhaps only then will it be possible to see with any clarity what these genres or forms were" (v). Still, O'Connor and Hoffman sense that the nonfiction they discuss was undergoing considerable change: "Our era, at least in the United States, has tended to ignore traditional assumptions about the nature of the literary essay, to merge biography with history, social theory, or literary criticism, and to break down the distinction between literature and journalism" (vi). This breakdown of boundaries is echoed thirty-seven years later by Dennis Rygiel when he takes note of the "growing critical interest over the past 20 years or so in nonfiction in general and twentieth-century nonfiction in particular, especially as the boundaries become blurred between literature and non-literature, fiction and nonfiction" ("Style" 567).

Literary journalism, as a subsidiary of a broader nonfiction, remains just as difficult to delineate. Indeed, in a statement remarkable for how much it echoes the critical position of Bakhtin, O'Connor and Hoffman note that "speculation about genres or forms which may be evolving within the enormous range of non-fiction would require highly detailed study, much beyond the scope of a brief survey" (vi). Bakhtin noted that his version of the "novel," or in this case nonfiction narrative, is fundamentally evolutionary because of its commitment to the "open-ended present" (40). In other words, narrative literary journalism cannot be brought to critical closure as a form. To be able to do so would be to clearly delineate its identity and thus to establish a critical certainty. Yet its nature alone—one that is open-ended—denies that possibility. It is, in effect, a critical moving target subject to the whims of a shaping consciousness.

The critical attitude toward nonfiction flip-flops in the same volume, however, when moving beyond O'Connor's and Hoffman's preface, James Gray presents his article "The Journalist as Literary Man." The name of the article is ironic because it reveals the extant critical confusion; Hoffman and O'Connor declare that the nonfiction "article" "carries no literary connotations" (v). To Gray, the journalist can be literary, while to Hoffman and O'Connor the journalist's article cannot. Gray, however, engages in little analysis as to aesthetic merit and instead presents a chronological accounting that takes in the broad range of a broad form. But in an acknowledgment of the reportage of the 1930s he does say of the literary journalist that "his chief subject, stated in the broadest way, is America" (96), thus echoing a similar position of Alfred Kazin, one of the form's few defenders, a decade earlier in *On Native Grounds* (485).

Under the New Critical banner, as a result, narrative literary journalism was excluded as literature because it insisted on accountability to the phenomenological world—however problematic that accountability might prove as an epistemological problem. MLA president Nitze was right: there is no totalizing principle of order in the subjective effort to record one's relations to an indeterminate world. The world is indeterminate if for no other reason than because of the inability of subjectivity to achieve omniscience, which is the point, or at least an important point, to narrative literary journalism. It bears repeating: narrative literary journalism is, depending upon the degree of reflex-

ivity in the production of the report, an attempt at personal engagement of one's subjectivity with what too commonly has been objectified. It is a practice that can only lead eventually to an acknowledgment
of subjectivity whose own limitations must reflect indeterminacy—all
expressed of course by means of the indeterminacy of language.

THE AESTHETIC essentializing of the literary modernists is only half
the equation, however, for why literary journalism has been neglected
during much of the twentieth century. The theorists of journalism and
of the mass communication academy were no less busy earlier in the
century reifying the concept of objectivity at the expense of subjectivity and ultimately to the exclusion of an indeterminate phenomenal
world. It is a point on which Phyllis Frus has also taken note: "Journalism shares the goal of objectivity which corresponds to the aesthetic
ones elevated by the modernists" (*Politics and Poetics* 91).

In the immediate aftermath of World War I the rise of the concept of
journalistic objectivity can be charted as a reinscription of a privileging
critical frame. By the 1920s the concept of "facts" as the basis of the
news story had fallen into disrepute because of two related factors, the
rise of public relations and wartime propaganda (Schudson 141). "It
was the astounding success of propaganda during the war . . . which
opened the eyes of the intelligent few in all departments of life to the
possibilities of regimenting the public mind," said the late Edward Bernays, who is credited as the founder of modern public relations (*Propaganda* 27). Michael Schudson adds: "Many journalists were directly
involved in World War I propaganda. On the one hand, American journalists found themselves the victims of military censorship as war correspondents in Europe. On the other hand, they themselves served as
agents of the American propaganda machine at home or abroad"
(141). The consequence, he notes, is that "nothing could have been
more persuasive than the war experience in convincing American newspapermen that facts themselves are not to be trusted. . . . In the war
and after, journalists began to see everything as illusion, since it ['factual' reporting] was so evidently the product of self-conscious artists
of illusion" (142).

One response was the call for objectivity in news reporting by Walter
Lippmann, among others. Schudson has characterized Lippmann as

"the most wise and forceful spokesman for the ideal of objectivity" (151). In 1922 Lippmann published *Public Opinion* in which he notes: "As our minds become more deeply aware of their own subjectivism, we find a zest in objective method that is not otherwise there" (256). Zest as a "keen enjoyment" and akin to the romantic concept of "gusto," according to one definition (*Webster's* 1039), amounts to little more than critical voodoo out of which effervesces Lippmann's conception of "objectivity," which inexplicably transcends subjectivity. In what becomes an implicit indictment of his own indictment of subjectivity even as he uses a critical terminology as subjective and value-laden as "zest," Lippmann, observes: "The greater the indictment against the reliability of human witnesses, the more urgent is a constant testing, as objectively as possible, of these results" (Lippmann and Merz 33). Thus Lippmann and Merz elide the problem of human subjectivity. In doing so, they take a leap of faith and place their faith, as did many moderns, in science. The effect was to reinscribe the practice of journalism in the positivist spirit, switching over from a positivist belief in facts to a positivist belief in objectivity. Lippmann's critical totalizing is reflected in his bald assertion of the need for a critical "unity": "There is but one kind of unity possible in a world as diverse as ours. It is a unity of method, rather than of aim; the unity of the disciplined experiment" (*Liberty and the News* 67). Lippmann's unity would be achieved by science, Schudson adds, because for Lippmann, "pure science was the modern incarnation of higher religion's best teachings. Virtue, as Lippmann defined it, is . . . the refusal to credit one's own tastes and desires as the basis for understanding the world" (154–55).

Lippmann would reiterate his position on objective reporting in 1931. The timing is important because at this point a reinvigorated Progressive narrative literary journalism, what William Stott calls "instrumental" documentary (238), began to emerge in response to the Depression and as part of an effort to prompt social action. Moreover, it was in response to the mainstream journalism establishment's "default," as James Boylan calls it, in covering the grim experience of that period in American life (159). In effect, by denying subjectivity Lippmann was placing himself squarely in a reactionary camp when he wrote: "The newer objective journalism is a less temperamental affair, for it deals with solider realities. . . . For the ability to present news objectively and to interpret it realistically is not a native instinct in the human species; it is a product of culture which comes only with knowledge of the past and acute awareness of how deceptive is our normal observation and how wishful is our thinking" ("Two Revolutions" 440). His thinking, too, one might add, in eliding the issue of subjectivity. It is a curiously contradictory statement, because in his elision Lippmann implicitly acknowledges his own subjectivity at work, his "acute awareness" determining that subjectivity, and presumably his own, is deceptive. Thus caught and compromised in his own critical duplicity, he reifies the concept of an external culture as the ground against which human activity must be judged, altogether ignoring that our understanding of human activity must also be negotiated and determined by such factors as subjectivity and language.

The call for journalistic objectivity had in common similar ideological concerns that would go beyond being critically reactionary to being reactionary in application as expressed by those who ultimately determined the newspaper culture, its editors and publishers. In 1937 the American Newspaper Publishers Association and the American Society of Newspaper Editors issued a statement designed to stymie efforts to unionize newspapers: "We do not deny that causes require champions, and that progress springs from the genius of advocates. Equally important to society, however, are those who report the controversial scene. It is the newspaperman's job to do that, not as a partisan but as an objective observer." Citing the cause of objectivity, newspaper owners opposed unionizing on the grounds that "any group already committed as an organization on highly controversial public questions" could not be objective (qtd. in Schudson 157). As a result, journalists were to deny the engagement of their own subjectivities in their means of production, which is a contradiction on its face.

To be sure, Lippmann acknowledged the power and influence of subjectivity, and it was for this reason that he called for a "constant testing" of the news. But he mistakes a constant testing or "unity of method" for presenting the news objectively, or what elsewhere he characterizes as "what actually is" (*Liberty and the News* 55). In "what actually is" he implies a cryptotheological transcendence of the meddling influences of subjectivity and language.

What remains remarkable is just how much Lippmann the journalist and Eliot the poet mirror each other in their critical essentializing, a point likely to horrify New Critics, namely that Eliot the aesthetic spiritualist could be reduced to the same class as Lippmann the material spiritualist. Coincidentally, their respective calls for a transcendent literature and a journalism that transcends subjectivity came at precisely the same time, 1920, in the aftermath of World War I, providing further evidence of the reinscription of totalized critical conceptions as the ground against which human activity must be enacted. In effect, both ultimately were members of the same critically catholic church, even if in one the liturgy were high church and in the other, low. When Eliot said a poem should "result in the production of a new object which is no longer purely personal, because it is a work of art itself," such a definition could aptly fit Lippmann's objective journalism. One could also say of journalism that it should "result in the production of a new object which is no longer purely personal, because it is a work of journalism itself." The same can be said of Eliot's concept of the "objective correlative," first articulated in 1919, which generations of undergraduates have had to accept as aesthetic gospel: "The only way of expressing emotion in art is by finding an 'objective correlative'" ("Hamlet" 48). This can be suitably reworded again to show the close relationship to Lippmann's view on journalistic objectivity: "The only way of expressing a journalistic account is by finding an 'objective correlative.'" Such were Eliot's and Lippmann's "zest" for finding the objective correlative that transcended personal experience in order to arrive at either art or journalism "itself," free of a meddling subjectivity. Or so their subjectivities believed in their own critical leaps of faith.

The result, then, of the rise of the concept of objectivity was, in a sense, a critical flimflam in which a journalism based on facts gave way to objective journalism based on wishful thinking uncannily similar to that of the literary modernists. Curiously, objective journalism was also, as Paul Many has noted, the result of the "*modern* age of journalism" (561, emphasis added). "Modernism" in the form of "objectivity" could only further sideline a narrative literary journalism and the attempt to narrow the gulf between subjectivity and objectification. In his call for objectivity, Lippmann unambiguously announced what mainstream journalistic practice had been doing all along: alienating subjectivity.

In fairness, however, it should be noted that despite the calls for objectivity, the age was marked by still another development in journalism, the resurgence of sensationalism in the founding of city tabloids such as the *New York Daily News* in 1919. This version of sensational or yellow journalism has been called "jazz journalism" (Emery and Emery 363). In the end, however, its epistemological ends were the same, not to narrow the distance between subjectivity and the object but rather to emphasize difference, to make a foreign object of the Other from which one could remain safely disengaged. In the sensational response sought in yellow journalism, the purpose, to cite again John Berger's definition, is "the reducing of the experience of the other into a pure framed spectacle from which the viewer, as a safe and separate spectator, obtains a thrill or a shock" ("Another Way" 63).

Meanwhile, much as the English academy was marching in step to the aesthetic modernists, the journalism academy was taking a similar line, strongly influenced by Lippmann, as was the later mass communication academy that eventually assumed journalism for its own. This was due in part to a small, close-knit group of individuals who were the major figures responsible for developing a journalism and mass communication academy and whose dominant critical paradigm could only exclude a journalism that made a claim to being literature.

In 1922 Willard Grosvenor Bleyer, who founded at the University of Wisconsin in Madison in 1906 one of the country's first journalism programs, began teaching a graduate seminar to doctoral students using Lippmann's *Public Opinion*. Bleyer, considered a pioneer in journalism education and scholarship (Durham 15), was an early advocate of the application of social scientific methods to the analysis of journalism. "These kinds of social scientific research, he asserted, could both improve the quality of newspapers and provide a stronger knowledge base for journalism teaching," Everett M. Rogers and Steven H. Chaffee write in a scholarly study that is instructive for understanding the origins of the journalism and mass communication academy (14). Indeed, Bleyer is described as having been a "missionary for his point of view" which thus dons once again a surplice of a cryptotheological nature (14). Bleyer helped to establish a social scientific approach as a dominant paradigm for journalistic study, one ultimately based, of course, in positivist assumptions.

It is Wilbur Schramm, however, whom Rogers and Chaffee charac-

terize as "undeniably the inventor of communication study" in the
1940s (36). Schramm, who had a Ph.D. in English (as did Bleyer) and
was an authority on Longfellow's *Song of Hiawatha,* had been involved
in the war effort in Washington, D.C. In 1943 he returned to the University of Iowa with ideas about a new academic discipline in communication studies. "Although Schramm's intellectual roots were in
the humanities, he conceived of communication as a new branch of
behavioral and social science" (7). It is perhaps one of those anomalies
of academic history that before he was converted to the scientific fold,
Schramm was appointed director in 1934 of the Iowa Writer's Workshop and was an accomplished short story writer, having won an
O. Henry Prize for fiction in 1942 (11). But by the time he returned to
Iowa after his propaganda work in Washington, he had embraced "the
promise that lay in empirical research" (10). At Iowa he was named
director of the university's School of Journalism where he began imple-
menting his program. In 1947 he moved to the University of Illinois
where he founded a program dedicated to the study of communication
as a science (7). Illinois would prove to be "the site where Schramm's
vision of communication study was first implemented on a full scale"
(7). In 1955 he went to Stanford University where he eventually became director of that institution's Department of Communication.

Schramm also saw mass communication study "as a graduate field
of interdisciplinary study" (7). But while his intention may have been
interdisciplinary, it is clear from the Rogers and Chaffee interpretation
that science and its underlying positivist assumption dominated the
study. Moreover, there is evidence that the interdisciplinary approach
was suspect. Wayne A. Danielson, who attended the Stanford program
from 1954 to 1957, received the institution's fourth Ph.D. in mass communication research, as Everett Rogers recounts in his history of communication study (458). Danielson recalled: "The doctoral program
was highly interdisciplinary. I took statistical methods in the Psychology Department from Quinn McNemar, and both he and Ernest Hil-
gard were on my doctoral committee. I also took doctoral psychology
courses from Robert Sears and Leon Festinger. . . . In the Sociology
Department, I enrolled in courses from Paul Wallin and R. T. LaPiere.
Students in communication consistently got top grades in these doctoral courses in psychology and sociology, helping to convince us that

we were competent" (qtd. in E. Rogers 458). Interdisciplinary study at Stanford was clearly framed within the context of social scientific study: psychology and sociology.

After Bleyer and Schramm came those who assumed leadership of many of the major mass communication programs in the country (Rogers and Chaffee 4). They included Fred Siebert, a student of Bleyer's who headed the Illinois program after Schramm left, and Ralph Casey, a student of Bleyer's who taught in the journalism program at the University of Minnesota but who also worked with Schramm in Washington, D.C., and joined him at Stanford in 1958. Ralph Nafziger was another Wisconsin alumnus and scholar who would eventually move on to Minnesota. Moreover, he too worked in Washington with Casey and Schramm. Finally, Chilton Bush, likewise from Wisconsin, taught at Stanford and eventually recruited Schramm to that institution.

How did such a close-knit group influence the prospects for the study of narrative literary journalism among some of the most highly esteemed mass communication programs in the country? As with the literary modernists, the evidence is paradigmatic. Indeed, it would be unfair to suggest that there was any conscious attempt to exclude the scholarly study of narrative literary journalism from mass communication studies. But it should be noted that Schramm did express his own antipathy toward literary study after he returned to Iowa from Washington. Observing that he had worked with Alfred North Whitehead at Harvard and studied psychology and statistics elsewhere, he said that "having such broad interests, it would have been hard coming back to Iowa and teaching the history of Chaucer" (qtd. in E. Rogers 17). Moreover, he appears to have soured on an affiliation with literary study for other reasons. When he returned to Iowa after his work in Washington, D.C., he declined to return to English studies because Norman Foerster, Schramm's former mentor when he was a doctoral student, had become dean of the School of Letters. As Rogers notes, "In 1943, Foerster and Schramm's relationship had ruptured, and this split was a major reason that Schramm did not wish to return to his old post" (17). Such circumstances could not bode well for the study of a journalism as literary in an academy dominated by social scientific methods.

In understanding the paradigmatic evidence, it is important to understand that mass communication study has largely claimed the study and teaching of journalism for its own, and to some extent journalism in the academy has countered the embrace with its own. One reason is because journalism study could find scholarly respectability in mass communication study. Until the 1940s journalism programs in universities "functioned as trade schools," according to James A. Crook, a communication scholar and editor of *Journalism and Mass Communication Educator* (6). He adds, "Although affiliated with universities, they were considered marginal members of the commonwealth of scholars. . . . They did not illuminate journalistic process by providing a body of literature and criticism for assessing the significance of this sector of the world" (6). Ejected earlier in the century from the literature academy and condemned by such critics as Julian Hawthorne and MLA president William A. Nitze, journalism study fended for itself until the emergence of mass communication study under the direction of Schramm and his colleagues. In that study, journalism could find scholarly respectability. Subsequently, as Crook notes, "the composition of journalism faculties changed from a predominance of ex-newspapermen to communication scholars educated in behavioral sciences" (7). Thus, too, came a shift from journalism as a fundamentally rhetorical study to one of the social sciences.

Everett Rogers corroborates Crook's assessment and adds that the consequences of communication study being reduced to a science would prove even more widespread: "Initially, communication study took over existing journalism schools, gradually shifting the teaching and study of communication in these schools from a professional perspective to a more scientific orientation. Similarly, communication study also began to invade departments of speech, changing them from the humanistic study of rhetoric toward a scientific analysis of interpersonal communication" (477–78). Largely by default, then, the study of journalism moved from being a humanistic and rhetorical enterprise to being a social science according to the paradigm under which it would be studied.

Still another measure of the paradigmatic evidence is to be found in the name change in Crook's publication, along with others associated with the Association for Education in Journalism and Mass Communication (AEJMC). In 1995 *Journalism Educator* became *Journalism and Mass Communication Educator,* confirming what had been a long-time process of assimilation (*Journalism Educator* verso front matter). The same happened to *Journalism Quarterly, Journalism Abstracts,* and *Journalism Monographs,* all adding "Mass Communication" to the "Journalism" in their titles (*AEJMC News* 1).

Journalism studies, lacking respect, accepted then the embrace of mass communication study founded on a behavioral emphasis. The behavioral emphasis based on quantifiable empirical evidence has continued to dominate much of this study, despite calls since at least the 1970s for other approaches, particularly cultural (Carey 177) and qualitative (Cooper, Potter, and Dupagne 54). This paradigmatic dominance can be detected in one study that found seven of the eight largest-circulation refereed communication journals with acceptance rates of less than 20 percent continued to be quantitative in nature: "From 1965 to 1989, the majority of published mass media research articles used quantitative methods" (Cooper, Potter, and Dupagne 58). The authors add, "Perhaps the most important finding is the lack of increase in qualitative research articles in the journals sampled. This finding contradicts assertions by recent authors that qualitative methods are reemerging in mass media research" (60). While there was one notable exception among the scholarly publications, *Critical Studies in Mass Communication* (60), the reality has been that most large-circulation scholarly journals in mass communication study remain quantitative, empirical, and behavioral in focus.

Furthermore, an effort has been made by some of the most prominent communication scholars to maintain communication study—and much journalism study through guilt by association—as a "science," which can only exclude paradigms that make no claim to being scientific. According to one interpretation of the communication discipline by Everett Rogers, "communication scholarship today is mainly empirical, quantitative, and focused on determining the effects of communication. This dominant perspective grew naturally out of the scholarly directions that Wilbur Schramm set in motion several decades ago and out of earlier communication research in sociology, social psychology, and political science. These fields, and communication study, were shaped by the social sciences' mimicking the quantification of the natural sciences, motivated by a desire for scientific respectability" (491).

In addition, in 1987 Steven Chaffee and Charles Berger published their *Handbook of Communication Science* in which they provide a definition for what qualifies as a scientific study of communication, altogether eliding it as rhetorical and humanistic study: "Communication science seeks to understand the production, processing and effects of symbol and signal systems by developing *testable* theories, containing *lawful generalizations,* that explain phenomena associated with production, processing and effects" (17, emphasis added). In the "testable theories" and the "generalizations" conforming to a higher "law," they have reinscribed communication study within the cryptotheological rhetoric of science, or rather faith that science provides all answers. Thus they effectively exclude analysis that makes no claim to being empirical. Moreover, "lawful generalizations" based on empirical evidence is an oxymoron, because as physicist Werner Heisenberg well understood in 1926, no generalization can incorporate all empirical evidence; fundamentally, there can be no fixity to the evidence of the universe (Hawking 55). Instead, there must always be some excess, some empirical Other, waiting to disprove the limited evidence of the "generalized law."

More to the point, Berger's and Chaffee's definition excludes the possibility of interpretation based on critical, not empirical, induction and deduction. In turn, they miss the point that all texts, even scholarly empirical texts, are fundamentally interpretive given the specular nature of language (as well as because of the ultimately indeterminate nature of temporal phenomena). Indeed, Rogers is perhaps unintentionally not far from the mark when he acknowledges that communication study was "shaped by the social sciences' mimicking the quantification of the natural sciences, motivated by a desire for scientific respectability." His observation is uncannily reminiscent of one by deconstructionist Paul de Man who would take a darker view of communication-as-language when he observed of the tropological nature of language that it "mimics the presumed attributes of authenticity when it is in fact just the hollow mask with which a frustrated, defeated consciousness tries to cover up its own negativity" (12).

Within the larger critical argument, then, it should be evident what the paradigmatic consequences would be for the narrower study of a literary journalism, either by doctoral students in the programs associated with Bleyer's and Schramm's efforts or by journalism students whose study has been contextualized within the larger arena of mass communication study as a social "science." Among some of the most highly esteemed mass communication programs in the country, a small group of individuals dedicated to mass communication largely as a scientific study helped to determine, according to the prevailing critical paradigm they operated under, what would be journalism. Literature, which shares half the discourse of literary journalism, clearly makes no claims to being a science. As a result, the paradigm of science has been necessarily if unintentionally exclusionary, especially given that science by definition attempts to isolate the subject in order to measure it as alienated object, the opposite of one modus that accounts for what narrative literary journalism attempts to do.

But a narrative literary journalism differs, still again, because it resists coming to critical closure. Science historically has sought closure, as can be detected in the Berger-Chaffee call for "lawful generalizations" that would "lawfully" determine the essential motions of the mass media. As literary critic Mark Edmundson notes, literature as a discourse ultimately escapes critical closure because it "resists being explained away" (31). As such, he is only one in a long line of critics who have taken up the theme that literature is fundamentally suggestive of possibilities of meaning—or allegory—but not fundamentally definitive of closed meanings. Literature examines and acknowledges ambiguity as ambiguity, while science, or at least Laplacian science, claims that ambiguity is decipherable and determinant within critical closure. Literature and its criticism are an ongoing negotiation of only approximate meaning.

Moreover, such exclusionary politics are reflected in conventional journalism historiography. When journalism historian Paul Many suggests measuring the history of narrative literary journalism according to conventional journalism historiography, he has attempted to make the form fit an already determined historical mold (561). In consequence he ignores altogether the active period of narrative literary journalism practiced in the 1930s and early 1940s when he calls the period from 1915 to 1960 the "modern" period. When he mentions only in passing Ernest Hemingway and John Hersey, one could conclude that literary journalism during the modern period was the exception rather than the rule (566). What Many fails to perceive is that there are critical reasons for why conventional journalism study has historically excluded literary journalism from serious scholarly consideration, reasons that justify the application of "modern" to both mainstream journalistic practice of the period as well as belletristic practice during this time as a hegemonic appellation that tended to marginalize narrative literary journalism. In doing so Many echoes a fundamental assumption in U.S. journalism history that characterizes the development of objective mainstream news style as a triumph over other modes of journalism. As Frank Luther Mott noted, "From the time of the success of the penny papers in the thirties, it was inevitable that news should triumph over editorial comment as the leading function of the American newspaper (384). The "triumph" was "inevitable" and therefore indisputable.

The unfortunate consequence of such a historiographic conceptualization is that when historians have confronted narrative literary journalism in whatever guise, most have tended to be unaware of the form, and in at least one instance, have disdained it. In one widely used text on the history of American journalism, the authors note that during the post–Civil War period when modern narrative literary journalism was asserting itself, "an increased number of editions caused pressure for more rapid handling of local news, and the summary lead gained favor as a means of condensing stories. (But the literary stylists and writers of rambling chronological stories were still numerous)" (Emery and Emery 264). Aside from the disdain implicit in the parenthetical insertion, implicit too is that if such stylists and writers *were* still numerous, the summary news lead, as one rhetorical measure of factual or objective journalism, was ascendant at their expense. In lockstep with Mott, the authors assert that the "story" of the history of American journalism is one in which "news should triumph over editorial comment as the leading function of the American newspaper."

A FEW critical voices, as James Gray's article suggests, found something redeeming in the form and defended it in the face of the rise of a critical ostracism from the end of World War I to the 1960s and the advent of the new journalism. The observation is important, because if in situating the form it is only defined during this period by the presence it was not permitted to have, then it is open to charges by critics that that is exactly what it was, a "nought." But to also define it according to the terms of its outnumbered critical supporters establishes a dialectic with the opposition that adds to siting the form historically as an ongoing discussion.

After the first major period of the form at the turn of the century, the next major period during which it was practiced was the 1930s and 1940s. During this period, Joseph North, editor of the *New Masses* in the 1930s, was one of the form's critical supporters, having observed that "the writer of reportage must . . . do more than tell his reader what has happened—he must help the reader experience the event. Herein reportage becomes durable literature. Reportage is three-dimensional reporting. The writer not only condenses reality, he helps the reader feel the fact. The finest writers of reportage are artists in the fullest sense of the term. They do their editorializing through their imagery" (120–21). In the editorializing can be detected the shaping subjectivity of the journalist attempting to help the reader feel the experience or, ultimately, narrow the gulf between subjectivities.

Another supporter from the thirties is the now largely forgotten Edwin H. Ford of the University of Minnesota who in 1937 perhaps most clearly made the claim that the enterprise workaday journalists engaged in could result in a narrative literary journalism. In the foreword to his 1937 bibliography he alludes to the marginalized status of the form, as well as the plebeian status of journalism broadly defined, and pleads for a reconsideration: "Literary journalism as conceived for the purpose of this bibliography might be defined as writing which falls within the twilight zone that divides literature from journalism. If literature is distinguished by its quality of permanence, and journalism is ephemeral, there has been much significant writing, surely, which does not attach itself wholeheartedly to either standard; writing which has the interpretative cast of literature as well as the contemporary interest of journalism" (*Bibliography* n. pag.). If the way his bibliography was published is any indication, Ford was indeed a lone voice; the text was not typeset but printed instead directly from a typescript.

In "The Art and Craft of the Literary Journalist" (originally published in 1937) Ford raises the issue of journalistic subjectivity and uses the terminology "reportage" when he notes that the literary journalist's

job "is to make people . . . feel through their senses . . . in his attempt
to create an emotional tone. . . . Reportage, then, may be defined as
the presentation of a particular fact or facts, a specific event, a setting
that aids the reader to experience those facts or that event. Reportage
becomes literary journalism when a John Dos Passos writes 'Anacostia
Flats'" (310). The reference to Dos Passos is telling because it forges
once again a connection between the temporal and epistemological
politics of a form widely adopted by political Progressives.

But what is perhaps most remarkable about Ford is that as a member
of the journalism academy he all but attacks the dictate enunciated by
Lippmann that journalists should attempt to remove their subjectivities
from their reporting to realize the gospel of objectivity. Additionally,
Ford, whether consciously or not, takes note of the rising social scientific hegemony in the following reference to the "political scientist"
and observes that different critical perspectives result in different interpretations of reality:

> The literary journalist personalizes his writing. That is to say, he is more
> interested in people and their relationship to one another than he is in
> principles or abstract comment. The newspaperman with the point of
> view of the political scientist sees news from the angle of its relation to
> theories and practices of government. The literary journalist sees news
> in relation to its human quality, its possibilities of showing people in the
> midst of life, a life that may seem comic, tragic, pathetic, farcical. (311)

To do this, Ford adds, the literary journalist "must take sides in portray-
ing human relationships" (311). In effect, narrative literary journalists must help readers make the choices Hurstwood was afraid to make,
help them engage subjectivities, eschewing an objective discourse
determined by what Ford calls "principles" reflected in "abstract" or,
better, *abstracted* commentary. In such abstraction can a subjectivity
smugly disengage.

Another supporter in criticism but from the other side of letters,
that of literature, was Alfred Kazin. In *On Native Grounds*, which appeared in 1941, Kazin perhaps prematurely saw a promising future for
the form when he noted: "That literature has hardly run its course, and
it may even dominate the scene for many years to come; but for all its
shapelessness and often mechanical impulse, it is a vast body of writing

that is perhaps the fullest expression of the experience of the American consciousness after 1930, and one that illuminates the whole nature of prose literature in those years as nothing else can" (485). Moreover, he characterized literary journalist and critic Edmund Wilson as "not a reporter but a literary artist driven by historical imagination" (485). In the 1950s, during the height of the New Critical hegemony, Kazin acknowledged that he missed "the frankly 'literary' reportage of national events that used to be done by writers like Theodore Dreiser, H. L. Mencken, John Dos Passos, [and] Edmund Wilson" during the Depression ("Edmund Wilson" 405). (However, Kazin would remark of the new journalism in 1973 that "it went through a whole cycle in the Sixties and no longer astonishes" ["Imagination" 240].) Other voices in support of the form during this period include Steffens and Hapgood in their autobiographies that appeared in the 1930s. But they of course were hearkening back to an earlier era, the 1890s. Still another lone advocate was James Gray from the early 1950s.

By the late 1950s critical opinion shows signs of shifting. In a direct challenge to Hoffman and O'Connor that nonfiction could not have "literary connotations," the young critic Norman Podhoretz took up advocacy of a literary journalism or nonfiction in a 1958 *Harper's* article called "The Article as Art." Podhoretz notes that often autobiographical "writing of people who think of themselves primarily as novelists turns out to be more interesting, more lively, more penetrating, more intelligent, more forceful, more original—in short, better—than their fiction, which they and everyone else automatically treat with greater respect." In the "greater respect" for fiction, Podhoretz detects the literary establishment's contempt for nonfiction when its writers condescend to engage in the form. He continues: "Indeed, some novelists (and this applies to many poets too) tend to express their contempt or disdain for [nonfiction] prose in the very act of writing it. You can hear a note of condescension toward the medium they happen to be working in at the moment" (74). Podhoretz is of course assaulting the New Critical hegemony. And *Harper's* editors, perhaps mindful of the critical climate of the time, add by way of disclaimer an editorial preface that acknowledges the second-class status of the form: "One of the most unconventional of the young American critics takes a hard look at a kind of writing usually considered beneath a critic's contempt" (74).

On the one hand, the comment reveals the near totalitarian sway of the New Criticism. At the same time, the disclaimer suggests the coming assault against the totalitarian facade.

Podhoretz's 1958 comments anticipate the new journalism of the sixties and the critical furor that arose over it. The furor was reflected in Powers's smug contempt for the new journalism when he crowed that "journalism, alas . . . is still journalism" (499). It would be stating the obvious to note that literary critics were left uncomfortable by the new journalism because of its clear challenge to prevailing literary and journalistic correctness. But Powers's dismissiveness already reflected a swan song, given that Derrida had detonated his linguistic charge in 1966 at Johns Hopkins University, around the same time Truman Capote detonated his with *In Cold Blood*. Each was, in his own fashion, engaging in assaults on epistemological assumptions: Capote's a challenge to the mythology of the American dream; Derrida's a challenge to assumptions about what language could accomplish. They would be followed by critics and scholars who would insist that the form could not be dismissed, despite the pronouncements of Powers and other conservators of the ancien régime.

THE "FALL," then, of journalism—and by extension narrative literary journalism—from literary grace was largely the result of the invention of a high literature in the nineteenth century. That fall would be complete with the rise of aesthetic modernism and the New Criticism. Moreover, journalism would be condemned as a merely utilitarian exercise by the rise of the concept of objectivity and the scientific direction mass communication study would take, both of which are founded on positivist assumptions about what we can and are permitted to know about the world, a world that could not be literary.

There is a critical irony to this. As Barbara Lounsberry observes, "our age has stopped subscribing to the belief that the novel is the highest form of the literary imagination" (xi). Instead, she suggests, narrative literary journalism has emerged as one of our extant contemporary literatures, its practice doing justice to the journalistic enterprise because it engages in a compelling examination of issues—philosophical, aesthetic, and social among others—that are of profound concern to society and the individual. Yet as Lounsberry has noted, the form has remained "the great unexplored territory of contemporary criticism" (xi), in the end largely ignored, except for a few voices, by the academy during the course of the twentieth century. And no wonder: the form has existed largely outside the calipers of the critical paradigms of scholarship and criticism that have so much dominated that century.

Coda

To be sure, much has been left out of this history, in part because that is the nature of history. What can be determined is that there is a long tradition of narrative literary journalism. Moreover, this effort at historicizing intentionally halts with the new journalism of the 1960s because it is much more difficult to assess what is "literary" among contemporary writers of our own era. For example, *Confederates in the Attic* by Tony Horwitz strikes me as an eligible candidate because of its nonjudgmental sensitivity in its examination. One consequence is that it qualifies as social allegory. On the other hand, Neil Sheehan's *Bright Shining Lie*, which won the Pulitzer Prize, is more problematic because its prose is, in my view, more flaccid and objectified. That said, the last quarter or so of the twentieth century remains to be explored, and perhaps that enterprise will be better off in the hands of someone a quarter century from now.

In any event, as a coda it can be said that modern American literary journalism, narrative in its nature, emerged during the post–Civil War period and by the 1890s had achieved critical recognition. Evidence for situating the modern form to this time frame includes the adaptation of rhetorical techniques traditionally associated with novel-writing to journalistic discourse by professional journalists and the acknowledgment of that discourse, directly or indirectly, by critics. It is at the nexus of such factors that the form can be situated as having come of age by the 1890s at the latest.

Citing external evidence of the form's presence in the post–Civil War period does not, however, explain why it should emerge then or the consequences of what it was attempting to do. Critics have noted that the rise of objectified styles in the modern newspaper fundamentally alienated readers from experience. American narrative literary journalism, I suggest, was a response to that alienation because it attempted to engage readers' subjectivities by means of the journalist's own subjectivity. The result was a journalistic form whose narrative ambition was the opposite of mainstream practices that attempted to objectify the world. Moreover, the attempt to narrow the gulf between subjectivity and the object suggests a larger thesis: narrative literary journalism works on a narrative spectrum or continuum somewhere between an unattainable objectified world and an incomprehensible solipsistic subjectivity.

The results reflect profound epistemological and existential consequences. Such heightened subjectivity could only conclude with a report that implicitly acknowledges its epistemological limitations: subjectivity by definition cannot be omniscient. The result is that the more subjectivity is acknowledged in the attempt to narrow the gulf between consciousness and an objectified world, the more there must be a portrait of a contingent or indeterminate world. A narrative presenting a portrait of a contingent world inherently resists critical closure. Paradoxically, this suggests not only a consequence of the form but also another potential modus or ambition for it—the intention at whatever level of consciousness to challenge smug critical totalizations of how our phenomenal life is to be prescribed. Fundamentally, then, narrative literary journalism is a version of what Mikhail Bakhtin calls the novel of the "inconclusive present," eschewing a narrative framed or prescribed in the "distanced image of the past." One further consequence that emerges in such an examination of the historical material is that the increased engagement of the subjectivity of the journalist in experience in order to engage the subjectivity of readers not infrequently politicized many of those journalists so that they became activists in Progressive politics or other political issues.

An examination of the origins of the form suggests that there are both older and immediate precursors. Older precursors can be researched back at least to the Roman *acta* and from there traced up through the eighteenth century to James Boswell's announced ambition to write a biography like a novel. More immediate precursors derive from the nineteenth century when we begin to see the emergence of two kinds of journalism, or what have been characterized as the "story" and "information" models.

One of the outstanding issues concerning the emergence of narrative literary journalism by 1900 is its relationship to sensational and muckraking journalism. At the heart of the matter in differentiating between sensational journalism and literary journalism lies the success or lack of success of journalists in utilizing rhetorical strategies to narrow the gulf between subjectivity and the object. The rhetorical success of overcoming the difference between self and Other, of avoiding reinforcing difference and of showing commonalties instead, provides one measure for determining what qualifies as narrative literary journalism and a measure for what separates it from sensational journalism. As for muckraking journalism, it can reenact the same epistemological problems of literary or sensational journalisms in a narrative mode, reinforcing the differences between subject and object or attempting to close the distance between them. If the latter, it can overlap with narrative literary journalism.

The attempt to overcome the alienation of human consciousness because of the emergence of objectified news styles, as well as the recognition of an indeterminate world, results in still larger historiographic consequences by offering a modus for explaining the continuing publication and appeal of the form in the twentieth century. Using Thomas B. Connery's historical template, this evidence can be traced through the Depression era of the 1930s and the new journalism of the 1960s and 1970s. But narrative literary journalism never entirely disappeared during the lulls between these periods. During the past century there have always been examples of literary journalism that attempted to narrow the gulf between subjectivity and the alienated object.

What remains troubling is why the form has been largely ignored by literary and journalistic practitioners and by the academy. Such an accounting is necessary in order to further delineate the form historically by the historical presence it was not permitted to have, much as women's and ethnic literatures were for long denied a historical presence. To that end, evidence exists that during the nineteenth century the evolution of journalism as a "nonliterary" enterprise stemmed from the demise of the elitist partisan press whose forms had origins in a neoclassical and thus a proper class-determined rhetoric. Such a consideration ultimately helps to account for why journalism broadly conceived but including narrative literary journalism would later be marginalized by the English academy.

In the twentieth century, narrative literary journalism was further marginalized by the dominant underlying paradigm that led to an aesthetic hegemony by literary modernists as to what was considered literature. In the end it was a paradigm that could only exclude a narrative literary journalism from consideration as a literature. Likewise, a similar hegemony was established by the New Critics in response to calls by literary modernists for an art that transcended the means of production.

In the case of journalism, the underlying paradigm that came to dominate the practice of most American journalism in this century, that of the concept of "objectivity," could also only exclude from serious consideration a discourse as openly subjective as narrative literary journalism. A similar paradigmatic hegemony was practiced by the journalism academy and the later mass communication academy, a critical hegemony based on the concept of "objectivity" and the larger positivist paradigm upon which it is ultimately based. Thus the form was excluded from serious consideration largely because of the critical straitjackets donned by practitioners and academicians in both camps.

Appendix

Scholarship of Literary Journalism / Nonfiction

As BARBARA LOUNSBERRY notes in her *Art of Fact,* literary journalism or nonfiction is "the great unexplored territory of contemporary criticism" (xi). While her statement may tend toward hyperbole, nonetheless her position is one generally echoed by Thomas B. Connery, one of the form's most notable scholars, in his "Research Review" (2). The result is that scholarship directly addressing the form is relatively meager when compared with more traditional areas of literary research. Part of the difficulty is that "literary journalism" and "literary nonfiction" are by no means universal as the nomenclatures for the form. Moreover, any examination of the form must acknowledge that it has, as Connery observes in "Research Review," no academic home or center. While Connery, for example, is identified with journalism studies, Lounsberry's academic allegiance is to English. Nor is literary journalism, or literary nonfiction as it may be called, the possession of only those two academies. Ronald Weber, who teaches at the University of Notre Dame, is another of the form's prominent scholars, and his background is in American studies. Nor, ultimately, is there any critical agreement on what belongs in a form with no clear identity that is being critiqued in different academies. These are only some of the difficult issues reflected in the scholarship of the form.

Accounting for the scholarship, then, requires searching beyond just narrow disciplinary concerns, as well as an open mind about what to call the form and of what works it consists. Any consideration of the scholarship, aside from the limited historical scholarship discussed in the introduction, must confront the reality that what is said of literary journalism can, theoretically, often be said of literary nonfiction and vice versa. For example, works that Lounsberry calls "literary nonfiction" Connery elsewhere calls "literary journalism." It is not my intention to argue which terminology is preferable other than to note that there is a body of work by professional journalists—those whose means of production was largely the newspaper and magazine press—that can be characterized as a "literary journalism" and that can fit comfortably into a larger nonfiction category. Such a distinction is important if narrative literary journalism is to emerge from the marginalizing shadow of the larger category and receive

251

the recognition it has been denied—that it is a compelling discourse attempting to speak profoundly to the human condition as any literature that moves us will attempt to do.

Acknowledging the similar theoretical concerns literary journalism and literary nonfiction raise, I briefly examine representative popular criticism that places the form in a more contemporary context; explore the very limited recent scholarship that provides an overview of the form's critical concerns and scholarship; note early examples of scholarship that attempted to account for the new journalism of the 1960s and that provide the initial scholarly stances around which the form is still largely discussed today; and finally, examine more recent efforts in light of those initial stances. Such an organizing principle is of course somewhat arbitrary. But given just how much the form is ill-defined and poorly understood, such an organization hopefully can only contribute to the process of trying to give the scholarship some semblance of order. By way of a working definition of literary journalism and literary nonfiction, I mean those texts of true-life stories that read like novels or short stories.

THE CONTEMPORARY CRITICAL CONTEXT

There is ample evidence that narrative literary journalism/nonfiction is not just the passing invention of a few scholars. One example is an article by Jack Hart, writing coach for the *Portland Oregonian,* in the September 1995 issue of *Writer's Digest* that examines what he calls "literary nonfiction" in newspapers. According to Hart, freelancers can find a ready market for the form in contemporary newspapers (29–33). Similarly, Chris Harvey in "Tom Wolfe's Revenge" in a 1994 issue of *American Journalism Review* notes that "literary journalism," as he calls it, has become commonplace as a practice, and the growth in interest in the form is reflected in the founding of a joint journalism and English department program in literary journalism at the University of Oregon (40, 46). Similarly, a 1992 article in the *Nieman Reports,* "Journalism's Guilty Secret," suggests that the guilty secret is the important role writing imaginatively plays in journalism's most compelling stories, in other words, those stories that utilize the techniques commonly associated with novel-writing (Kirkhorn 36). The degree to which the form's boundaries are uncertain is reflected in Judith Paterson's "Literary Journalism's Twelve Best" in the October 1992 *Washington Journalism Review.* The article is little more than a listing of what Paterson deems "best." Nonetheless, it is one more popular critique that acknowledges what the academy has long overlooked.

Not all recent considerations are designed for popular audiences, however. One example is Maureen Ryan's "Green Visors and Ivory Towers: Jean Stafford and the New Journalism" in a 1994 issue of the respected *Kenyon Review.* The article is important not only for how it reinterprets Stafford as a "new journalist" but also for how it reflects the glacial shift in the academy in recognizing literary journalism or literary nonfiction as a form worthy of serious scholarly

consideration. Ryan's bibliography is also revealing in that it cites the first generation of new journalism critics and scholars, such as John Hollowell, Tom
Wolfe, and Mas'ud Zavarzadeh. Ryan thus helps establish their work as standards of criticism of the form.

These are only selected examples from what has been at the close of the
twentieth century a spate of criticism or scholarship on literary journalism/
nonfiction or on the related issue of drafting literary technique in the writing
of journalism. (Jack Hart, for one, is a columnist for *Editor and Publisher* and
frequently takes up the subject of using literary technique in journalism.) What
they demonstrate is that the form, long ignored by the academy, is not just a
passing phenomenon.

SCHOLARSHIP PROVIDING AN OVERVIEW OF THE SCHOLARSHIP

Two attempts at providing an overview of the issues the form raises and of its
scholarship are Connery's "Research Review" and his "Discovering a Literary
Form," the latter in *A Sourcebook of American Literary Journalism,* a collection that
historicizes the form with articles on thirty-five literary journalists from Mark
Twain to Tracy Kidder. "Research Review" examines primarily those questions
that in Connery's view need further exploration in order to better situate the
form. Among others, he identifies the problem of the relationship between
narrative literary journalism and autobiography and, by implication, between
narrative literary journalism and other nonfiction forms. A not-unrelated issue,
Connery suggests, is the role of reflexive subjectivity in such texts (6–7).

"Research Review" is aimed at encouraging scholarship that examines primarily American magazine journalism, but the issues it raises apply to the form
at large, whether in newspaper or book-length texts. Connery's "Discovering a
New Literary Form" provides an overview of scholarship. In addition, Connery
provides some historicizing of the form (5–12). More important, however, he
acknowledges that given the lack of scholarship on the form, much research
must yet be done that requires examining broader areas of inquiry (20, 36–
37). That is what I attempt to do in this book—by examining intellectual, literary, and cultural history that can help frame and locate the form historically.

SCHOLARSHIP ON THE "NEW JOURNALISM"

Connery notes in the abstract to his "Research Review" that there are only a
few book-length efforts that examine the form. Indeed, since the rise of the
new journalism they can be counted on the digits of two hands. Add critical
articles from that period to the book-length efforts and what emerges are the
different threads of scholarship still prevalent in the scholarship of the late
1980s and 1990s. Perhaps not surprisingly, what also emerges is that the form
reflects something of the range—and perhaps chaos—of criticism today. What

can be detected are three general theoretical approaches, all arising in response to the new journalism.

In 1973 Tom Wolfe was one of the first to attempt to theorize his version of literary journalism/nonfiction, and in so doing he established a direct line of scholarship that can be traced down to Lounsberry, a line based on unambiguous rhetorical technique and authorial intention. Wolfe provides a taxonomy in which he identifies four characteristics that go into the making of new journalism. They are "scene-by-scene construction" similar to that of the realistic novel; using third-person point-of-view as a way to give the reader the feeling of being inside the character's mind; recording full dialogue instead of the selective use of quotation found in objectified mainstream journalism; and providing what Wolfe calls "status" details, meaning such characteristics as a person's gestures, or styles of furniture and clothing that result in "symbolic details" ("New Journalism" 31–32).

A second broad category of theorizing is what Connery calls "literary" but which might also be characterized as rhetorical ("Discovering" 22). Such approaches are different from Wolfe's in that they focus on more sophisticated analysis of rhetorical strategies. Two book-length efforts that approach the form as a literary study are John Hollowell's *Fact and Fiction* (1977) and John Hellmann's *Fables of Fact* (1981). Hollowell's acknowledged purpose is to examine the changes in journalism style, in the role of the artist and the production of art, and ultimately in changes in imaginative writing as reflected in the new journalism (x). He also proposes a continuum into which he places the new journalism somewhere between fantasy and history that helps to situate the form (20). In addition, he takes note of the heightened subjectivity of the form, both in terms of the greater role the writer's subjectivity occupies in the text and in the attempt by the writer to convey the psychological depth of the "subject" he or she is writing about (22, 52–53, 25). Hellmann argues that the new journalism is fundamentally an example of the "new fiction" that was current in the 1960s. His thesis is that the form engages in a fabulist "pattern-making" derived from a "collective consciousness" that is then imposed on experience as the only way to make sense of our postmodern world (xi, 140).

The third broad critical approach under which the form was theorized in early scholarship is that of cultural studies. One of the first attempts to do so was Michael Johnson's 1971 *New Journalism,* which examines the "artists of nonfiction" as well as the rise of the underground press and changes in the mainstream media. Johnson places the new journalism in the context of broader cultural turmoil in the 1960s. Thus he establishes an approach that would be taken up later by Connery, among others. Still another book-length effort is Ronald Weber's 1980 *Literature of Fact,* which straddles the boundary between a literary study, as Connery notes ("Discovering" 22), and a cultural study, as I suggest. Weber observes that a reflexive author's subjectivity heightens the credibility of a new journalism narrative. One example he cites is C. D. B. Bryan's *Friendly Fire* (159, 164). But Weber also places the new journal-

ism in a cultural context by noting the critical debate many of the new journalists engaged in, whether implicitly or explicitly. Wolfe's challenge to elitist literary attitudes in his essay "The New Journalism" is one example Weber cites
(16–21).

Weber's cultural studies orientation is reflected again in *The Reporter as Artist*. The collection contains a potpourri of different early critical positions on
the new journalism, and Weber provides a useful overview of those positions
in his introductory essay to the volume. Two themes he identifies are that the
new journalism appeared during and was a response to a time of social upheaval, picking up on Michael Johnson's thesis, and that heightened if not
reflexive subjectivity has been a common denominator of the form. Among
some of the writers and critics in the collection, Dan Wakefield discusses in
a reprinted *Atlantic* article the impossibility of avoiding one's subjectivity in
attempting to provide a portrait of the phenomenal world. He goes so far as to
propose that the future of reporting lies in greater acknowledgment of subjectivity, or "personal territories of feeling" (46, 48). Theodore Solotaroff notes
that such nonfictional accounts seem to appear in times of cultural and social
change and upheaval (163). Meanwhile, Dwight Macdonald and Herbert Gold
attack the new journalism. Gold assaults the form's "epidemic first-personism"
(283–87); Macdonald characterizes the form as "parajournalism" and describes Tom Wolfe's writing as "kitsch." Macdonald calls instead for a more
responsible "objective" or "information" journalism (223, 227).

Uncertainty over what to call the form is reflected in other articles in the
collection, such as Donald Pizer's "Documentary Narrative as Art." Pizer's
preferred terminology for the form is reflected in the article's title, and he
discusses the difference between William Manchester's *Death of a President*
and Truman Capote's *In Cold Blood*. Pizer characterizes Manchester's work as
merely "narrative documentary" but in an act of critical ordination crowns Capote's effort with the appellation of "art" (207). Ultimately, Pizer's argument
reflects the unclear boundaries in nonfictional forms of which scholarship until the 1960s had treated little.

While Weber's collection today is dated, its importance may well lie in its
sum effect: it reveals a cultural slice of life on the form as it was practiced in
the 1960s, not the least of which was the general uncertainty as to how to treat
the form.

MORE RECENT EXAMINATIONS OF THE FORM

From these early examinations of the new journalism can be traced the strands
of the various critical positions on the form up to the present. In "Literary
Newswriting: The Death of an Oxymoron" (1986), R. Thomas Berner picks up
where Wolfe left off when he notes in a survey of newspapers that the combin-
ing of fictional technique with in-depth reporting has become all but commonplace. What he found was that like Wolfe's taxonomy the newspaper articles

had "narration and scene" and "dialogue" (3). But Berner adds process, point of view, drama, foreshadowing, metaphor, and irony among others to the taxonomy. As Connery notes, perhaps Berner's most important contribution was that he conducted a survey of newspapers (although the survey was limited), a medium that has been largely ignored as a vehicle for (Berner's preferred usage) "literary newswriting" (Connery, "Discovering" 26). Most often such writing had been examined in magazine journalism or book-length texts.

Norman Sims continues in this tradition by attempting to delineate what he calls the "boundaries of the form" ("Literary Journalists" 8) based on interviews with well-known literary journalists such as John McPhee, Sara Davidson, Tracy Kidder, and Richard Rhodes. He arrives at six characteristics of the form that depend heavily on authorial intention and conventional understandings of rhetorical construction. The first is "immersion" in the subject matter (8–12), or what Wolfe called "saturation" reporting but which is not included in the Wolfean taxonomy. Sims's second characteristic is that every narrative of the form has a "structure" (12–15), which bears some resemblance to Wolfe's scene-by-scene construction. The third is that such narratives must be informed by journalistic "accuracy" in order to have credibility with the reader (15–16). The fourth is that such narratives usually express the individual "voice" of the journalist, unlike mainstream journalism (16–18). In effect, the reporter can have a presence in the narrative. The fifth is that literary journalists must demonstrate "responsibility" to the characters of the narrative (18–21). The final characteristic is that such narratives are informed with symbolism or underlying meanings (21–25).

Barbara Lounsberry identifies four defining characteristics of the form, three of which are derived from Wolfe and Sims. The derivative characteristics are documentable subject matter, exhaustive research, and creation of the scene (xv). The fourth—and her original contribution to a taxonomy—is perhaps the most problematic to a postmodern position. Lounsberry suggests that a work of literary journalism should be infused with what Annie Dillard calls "fine writing" and Gay Talese characterizes as "writing with style." Ultimately, Lounsberry suggests, literary journalism/nonfiction's "polished language reveals that the goal all along has been literature" (xv).

Because these attempts to theorize the form address what I characterize as "external" rhetorical and intentional characteristics, much of course is open to debate, not the least of which is what constitutes "fine writing." But Lounsberry also goes beyond such "external" characteristics in providing her taxonomy, and her effort crosses into the category of literary or rhetorical criticism designed to seek out "internal" mechanisms for how the form works. By her own account she takes a formalist approach, noting for example that Tom Wolfe is an American "Jeremiah" preaching hellfire (64), while Norman Mailer writes on an "epic" scale (139, 188). But despite classical references, she sprinkles her formalist approach liberally with biographical and psychoanalytical observations, claiming for example that Gay Talese explores the issue of father-son conflict (3, 35).

In this second group that is "literary" in orientation falls not only Lounsberry the announced formalist but also Hugh Kenner. Kenner notes that the rhetoric of what he calls the "plain style," which has been adopted by journalism at large—and used for telling effect by literary journalist George Orwell in *Homage to Catalonia*—is deceptively simple and simply deceptive because in its rhetorical forthrightness it persuades the reader that if the truth can be told simply it must be true (186–87).

Narrative literary journalism or nonfiction as fundamentally a rhetorical enterprise is taken up in Chris Anderson's collection of criticism *Literary Nonfiction*. In his introductory essay, Anderson notes the concerns the form and the teaching of composition appear to share. One of the common denominators between the two, he suggests, is the theme of indeterminacy that can only be negotiated rhetorically (xxi–xxii). Thus Anderson echoes a similar position of Hellmann's that rhetorical "pattern-making" is necessary for imposing some sense of order in a seemingly absurd world. Although the essays in the collection generally fall within the parameters of rhetorical analysis, they vary as much as rhetorical theory can vary. For example, Charles I. Schuster examines the prose of Richard Selzer by engaging in what he calls an "aesthetic analysis" by means of a New Critical discourse, referring for example to the "poet's vision" (3–4). Curiously, however, Schuster is not above invoking a little postmodern theory when he applies Mikhail Bakhtin's definition of the novel of the "inconclusive present"—or the indeterminate novel—to Selzer's work (23, 26–27). In sharp contrast to Schuster is Dennis Rygiel who advocates a stylistics approach or a counting of stylistic conventions as a means for analyzing his preferred usage, "literary nonfiction" ("Stylistics" 29).

Among those in the literary camp who focus on literary journalism as largely a fiction is Kathy Smith. In "John McPhee Balances the Act" she proposes that the "true story" as represented by the writings of McPhee is a contradiction in terms because of its use of fictional technique (226). Thus she provides ammunition for those descended in the line from Hellmann and Hollowell who would characterize true stories as fictions in disguise. So does Lars Ole Sauerberg in *Fact into Fiction*. Sauerberg takes a position close to Hellmann's when he notes that literary journalism/nonfiction remains fundamentally a "narrative fiction" (vii). He then proceeds to altogether break down the boundary between a narrative literary journalism and traditional fiction, discussing in the same context works traditionally considered fiction, such as James Michener's *Texas*, and those considered nonfiction, such as Capote's *In Cold Blood*.

In the cultural studies group belongs John J. Pauly, whose article "The Politics of the New Journalism" characterizes the form as a "realm of symbolic confrontation" reflecting larger cultural confrontation in an attempt to engage in cultural negotiation (111). David Eason, in "The New Journalism and the Image-World," differentiates between what he calls "realist" texts of literary journalism such as Gay Talese's, in which "conventional ways of understanding still apply," and "modernist" texts such as Joan Didion's, "where there is no consensus about a frame of reference" (192). Another example of the cultural studies approach is Shelley Fisher Fishkin's "Borderlands of Culture." Fishkin, who comes from an American studies background, notes that dominant generic forms, because of cultural constraints, proved inadequate for some writers who turned to experimental nonfiction that permitted them to more openly acknowledge the marginalization of other voices (133–35). Thus W. E. B. Du Bois in *The Souls of Black Folk* included passages of African American spirituals, and James Agee abandoned an assignment for *Fortune* in order to more fully explore the subjectivities of the Gudger family by exploring his own subjectivity. According to Fishkin, Gloria Anzaldúa wrote in both English and Spanish and included lines of verse in her nonfictional account to reflect how she inhabited the cultural and sexual "borderlands," while Tillie Olsen wrote the stories of women writers such as Rebecca Harding Davis who had been largely marginalized by the elitist literary establishment (133–82).

Similar to those in the cultural studies grouping is Phyllis Frus, whose postmodern Marxist interpretation of literary journalism, *The Politics and Poetics of Journalistic Narrative*, examines the means of production to account for the texts. Frus challenges elitist literary assumptions in books like *Hiroshima* and *In Cold Blood*, works that respectively marginalize, she says, the Japanese (93–95) or homicidal drifters (184) as Other.

Finally, among other efforts that do not fall comfortably into any of the categories I describe are Mas'ud Zavarzadeh's *Mythopoeic Reality* and Eric Heyne's "Toward a Theory of Literary Nonfiction." Zavarzadeh acknowledges subjectivity in language but also notes that the phenomenalist status of the world cannot be denied (226). As an ultimate consequence, "the tension between the centrifugal energies of reality and the centripetal forces of fiction produce double fields of reference in the nonfiction novel and distinguish the genre through its bi-referentiality from such mono-referential narratives as the fictive novel or factual history" (226). Out of this, he suggests, derives a neutral narrative of "zero interpretation" whose ambition in its neutrality is to reflect the absurdity of the world (40).

As the title to Heyne's examination suggests, the author is fully cognizant of the problematic nature of the form: he is only moving "toward" a theory of the form. He proposes a distinction between what he calls "factual status"— the author's intention that a narrative is a transcription of reality—and "factual adequacy"—a question that "readers would have to resolve individually or by debate" (480–81). Narrative literary journalism/nonfiction then has a binary nature and Heyne cites as an illustration *In Cold Blood*. The book has factual status according to the intentions Capote announces in the book's subtitle, *A True Account. . . .* Moreover, that factual status is reflected in the book's prefatory acknowledgments, when the author says all the material is taken either from his own observations, interviews, or transcripts. However some critics, Heyne notes, have since offered evidence that Capote invented or fictionalized passages in the book. Such findings would diminish the work's "factual adequacy" but would not change the status of *In Cold Blood* from nonfiction to fiction, Heyne says, because according to him the book is not a "triumph" of fiction over nonfiction but of lying over "truth-telling." Authorial intention and audience response are key then to situating literary journalism/nonfiction among literary forms, according to Heyne.

SUCH A critically fluid and uncertain form may raise the issue of course as to whether there is indeed a form called literary journalism or literary nonfiction. Moreover, the attempt to situate the scholarship of the form is admittedly problematic, if for no other reason than that its nomenclature is by no means established. Also, because there are only a few book-length examinations of literary journalism and the scholarship is generally meager, the form's study lacks a critical or scholarly mass. Such a problematic conclusion might suggest in more traditional academic circles that literary journalism/nonfiction cannot be critiqued because it appears to lack focus and weight, with the result that such a position can only continue to marginalize the form. Yet as I attempt to demonstrate, the form—by whatever name—is alive and well given the ongoing critical acknowledgment of it. More important, to further marginalize the form would fail to recognize one compelling circumstance, that texts of narrative literary journalism/nonfiction or whatever they are called are being produced.

Bibliography

Ade, George. *In Babel: Stories of Chicago.* New York: McClure, Phillips, 1903.
———. *The Permanent Ade.* Ed. Fred C. Kelly. Indianapolis: Bobbs, 1947.
[Addison, Joseph.] *Spectator* 7 May 1711: 1. Research Publications (n.d): 596. Charles Burney Collection of Early English Newspapers from the British Library.
AEJMC News. "Journals Undergo Name, Design Change" 28.2 (1995): 1.
Agee, James, and Walker Evans. *Let Us Now Praise Famous Men.* Boston: Houghton, 1941.
Anderson, Chris, ed. Introduction. *Literary Nonfiction: Theory, Criticism, Pedagogy.* Carbondale: Southern Illinois UP, 1989.
Anderson, Sherwood. *Puzzled America.* 1935. Mamaroneck, NY: Paul P. Appel, 1970.
Andrews, Alexander. *The History of British Journalism, from the Foundation of the Newspaper Press in England, to the Repeal of the Stamp Act in 1855 with Sketches of Press Celebrities.* 1859. Vol. 1. New York: Haskell House, 1968.
A[nger], Ja[ne]. *Jane Anger: Her Protection for Women.* 1589. Rpt. in *By a Woman Writt: Literature from Six Centuries by and about Women.* Ed. Joan Susan Goulianos. Indianapolis: Bobbs, 1973. 23–29.
Anson, Robert Sam. "The Rolling Stone Saga: Part 2." *New Times* 10 Dec. 1976: 22–37, 54–61.
Anthony, Ted. "Author Depicts Town Life in New Book." *Cortland Standard* 26 June 1999: 16. Associated Press Report.
Applegate, Edd, ed. *Literary Journalism: A Biographical Dictionary of Writers and Editors.* Westport, CT: Greenwood, 1996.
Asch, Nathan. Review. *New Republic* 4 Sept. 1935: 108.
Bakhtin, M[ikhail]. M. *The Dialogic Imagination.* Ed. Michael Holquist. Trans. Caryl Emerson and Michael Holquist. Austin: U of Texas P, 1981.
Ball, John. Introduction. *Children of the Levee.* By Lafcadio Hearn. Ed. O. W. Frost. N.p.: U of Kentucky P, 1957. 1–8.
Barrett, William. *Irrational Man.* Garden City, NY: Anchor, 1962.
Baym, Nina, et al., eds. *The Norton Anthology of American Literature.* 2d ed. 2 vols. New York: Norton, 1986.
Beals, Carleton. *Banana Gold.* Illustrations by Carlos Merida. Philadelphia: Lippincott, 1932.

261

————. *Brimstone and Chili: A Book of Personal Experiences in the Southwest and in Mexico.* New York: Knopf, 1927.

Beilin, Elaine V. *Redeeming Eve: Women Writers of the English Renaissance.* Princeton: Princeton UP, 1987.

Benjamin, Walter. "On Some Motifs in Baudelaire." *Illuminations.* Ed. Hannah Arendt. Trans. Harry Zohn. New York: Schocken, 1969. 155–200.

————. "The Storyteller: Reflections on the Works of Nikolai Leskov." *Illuminations.* Ed. Hannah Arendt. Trans. Harry Zohn. New York: Schocken, 1969. 83–110.

Bennett, H. S. *Chaucer and the Fifteenth Century.* Oxford: Clarendon, 1958.

Bennett, J. A. W. *Middle English Literature.* Ed. and completed by Douglas Gray. Oxford: Clarendon, 1986.

Berger, Charles R., and Steven H. Chaffee, eds. *Handbook of Communication Science.* Beverly Hills: Sage, 1987.

Berger, John. "Another Way of Telling." *Journal of Social Reconstruction* 1.1 (1980): 57–75.

————. "Stories." *Another Way of Telling.* New York: Pantheon, 1982. 277–89.

Berger, Meyer. Acknowledgments. *The Eight Million.* New York: Simon, 1942. xi.

————. "Al Capone Snubs de Lawd." *The Eight Million.* New York: Simon, 1942. 180–85.

————. *Meyer Berger's New York.* New York: Random, 1960.

Bernays, Edward. *Propaganda.* New York: Horace Liveright, 1928.

Berner, R. Thomas. "Literary Newswriting: The Death of an Oxymoron." *Journalism Monographs* 99 (Oct. 1986).

————. "Literary Notions and Utilitarian Reality." *Style* 16: 452–57.

Berreby, David. "Unabsolute Truths: Clifford Geertz." *New York Times Magazine* 9 Apr. 1995: 44–47.

Bickerstaff, Isaac [Richard Steele]. *Tatler* 12 Apr. 1709: 1. Research Publications (n.d.): 265. Charles Burney Collection of Early English Newspapers from the British Library.

Bierce, Ambrose. *The Collected Works of Ambrose Bierce.* 1909. Vol. 1. New York: Gordian, 1966.

Blair, Hugh. *Lectures on Rhetoric and Belles Lettres.* 1783. Abridged in *The Rhetoric of Blair, Campbell, and Whately.* Ed. J. L. Golden and E. P. J. Corbett. New York: Holt, 1968. 30–137.

Bly, Nellie [Elizabeth Cochrane]. *Nellie Bly's Book: Around the World in Seventy-Two Days.* Ed. Ira Peck. Brookfield, CT: Twenty-First Century Books, 1998.

————. *Ten Days in a Mad-House: or, Nellie Bly's Experience on Blackwell's Island.* New York: N. L. Munro, 1887. Library of Congress Microfilm 24142.

Bond, R. Warwick, ed. *The Complete Works of John Lyly.* 1902. Vol. 1. Oxford: Clarendon, 1967.

Bordelon, Pamela, ed. Biographical essay. *Go Gator and Muddy the Water: Writings by Zora Neale Hurston from the Federal Writers' Project.* New York: Norton, 1999.

"The Borderland of Literature." *Spectator* 14 Oct. 1893: 513–14.

Borus, Daniel H. *Writing Realism: Howells, James, and Norris in the Mass Market.* Chapel Hill: U of North Carolina P, 1989.

Boswell, James. *Boswell's London Journal: 1762–1763.* Ed. Frederick A. Pottle. Yale Editions of the Private Papers of James Boswell. New Haven: Yale UP, 1950.

———. *The Journal of a Tour to the Hebrides with Samuel Johnson LL.D.* 1786. Rpt. as *The Journal of a Tour to the Hebrides* and *A Journey to the Western Islands of Scotland.* 1775. Samuel Johnson. New York: Penguin, 1984.

———. "Memoirs of James Boswell, Esq." *European Magazine and London Review* May 1791: 323–26. Rpt. in *The Literary Career of James Boswell, Esq.: Being the Bibliographical Materials for a Life of Boswell.* By Frederick Albert Pottle. 1929. Oxford: Clarendon, 1965. xxxi–xliv.

Bowden, Mark. *Black Hawk Down: A Story of Modern War.* New York: Atlantic Monthly, 1999.

Boylan, James. "Publicity for the Great Depression: Newspaper Default and Literary Reportage." *Mass Media between the Wars: Perceptions of Cultural Tension, 1917–1941.* Ed. Catherine Covert and John Stevens. Syracuse: Syracuse UP, 1984. 159–79.

Boynton, H. W. "The Literary Aspect of Journalism." *Atlantic* 93 (1904): 845–51.

Bradford, William. *Of Plymouth Plantation, 1620–1647.* New York: Knopf, 1952.

Bradley, Patricia. "Richard Harding Davis." *A Sourcebook of American Literary Journalism: Representative Writers in an Emerging Genre.* Ed. Thomas B. Connery. New York: Greenwood, 1992. 21–52.

Braman, Sandra. "Joan Didion." *A Sourcebook of American Literary Journalism: Representative Writers in an Emerging Genre.* Ed. Thomas B. Connery. New York: Greenwood, 1992. 353–58.

Bromwich, David. "What Novels Are For." *New York Times Book Review* 30 Oct. 1994: 7.

Brown, Edith Baker. "A Plea for Literary Journalism." *Harper's Weekly* 46 (1902): 1558.

Bryan, C. D. B. *Friendly Fire.* New York: Putnam's, 1976.

Bunyan, John. *The Pilgrim's Progress from this World to That Which Is to Come.* Ed. James Blanton Wharey. 2d ed. Oxford: Oxford UP, 1960.

Bush, Douglas. *English Literature in the Earlier Seventeenth Century, 1600–1660.* 2d rev. ed. Oxford: Oxford UP, 1962.

Cahan, Abraham. "Can't Get Their Minds Ashore." *Commercial Advertiser* 11 Nov. 1898. *Grandma Never Live in America: The New Journalism of Abraham Cahan.* Ed. and intro. Moses Rischin. Bloomington: Indiana UP, 1985. 113–16.

———. "Pillelu, Pillelu!" *Commercial Advertiser* 1 Apr. 1899. *Grandma Never Live in America: The New Journalism of Abraham Cahan.* Ed. and intro. Moses Rischin. Bloomington: Indiana UP, 1985. 56–59.

Caldwell, Erskine. *Some American People.* New York: Robert M. McBride, 1935.

Cannon, Jimmy. *Nobody Asked Me.* New York: Dial, 1951.

Capote, Truman. *In Cold Blood: A True Account of a Multiple Murder and Its Conse-quences*. Signet ed. New York: Random, 1965.

Carey, James. "Culture and Communications." *Communication Research* 2 (1975): 173–91.

Carmer, Carl. *Stars Fell on Alabama*. New York: Literary Guild, 1934.

Casey, Robert J. *Torpedo Junction: With the Pacific Fleet from Pearl Harbor to Midway.* Indianapolis: Bobbs, 1942.

Chekhov, Anton. "Vanka." *The Portable Chekhov.* Ed. Avrahm Yarmolinsky. New York: Viking, 1968. 34–39.

Childers, Joseph, and Gary Hentzi, gen. eds. *The Columbia Dictionary of Modern Literary and Cultural Criticism.* New York: Columbia UP, 1995.

"Chronicle and Comment." *Bookman* 14 (Oct. 1901): 110–11.

Churchill, Allen. *Park Row.* 1958. Westport, CT: Greenwood, 1973.

Clarendon, Edward [Hyde], Earl of. *The History of the Rebellion and Civil Wars in England Begun in the Year 1641.* 1702–4. Ed. W. Dunn Macray. 6 vols. Oxford: Clarendon, 1888/1958.

Colvert, James B. Introduction. *Great Short Works of Stephen Crane.* New York: Harper, 1968.

The Compact Edition of the Oxford English Dictionary. Vol. 1. 1971 ed.

"The Confessions of 'a Literary Journalist.'" *Bookman* 26 (Dec. 1907): 370–76.

Connery, Thomas B. "Discovering a Literary Form." *A Sourcebook of American Literary Journalism: Representative Writers in an Emerging Genre.* Ed. Thomas B. Connery. New York: Greenwood, 1992. 3–37.

———. "Hutchins Hapgood." *A Sourcebook of American Literary Journalism: Repre-sentative Writers in an Emerging Genre.* Ed. Thomas B. Connery. New York: Greenwood, 1992. 121–29.

———. Preface. *A Sourcebook of American Literary Journalism: Representative Writers in an Emerging Genre.* Ed. Thomas B. Connery. New York: Greenwood, 1992. xi–xv.

———. "Research Review: Magazines and Literary Journalism, an Embar-rassment of Riches." *Electronic Journal of Communication/La Revue Electronique de Communication.* 4 (1994): 1–12.

———. "A Third Way to Tell the Story: American Literary Journalism at the Turn of the Century." *Literary Journalism in the Twentieth Century.* Ed. Norman Sims. New York: Oxford UP, 1990. 3–20.

———, ed. *A Sourcebook of American Literary Journalism: Representative Writers in an Emerging Genre.* New York: Greenwood, 1992.

Connors, Robert. "The Rise and Fall of the Modes of Discourse." *The St. Mar-tin's Guide to Teaching Writing.* Ed. Robert Connors and Cheryl Glenn. New York: St. Martin's, 1992. 362–75.

Cooper, R., W. Potter, and M. Dupagne. "A Status Report on Methods Used in Mass Communication Research." *Journalism Educator* 48.4 (1994): 54–61.

Corson, Hiram. *The Aims of Literary Study.* 1895. Excerpt in *The Origins of Literary*

Studies in America: A Documentary Anthology. Ed. Gerald Graff and Michael Warner. New York: Routledge, 1989. 90–95.

Crane, Stephen. "An Experiment in Misery." *New York Press* 22 Apr. 1894. Rpt. in *The New York City Sketches of Stephen Crane and Related Pieces.* Ed. R. W. Stallman and E. R. Hagemann. New York: New York UP, 1966. 33–43.

———. "In the Depths of a Coal Mine." *McClure's Magazine* (1894). Rpt. in *Tales, Sketches, and Reports.* Charlottesville: UP of Virginia, 1972. Vol. 8 of *The University of Virginia Edition of the Works of Stephen Crane.* Ed. Fredson Bowers. 590–607.

———. "A Lovely Jag in a Crowded Car." *New York Press* 6 Jan. 1895. Rpt. in *The New York City Sketches of Stephen Crane and Related Pieces.* Ed. R. W. Stallman and E. R. Hagemann. New York: New York UP, 1966. 125–28.

———. "The Men in the Storm." *Arena* Oct. 1894. Rpt. in *The New York City Sketches of Stephen Crane and Related Pieces.* Ed. R. W. Stallman and E. R. Hagemann. New York: New York UP, 1966. 91–96.

———. *The New York City Sketches of Stephen Crane and Related Pieces.* Ed. R. W. Stallman and E. R. Hagemann. New York: New York UP, 1966.

———. "The Open Boat." *Scribner's Magazine* June 1897. Rpt. in *Great Short Works of Stephen Crane.* Intro. James B. Colvert. New York: Harper, 1968. 277–302.

———. "Regulars Get No Glory." *New York World* 20 July 1898. Rpt. in *Reports of War: War Dispatches: Great Battles of the World.* Charlottesville: UP of Virginia, 1971. Vol. 9 of *The University of Virginia Edition of the Works of Stephen Crane.* Ed. Fredson Bowers. 170–73.

———. "Stephen Crane's Own Story." *New York Press* 7 Jan. 1897. Rpt. in *Reports of War: War Dispatches: Great Battles of the World.* Charlottesville: UP of Virginia, 1971. Vol. 9 of *The University of Virginia Edition of the Works of Stephen Crane.* Ed. Fredson Bowers. 85–94.

———. "To William H. Crane." 29 Nov. 1896. Letter 285 of *The Correspondence of Stephen Crane.* Ed. Stanley Wertheim and Paul Sorrentino. Vol. 1. New York: Columbia UP. 264–66.

———. "When Man Falls a Crowd Gathers." *New York Press* 9 Dec. 1894. Rpt. in *The New York City Sketches of Stephen Crane and Related Pieces.* Ed. R. W. Stallman and E. R. Hagemann. New York: New York UP, 1966. 102–11.

Creative Nonfiction. 1 (1993): ii.

———. 13 (1999): iv.

Crèvecoeur, Hector St. John de. *Letters from an American Farmer.* 1782. Intro. Warren Barton Blake. London: J. M. Dent and Sons, 1912, 1945.

Crook, James A. "1940s: Decade of Adolescence for Professional Education." *Journalism and Mass Communication Educator* 50.1 (1995): 4–15.

Cummings, E. E. *The Enormous Room.* 1922. New York: Modern Library, 1934.

Dana, Richard Henry, Jr. "Cruelty to Seamen." *American Jurist and Law Magazine* 22 (Oct. 1839): 92–107.

————. *The Seaman's Friend.* 1841. 14th ed. (1879). Mineola, NY: Dover, 1997.

————. *Two Years before the Mast.* 1840. New York: Harper, 1936.

Davidson, Cathy N. "Ideology and Genre: The Rise of the Novel in America." *Proceedings of the American Antiquarian Society* 96 (1986): 295–321.

Davidson, Sara. *Real Property.* Garden City, NY: Doubleday, 1980.

Davis, Lennard J. *Factual Fictions: The Origins of the English Novel.* Philadelphia: U of Pennsylvania P, 1983.

Davis, Richard Harding. "The Death of Rodriguez." 1897. *Notes of a War Correspondent.* New York: Scribner's, 1911.

————. "The German Army Marches through Brussels, 21 August 1914." *London News Chronicle* 23 Aug. 1914. Rpt. in *Eyewitness to History.* Ed. John Carey. New York: Avon, 1987. 445–48.

————. *With the Allies.* New York: Scribner's, 1915.

Day, Dorothy. *By Little and by Little.* Ed. Robert Ellsberg. New York: Knopf, 1983.

Defoe, Daniel. *A Journal of the Plague Year.* 1722. Oxford: Shakespeare Head Press, 1928.

————. *The Life and Strange Surprising Adventures of Robinson Crusoe.* 1719. Vol. 1. Oxford: Shakespeare Head Press, 1927.

————. *The Storm: Or, a Collection of the Most Remarkable Casualties and Disasters Which Happen'd in the Late Dreadful Tempest Both by Sea and Land.* London: 1704.

————. *The True and Genuine Account of the Life and Actions of the Late Jonathan Wild.* London: 1725. Photocopy of original in British Museum. London: University Microfilms, Remax House, [1966?].

Dekker, Thomas. *Lanthorn and Candlelight; or, the Belman's Second Nights-Walke.* 1609. *The Non-Dramatic Works of Thomas Dekker.* 1884. Ed. Alexander B. Grossart. 5 vols. New York: Russell and Russell, 1963.

————. *The Wonderfull Yeare, 1603.* 1603. *The Non-Dramatic Works of Thomas Dekker.* 1884. Ed. Alexander B. Grossart. 5 vols. New York: Russell and Russell, 1963.

de Man, Paul. "Criticism and Crisis." *Blindness and Insight.* Minneapolis: U of Minnesota P, 1983. 3–19.

Didion, Joan. *Salvador.* New York: Simon, 1983.

————. *Slouching towards Bethlehem.* New York: Noonday, 1990.

Dobrée, Bonamy. *English Literature in the Early Eighteenth Century, 1700–1740.* New York: Oxford UP, 1959.

Dreiser, Theodore. "Curious Shifts of the Poor." *Demorest's* 36 (Nov. 1899): 22–26. Rpt. in *Selected Magazine Articles of Theodore Dreiser.* Ed. Yashinobu Hakutani. Rutherford, NJ: Fairleigh Dickinson UP, 1985. 170–80.

————. *Newspaper Days.* 1922. Ed. T. D. Nostwich. University of Pennsylvania Dreiser Edition. Gen. ed. Thomas P. Riggio. Philadelphia: U of Pennsylvania P, 1991.

————. *Sister Carrie.* 1900. Ed. Donald Pizer. New York: Norton, 1970.

Dryden, John. "Life of Plutarch." *The Works of John Dryden*. Ed. Samuel Holt Monk. Vol. 17. Berkeley: U of California P, 1971. 226–88.

Du Bois, W. E. B. *W. E. B. Du Bois: Writings*. Ed. Nathan Huggins. New York: Library of America, 1986.

Dunne, Finley Peter. *Mr. Dooley in Peace and in War*. Boston: Small, Maynard, 1899.

Durham, Frank. "History of a Curriculum: The Search for Salience." *Journalism Educator* 46.4 (1992): 14–21.

Duyckinck, Evert A., and George L. Duyckinck. *Cyclopaedia of American Literature*. 2 vols. New York: Scribner's, 1855.

Earle, John. *Microcosmography: Or a Piece of the World Discovered in Essays and Characters*. 1628–29. Ed. Harold Osborne. London: University Tutorial, 1933.

Eason, David. "The New Journalism and the Image-World." *Literary Journalism in the Twentieth Century*. Ed. Norman Sims. New York: Oxford UP, 1990.

Easterbrook, Gregg. "Toxic Business." *New York Times Book Review* 10 Sept. 1995: 13.

Easthope, Anthony. "Can Literary Journalism Be Serious?" *Times Literary Supplement* 20 May 1994: 17.

Edmundson, Mark. "Theory's Battle against the Poets." *Harper's Magazine* Aug. 1995: 28–31.

Eisenstein, Elizabeth L. *The Printing Press as an Agent of Change: Communications and Cultural Transformations in Early-Modern Europe*. 2 vols. Cambridge: Cambridge UP, 1979.

Eliot, T. S. "Hamlet." *Selected Prose of T. S. Eliot*. Ed. Frank Kermode. New York: Harcourt; Farrar, 1975. 45–49.

———. "The Perfect Critic." *Selected Prose of T. S. Eliot*. Ed. Frank Kermode. New York: Harcourt; Farrar, 1975. 50–58.

Emerson, Ralph Waldo. "The American Scholar." 1837. Rpt. in *The Collected Works of Ralph Waldo Emerson*. Vol. 1. *Nature, Addresses, and Lectures*. Gen. ed. Alfred R. Ferguson. Cambridge, MA: Belknap P of Harvard UP, 1971. 52–70.

Emery, Edwin, and Michael Emery. *The Press and America: An Interpretative History of the Mass Media*. Englewood Cliffs, NJ: Prentice, 1978.

Evelyn, John. *The Diary of John Evelyn*. Ed. William Bray. Vol. 2. New York: M. Walter Dunne, 1901.

Evensen, Bruce J. "Abraham Cahan." *A Sourcebook of American Literary Journalism: Representative Writers in an Emerging Genre*. Ed. Thomas B. Connery. New York: Greenwood, 1992. 91–100.

Fedler, Fred. *Reporting for the Print Media*. 5th ed. New York: Harcourt, 1993.

Fishkin, Shelley Fisher. "The Borderlands of Culture: Writing by W. E. B. Du Bois, James Agee, Tillie Olsen, and Gloria Anzaldúa." *Literary Journalism in the Twentieth Century*. Ed. Norman Sims. New York: Oxford UP, 1990. 133–82.

FitzStephen[, William]. "Prelude to FitzStephen's 'Life of Becket.'" [ca.

1180?]. *Documents Illustrating the History of Civilization in Medieval England (1066–1500)*. 1926. Ed. R. Trevor Davies. New York: Barnes, 1969. 115–22.

Folkerts, Jean, and Dwight L. Teeter Jr. *Voices of a Nation: A History of Media in the United States*. New York: Macmillan, 1989.

Ford, Edwin H. "The Art and Craft of the Literary Journalist." *New Survey of Journalism*. Ed. George Fox Mott. New York: Barnes, 1950. 304–13.

———. *A Bibliography of Literary Journalism in America*. Minneapolis: Burgess, 1937.

Foster, Mike. "Ancient Scroll Provides a Description of Heaven:—And a Secret Formula for Resurrecting the Dead!" *Weekly World News* 4 Jan. 2000: 6.

———. "Demon's Body Found in Holy Land." *Weekly World News* 4 Jan. 2000: 13.

Foxe, John. *Acts and Monuments of Matters Most Special and Memorable Happening in the Church, Especially in the Realm of England*. 1596–97. 5th ed. *Foxe's Book of Martyrs*. Ed. and abr. G. Williamson. Boston: Little, 1965.

Francke, Warren T. "W. T. Stead: The First New Journalist?" *Journalism History* 1.2 (1974): 36, 63–66.

Frus, Phyllis. *The Politics and Poetics of Journalistic Narrative: The Timely and the Timeless*. New York: Cambridge UP, 1994.

———. "Two Tales 'Intended to Be after the Fact': 'Stephen Crane's Own Story' and 'The Open Boat.'" *Literary Nonfiction: Theory, Criticism, Pedagogy*. Ed. Chris Anderson. Carbondale: Southern Illinois UP, 1989. 125–51.

Fuller, Thomas. *The Worthies of England*. 1662. Ed. Thomas Fuller. London: George Allen & Unwin, 1952.

Furtwangler, A. *The Authority of Publius: A Reading of the Federalist Papers*. Ithaca, NY: Cornell UP, 1984.

Garland, Hamlin. *Crumbling Idols*. 1894. Cambridge, MA: Harvard UP, 1960.

Gobright, Lawrence A. Fifth dispatch. *New York Tribune* 15 Apr. 1865. Rpt. in *A Treasury of Great Reporting: "Literature under Pressure" from the Sixteenth Century to Our Own Time*. Ed. Louis L. Snyder and Richard B. Morris. Pref. Herbert Bayard Swope. 2d rev. ed. New York: Simon, 1962. 150–54.

Gold, Herbert. "On Epidemic First Personism." *The Reporter as Artist: A Look at the New Journalism Controversy*. Ed. Ronald Weber. New York: Hastings House, 1974. 283–87.

Golden, J. L., and E. P. J. Corbett, eds. *The Rhetoric of Blair, Campbell, and Whately*. New York: Holt, 1968.

Good, Howard. "Jacob A. Riis." *A Sourcebook of American Literary Journalism: Representative Writers in an Emerging Genre*. Ed. Thomas B. Connery. New York: Greenwood, 1992. 81–90.

Graff, Gerald. *Professing Literature: An Institutional History*. Chicago: U of Chicago P, 1987.

Gray, James. "The Journalist as Literary Man." *American Non-Fiction, 1900–1950*. Ed. William Van O'Connor and Frederick J. Hoffman. 1952. Westport, CT: Greenwood, 1970. 95–147.

Griffin, John Howard. *Black like Me*. 2d ed. Boston: Houghton, 1977.

Hakluyt, Richard. *Hakluyt's Voyages*. 1598–1600. 8 vols. [Ed. S. Douglas Jackson.] Intro. John Masefield. New York: Dutton, 1907.

———. *The Principall Navigations Voiages and Discoveries of the English Nation.* 1589. 2 vols. New York: Cambridge UP, 1965.

Hakutani, Yashinobu, ed. Introduction. *Selected Magazine Articles of Theodore Dreiser.* Rutherford, NJ: Fairleigh Dickinson UP, 1985. 15–38.

———. Preface. *Selected Magazine Articles of Theodore Dreiser.* Rutherford, NJ: Fairleigh Dickinson UP, 1985. 9–11.

Hall, William Henry. *Hall's Encyclopaedia*. London: [ca. 1795?].

Hapgood, Hutchins. "A New Form of Literature." *Bookman*. 21 (1905): 424–47.

———. *The Spirit of the Ghetto*. 1902. Ed. Moses Rischin. Cambridge: Belknap P of Harvard UP, 1967.

———. *A Victorian in the Modern World*. New York: Harcourt, 1939.

Hard, William. "Cannon: The Proving." *New Republic* 15 (1 June 1918): 136–38.

———. "In Judge Anderson's Courtroom." *New Republic* 20 (26 Nov. 1919): 373–77.

Harding, Rebecca. "Life in the Iron-Mills." *Atlantic Monthly* 7 (Apr. 1861): 430–51.

———. "A Story of To-Day." Part 1. *Atlantic Monthly* (Oct. 1861): 471–86.

Hardy, Thomas. "The Convergence of the Twain." *Modern Poetry: American and British*. Ed. Kimon Friar and John Malcolm Brinnin. New York: Appleton, 1951.

Hart, Jack. "Stories in the News." *Writer's Digest* Sept. 1995: 29–33.

Hart, James D., ed. *The Oxford Companion to American Literature*. 6th ed. Rev. and additions Phillip W. Leininger. New York: Oxford UP, 1995.

Hartsock, John C. "'Literary Journalism' as an Epistemological Moving Object within a Larger 'Quantum' Narrative." *Journal of Communication Inquiry* 23 (Oct. 1999): 432–47.

Harvey, Chris. "Tom Wolfe's Revenge." *American Journalism Review* Oct. 1994: 40–45.

Hawking, Stephen. *A Brief History of Time: From the Big Bang to Black Holes*. Intro. Carl Sagan. New York: Bantam, 1988.

Hawthorne, Julian. "Journalism the Destroyer of Literature." *The Critic* 48 (1906): 166–71.

Hearn, Lafcadio. "All in White." *New Orleans Item* 14 Sept. 1879. Rpt. in *Stray Leaves from Strange Literature and Fantastics and Other Fancies*. Boston: Houghton, 1914. Koizumi Edition. Vol. 2 of *The Writings of Lafcadio Hearn*. 217–19.

———. "At a Railway Station." *Kokoro*. 1896. Rpt. in *The Selected Writings of Lafcadio Hearn*. Ed. Henry Goodman. New York: Citadel, 1949. 347–50.

———. "A Child of the Levee." *Cincinnati Commercial* 27 June 1876. Rpt. in *Children of the Levee*. Ed. O. W. Frost. N.p.: U of Kentucky P, 1957. 9–12.

————. "Dolly: An Idyl of the Levee." *Cincinnati Commercial* 27 Aug. 1876. Rpt. in *Children of the Levee*. Ed. O. W. Frost. N.p.: U of Kentucky P, 1957. 13–22.

————. "Jot: The Haunt of the Obi Man." *Cincinnati Commercial* 22 Aug. 1875. Rpt. as "Jot" in *Children of the Levee*. Ed. O. W. Frost. N.p.: U of Kentucky P, 1957. 49–53.

————. "The Last of the Voudous." *Harper's Weekly* 7 Nov. 1885. Rpt. in *The Selected Writings of Lafcadio Hearn*. Ed. Henry Goodman. New York: Citadel, 1949. 268–73.

————. "Levee Life: Haunts and Pastimes of the Roustabouts: Their Original Songs and Dances." *Cincinnati Commercial* 17 Mar. 1876. Rpt. as "Levee Life" in *Children of the Levee*. Ed. O. W. Frost. N.p.: U of Kentucky P, 1957. 61–83.

————. "The Rising of the Waters." *Cincinnati Commercial* 18 Jan. 1877. Rpt. in *Children of the Levee*. Ed. O. W. Frost. N.p.: U of Kentucky P, 1957. 99–103.

————. "The Stranger." *New Orleans Item* 17 Apr. 1880. Rpt. in *Stray Leaves from Strange Literature and Fantastics and Other Fancies*. Boston: Houghton, 1914. Koizumi Edition. Vol. 2 of *The Writings of Lafcadio Hearn*. 237–38.

————. "Ti Canotie." *Martinique Sketches*. 1890. Rpt. in *The Selected Writings of Lafcadio Hearn*. Ed. Henry Goodman. New York: Citadel, 1949. 285–97.

————. "To H. E. Krehbiel." 1878. *Life and Letters of Lafcadio Hearn*. Ed. Elizabeth Bisland. Vol 1. Boston: Houghton, 1906. 191–97.

————. "To H. E. Krehbiel." 1880. *The Life and Letters of Lafcadio Hearn*. Ed. Elizabeth Bisland. Vol. 1. Boston: Houghton, 1906. 218–22.

————. "Voices of Dawn." 1881. Rpt. in *The Selected Writings of Lafcadio Hearn*. Ed. Henry Goodman. New York: Citadel, 1949. 266–68.

————. "Why Crabs Are Boiled Alive." *New Orleans Item* 5 Oct. 1879. Rpt. in *The Selected Writings of Lafcadio Hearn*. Ed. Henry Goodman. New York: Citadel, 1949. 266.

————. "Y Porque." *New Orleans Item* 17 Apr. 1880. Rpt. in *Stray Leaves from Strange Literature and Fantastics and Other Fancies*. Boston: Houghton, 1914. Koizumi Edition. Vol. 2 of *The Writings of Lafcadio Hearn*. 239–40.

Hecht, Ben. *A Child of the Century*. New York: Simon, 1954.

————. "The Dagger Venus." *A Thousand and One Afternoons in Chicago*. Chicago: Covici Friede, 1927. 189–92.

Heinz, W. C. *The Professional*. 1958. Intro. George Plimpton. New York: Arbor House, 1984.

Heisenberg, Werner. *Physics and Philosophy: The Revolution in Modern Science*. Ed. Ruth Nanda Anshen. Vol. 19 of *World Perspectives*. New York: Harper, 1958.

Hellmann, John. *Fables of Fact: The New Journalism as Fables of Fact*. Urbana: U of Illinois P, 1981.

Hemingway, Ernest. "Italy, 1927." *New Republic* 18 May 1927: 350–53.

————. *A Moveable Feast*. New York: Scribner's, 1964.

————. "A Situation Report." *Look* 4 Sept. 1956. Rpt. in *By-Line: Ernest Hemingway*. Ed. William White. New York: Scribner's, 1967. 470–78.

Herr, Michael. *Dispatches*. New York: Vintage, 1991.

Hersey, John. *Hiroshima*. 1946. New York: Bantam, 1986.

Hettinga, Donald R. "Ring Lardner." *A Sourcebook of American Literary Journalism: Representative Writers in an Emerging Genre*. Ed. Thomas B. Connery. New York: Greenwood, 1992. 161–67.

Heyne, Eric. "Toward a Theory of Literary Nonfiction." *Modern Fiction Studies* 23 (1989): 479–90.

Holinshed, Raphael, et al. *The First and Second Volumes of Chronicles*. . . . 1586. Rpt. as *Holinshed's Chronicles: England, Scotland, and Ireland*. 1807. New York: AMS, 1965.

Hollowell, John. *Fact and Fiction: The New Journalism and the Nonfiction Novel*. Chapel Hill: U of North Carolina P, 1977.

Hoover, Herbert. "The President's News Conference of November 29, 1929." Document 292 of *Public Papers of the Presidents of the United States: Herbert Hoover*. Washington, DC: GPO, 1974. 401–2.

Horwitz, Tony. *Confederates in the Attic: Dispatches from the Unfinished Civil War*. New York: Vintage, 1998.

Hough, George A. "How New?" *Journal of Popular Culture* 9 (1975): 114/16–121/23.

Howard, June. *Form and History in American Literary Naturalism*. Chapel Hill: U of North Carolina P, 1985.

Howells, William Dean. *Criticism and Fiction*. 1891. Cambridge, MA: Walker-de Berry, 1962.

———. *A Hazard of New Fortunes*. 1890. New York: Meridian, 1994.

———. *A Modern Instance*. 1882. Boston: Houghton, 1957.

———. *Years of My Youth*. 1916. Rpt. as *Years of My Youth and Three Essays*. Ed. David J. Nordloh. Bloomington: Indiana UP, 1975. Vol. 29 of *A Selected Edition of W. D. Howells*. Gen. ed. Edwin H. Cady et al. 32 vols. 1968–83.

Hudson, Frederic. *Journalism in the United States, from 1690 to 1872*. New York: Harper, 1873.

Hudson, Robert V. "Literary Journalism: A Case Study from the 'Abyss.'" Paper presented at conference, "Historical Points in Time: Structure, Subject, Object." Seventy-ninth annual meeting of the Association for Education in Journalism and Mass Communication. 13 Aug. 1996.

Humphrey, Robert E. "John Reed." *A Sourcebook of American Literary Journalism: Representative Writers in an Emerging Genre*. Ed. Thomas B. Connery. New York: Greenwood, 1992. 151–60.

Hunt, Theodore. "The Place of English in the College Curriculum." 1884–85. Rpt. in *The Origins of Literary Studies in America: A Documentary Anthology*. Ed. Gerald Graff and Michael Warner. Routledge: New York, 1989. 38–49.

Hurston, Zora Neale. "Eatonville When You Look at It." *Go Gator and Muddy the Water: Writings by Zora Neale Hurston from the Federal Writers' Project*. Ed. and biographical essay Pamela Bordelon. New York: Norton, 1999. 124–25.

Hutson, Charles Woodward. "Fantastics and Other Fancies: Introduction." *Stray Leaves from Strange Literature and Fantastics and Other Fancies*. Boston: Houghton, 1914. Koizumi Edition. Vol. 2 of *The Writings of Lafcadio Hearn*. 197–214.

Jane, John. "The Last Voyage of Thomas Cavendish . . . 6. John Jane." [1598–
    1600]. *Last Voyages: Cavendish, Hudson, Ralegh: The Original Narratives.* Ed.
    Philip Edwards. Oxford: Clarendon, 1988. 98–120.
Jensen, Jay. "The New Journalism in Historical Perspective." *Journalism History*
    1.2 (1974): 37, 66.
Johnson, Michael L. *The New Journalism: The Underground Press, the Artists of Non-
    fiction, and Changes in the Established Media.* Lawrence: UP of Kansas, 1971.
Johnson, Samuel. "Abraham Cowley" from *Lives of the Poets.* 1779. Rpt. in *Se-
    lected Writings.* Samuel Johnson. Ed. R. T. Davies. Evanston, IL: Northwestern
    UP, 1965. 323–24.
———. "Contemporary Novels." *Rambler* 4 (31 Mar. 1750). Rpt. in *Selected Writ-
    ings.* Samuel Johnson. Ed. R. T. Davies. Evanston, IL: Northwestern UP,
    1965. 76–80.
———. *A Journey to the Western Islands of Scotland.* 1775. James Boswell. *The Jour-
    nal of a Tour to the Hebrides with Samuel Johnson LL.D.* 1786. Rpt. as *The Journal
    of a Tour to the Hebrides.* New York: Penguin, 1984.
———. *Letters of Samuel Johnson, LL.D.* Comp. and ed. George Birkbeck Hill.
    Oxford: Clarendon, 1892.
Journalism Educator. "Call for Papers: Fiftieth Anniversary Year" 49.4 (1995):
    verso front matter.
Kaplan, Amy. *The Social Construction of American Realism.* Chicago: U of Chicago
    P, 1988.
Kaul, Arthur J., ed. *American Literary Journalists, 1945–1995.* First Ser. Diction-
    ary of Literary Biography 185. Detroit: Gale, 1997.
Kazin, Alfred. "Edmund Wilson on the Thirties." *Contemporaries: From the Nine-
    teenth Century to the Present.* Rev. ed. New York: Horizon, 1982.
———. "The Imagination of Fact." *Bright Book of Life.* Boston: Little, 1973.
    209–41.
———. *On Native Grounds: An Interpretation of Modern American Prose Literature.*
    New York: Reynal and Hitchcock, 1942.
Keats, John. "Ode on a Grecian Urn." *The Complete Poetry and Selected Prose of John
    Keats.* Ed. Harold Edgar Briggs. New York: Modern Library, 1951. 294–95.
Kemp, William. *Nine Daies Wonder: Performed in a Daunce from London to Norwich.*
    1600. Ed. G. B. Harrison. Elizabethan and Jacobean Quartos. Rpt. from
    Bodley Head Quartos. New York: Barnes, 1966.
Keneally, Thomas. *Schindler's List.* New York: Touchstone, 1982.
Kenner, Hugh. "The Politics of the Plain Style." *Literary Journalism in the Twenti-
    eth Century.* Ed. Norman Sims. New York: Oxford UP, 1990. 183–90.
Kerrane, Kevin, and Ben Yagoda, eds. *The Art of Fact: A Historical Anthology of
    Literary Journalism.* New York: Scribner's, 1997.
Kirkhorn, Michael J. "Journalism's Guilty Secret." *Nieman Reports* 46.2 (summer
    1992): 36–41.
Knight, Sarah Kemble. *The Journal of Madam Knight.* Ed. and intro. George Par-
    ker Winship. Boston: Small, Maynard, 1920. *The Private Journal of a Journey
    from Boston to New York.* 1825.

Kramer, Dale. *Ross and the New Yorker.* New York: Doubleday, 1951.

Kroeger, Brooke. *Nellie Bly: Daredevil, Reporter, Feminist.* New York: Times Books, 1994.

Kydde, Thomas. *The trueth of the most wicked & secret murthering of Iohn Brewen . . . committed by his owne wife through the prouocation of one Iohn Parker. . . .* 1592. *Illustrations of Early English Popular Literature.* 1863. Ed. J. Payne Collier. Vol. 1. New York: Benjamin Blom, 1966. iii–15.

Lardner, Ring. *Some Champions.* Ed. Matthew J. Bruccoli and Richard Layman. New York: Scribner's, 1976.

Laurie, Annie [Winifred Black]. *Roses and Rain.* Annie Laurie Ser. San Francisco: A. Laurie, 1920.

Lawrence, T. E. *Revolt in the Desert.* New York: George H. Doran, 1927.

Lee, Alfred McClung. *The Daily Newspaper in America: The Evolution of a Social Instrument.* New York: Macmillan, 1947.

Lee, Gerald Stanley. "Journalism as a Basis for Literature." *Atlantic* Feb. 1900: 231–37.

Legge, M. Dominica. *Anglo-Norman Literature and Its Background.* Oxford: Clarendon, 1963.

Levi, Peter. Introduction. *A Journey to the Western Islands of Scotland.* 1775. Samuel Johnson. *The Journal of a Tour to the Hebrides with Samuel Johnson, LL.D.* 1786. James Boswell. Rpt. as *The Journal of a Tour to the Hebrides.* New York: Penguin, 1984. 11–28.

Levin, Harry. "Novel." *Dictionary of World Literature.* Rev. ed. Paterson, NJ: Littlefield, Adams, 1962.

Lewis, C. S. *English Literature in the Sixteenth Century: Excluding Drama.* Oxford: Clarendon, 1954.

Lewis, Oscar. Introduction. *Frank Norris of "The Wave": Stories and Sketches from the San Francisco Weekly, 1893 to 1897.* San Francisco: Westgate, 1931. 1–15.

Library of Congress. *Subject Headings.* 22d edition. Vol. 4. Washington, D.C: Library of Congress, 1999.

Liebling, A. J. *Back Where I Came From.* 1938. Foreword by Philip Hamburger. San Francisco: North Point, 1990.

———. *The Earl of Louisiana.* Baton Rouge: Louisiana State UP, 1970.

———. *Mollie and Other War Pieces.* 1964. New York: Schocken, 1989.

———. *A Reporter at Large: Dateline — Pyramid Lake, Nevada.* 1955. Ed. Elmer R. Rusco. Reno: U of Nevada P, 1999.

Lippmann, Walter. *Liberty and the News.* New York: Harcourt, 1920.

———. *Public Opinion.* 1922. New York: Free, 1965.

———. "Two Revolutions in the American Press." *Yale Review* 20 (1931): 433–41.

Lippmann, Walter, and Charles Merz. "'A Test of the News': Some Criticisms." *New Republic* 8 Sept. 1920: 32–33.

London, Jack. *The People of the Abyss.* 1903. New York: Library of America, 1982.

———. "To Anna Strunsky." 22 Aug. 1902. *The Letters of Jack London.* Ed. Earle

Labor, Robert C. Leritz III, and I. Milo Shepard. Vol 1. Stanford, CA: Stanford UP, 1988. 308–9.

———. "To George and Caroline Sterling." 22 Aug. 1902. *The Letters of Jack London.* Ed. Earle Labor, Robert C. Leritz III, and I. Milo Shepard. Vol 1. Stanford, CA: Stanford UP, 1988. 306.

Longstreet, Augustus Baldwin. *Georgia Scenes, Characters, Incidents, &c., in the First Half Century of the Republic.* 2d ed. New York: Harper, 1854.

Lounsberry, Barbara. *The Art of Fact: Contemporary Artists of Nonfiction.* New York: Greenwood, 1990.

Lyly, John. *Euphues: The Anatomy of Wyt.* 1578. *The Complete Works of John Lyly.* 1902. Ed. R. Warwick Bond. Vol. 1. Oxford: Clarendon, 1967.

Macdonald, Dwight. "Hersey's 'Hiroshima.'" *Politics* 3 (Oct. 1946): 308.

———. "Parajournalism, or Tom Wolfe and His Magic Writing Machine." *The Reporter as Artist: A Look at the New Journalism Controversy.* Ed. Ronald Weber. New York: Hastings House, 1974. 223–33.

Magnusson, A. Lynne. "'His Pen with My Hande': Jane Anger's Revisionary Rhetoric." *English Studies in Canada* 17 (1991): 269–81.

Mailer, Norman. *The Armies of the Night: History as a Novel: The Novel as History.* New York: NAL, 1968.

———. *The Executioner's Song.* New York: Warner Books, 1979.

Manguel, Alberto. *A History of Reading.* New York: Viking, 1996.

Man in the Moon, Discovering a World of Knavery under the Sunne. 4 July 1649. Research Publications (n.d): Microfilm 1191. Charles Burney Collection of Early English Newspapers from the British Library.

Mann, Nick. "Face of Satan Seen over U.S. Capitol." *Weekly World News* 4 Jan. 2000: 1, 46–47.

——— . "National Air Alert Issued by NTSB: Passenger Jet Reports Near Miss with Winged Entities at 40,000 Feet." *Weekly World News* 4 Jan. 2000: 40–41.

Mansell, Darrel. "Unsettling the Colonel's Hash: 'Fact' in Autobiography." *Literary Journalism in the Twentieth Century.* Ed. Norman Sims. New York: Oxford UP, 1990. 261–80.

Many, Paul. "Toward a History of Literary Journalism." *Michigan Academician* 24 (1992): 359–69.

Markey, Morris. *Well Done! An Aircraft Carrier in Battle Action.* Foreword by Ralph A. Ofstie. New York: Appleton, 1945.

Marmarelli, Ronald S. "William Hard." *A Sourcebook of American Literary Journalism: Representative Writers in an Emerging Genre.* Ed. Thomas B. Connery. New York: Greenwood, 1992. 131–42.

Martin, Jay. *Harvests of Change: American Literature, 1865–1914.* Englewood Cliffs, NJ: Prentice, 1967.

Martin, John Bartlow. *My Life in Crime.* New York: Harper, 1952.

Matschat, Cecile Hulse. *Suwannee River: Strange Green Land.* Ed. Constance Lindsay Skinner. New York: Farrar, 1936.

McCarthy, Mary. "Artists in Uniform." *Harper's Magazine* Mar. 1953. Rpt. in *Lit-*

erary Journalism in the Twentieth Century. Ed. Norman Sims. New York: Oxford UP, 1990. 231–46.

———. "Settling the Colonel's Hash." *Harper's Magazine* Feb. 1954. Rpt. in *Literary Journalism in the Twentieth Century.* Ed. Norman Sims. New York: Oxford UP, 1990. 247–60.

McGill, Jennifer, ed. *Journalism and Mass Communication Directory* 13 (1995–96): 140, 278.

McKillop, Alan D. Introduction. *Eighteenth-Century Poetry and Prose.* Ed. Louis I. Bredvold, Alan D. McKillop, and Lois Whitney. Prepared by John M. Bullitt. 3d ed. New York: Ronald Press, 1973.

McNulty, John. *The World of John McNulty.* Garden City, NY: Doubleday, 1957.

McPhee, John. *Basin and Range.* New York: Farrar, 1981.

———. Preface. *A Sense of Where You Are.* 1965. 2d ed. New York: Farrar, 1978.

Mencken, H. L. "The National Letters." *Prejudices: Second Series.* New York: Knopf, 1920.

Mills, Nicolaus. *The New Journalism: A Historical Anthology.* New York: McGraw, 1974,

Mitchell, Joseph. Author's Note. *Up in the Old Hotel and Other Stories.* New York: Vintage, 1993. ix–xii.

———. "The Old House at Home." *Up in the Old Hotel and Other Stories.* New York: Vintage, 1993. 3–22.

Moley, Raymond. Letters. *Today* 2 Dec. 1933: 3.

Mott, Frank Luther. *American Journalism: A History of Newspapers in the United States through 260 Years, 1690 to 1950.* New York: Macmillan, 1962.

Nelson, Jack A. "Mark Twain." *A Sourcebook of American Literary Journalism: Representative Writers in an Emerging Genre.* Ed. Thomas B. Connery. New York: Greenwood, 1992. 39–42.

Nietzsche, Friedrich. "On Truth and Falsity in Their Ultramoral Sense." 1873. *Early Greek Philosophy and Other Essays.* 1911. Trans. Maximilian Mugge. Vol. 2 of *The Complete Works of Friedrich Nietzsche.* New York: Russell and Russell, 1964. 171–92.

Nitze, William A. "Horizons." *PMLA* 44, supplement (1929): iii–xi.

Norris, Frank. "Brute." *Collected Writings.* Comp. Charles G. Norris. Vol. 10. Garden City, NY: Doubleday, Doran, 1928. 80–81.

———. *Frank Norris of "The Wave": Stories and Sketches from the San Francisco Weekly, 1893 to 1897.* San Francisco: Westgate, 1931.

North, Joseph. "Reportage." *American Writer's Congress.* Ed. Henry Hart. New York: International, 1935. 120–23.

O'Brien, Frank M. *The Story of the Sun: New York, 1833–1918.* New York: George H. Doran, 1918.

O'Connor, William Van, and Frederick J. Hoffman, eds. Preface. *American Non-Fiction, 1900–1950.* 1952. Westport, CT: Greenwood, 1970. v–vii.

Orr, Linda. "The Revenge of Literature: A History of History." *New Literary History* 18.1 (autumn 1986): 1–22.

Paterson, Judith. "Literary Journalism's Twelve Best." *Washington Journalism Review* Oct. 1992: 61.

Pattee, Fred Lewis. *A History of American Literature since 1870*. New York: Century, 1915.

———. *The New American Literature, 1890–1930*. New York: Appleton, 1937.

Pauly, John J. "Damon Runyon." *A Sourcebook of American Literary Journalism: Representative Writers in an Emerging Genre*. Ed. Thomas B. Connery. New York: Greenwood, 1992. 169–78.

———. "George Ade." *A Sourcebook of American Literary Journalism: Representative Writers in an Emerging Genre*. Ed. Thomas B. Connery. New York: Greenwood, 1992. 111–20.

———. "The Politics of the New Journalism." *Literary Journalism in the Twentieth Century*. Ed. Norman Sims. New York: Oxford UP, 1990. 110–29.

Peacham, Henry. *Coach and Sedan*. 1636. London: Frederick Etchells and Hugh Macdonald, 1925.

Pegler, Westwood. *'T Ain't Right*. Garden City, NY: Doubleday, Doran, 1936.

Penkower, Monty Noam. *The Federal Writers' Project: A Study in Government Patronage of the Arts*. Urbana: U of Illinois P, 1977.

Pepys, Samuel. *The Diary of Samuel Pepys*. Ed. Robert Latham and William Matthews. Vol. 7. Berkeley: U of California P, 1970.

Pinkney, [Lt. Col.]. "Fete Champetre in a Village on a Hill at Montreuil." *Cyclopaedia of American Literature*. Ed. Evert A. Duyckinck and George L. Duyckinck. Vol. 1. New York: Scribner's, 1855. 676.

Pizer, Donald. "Documentary Narrative as Art: William Manchester and Truman Capote." *The Reporter as Artist: A Look at the New Journalism Controversy*. Ed. Ronald Weber. New York: Hastings House, 1974. 207–19.

———. *Realism and Naturalism in Nineteenth-Century American Literature*. Carbondale: Southern Illinois UP, 1966.

Plato. "The Death of Socrates, 399 B.C." *Phaedo*. Trans. H. N. Fowler. Rpt. in *Eyewitness to History*. Ed. John Carey. New York: Avon, 1987. 7–11.

Plimpton, George. "Capote's Long Ride." *New Yorker* 13 Oct. 1997: 62–70.

———. "The Story behind a Nonfiction Novel." *New York Times Book Review* 16 Jan. 1966: 2.

Pliny. *Natural History*. Trans. H. Rackham. Vol. 3. Cambridge, MA: Harvard UP, 1940.

Podhoretz, Norman. "The Article as Art." *Harper's Magazine* July 1958: 74–79.

"The Point of View: The Newspaper and Fiction." *Scribner's Magazine* 40 (1906): 122–24.

"Police Office." *Sun* 4 July 1834, morning ed.: n. pag. New York State Library microfilm 93–32024.

Pope, Walter. *The Memoires of Monsieur Du Vall*. London: 1670. University Microfilms International 819 (1977): 26.

Pottle, Frederick A. Introduction. *Boswell's London Journal, 1762–1763*. By

James Boswell. Yale Editions of the Private Papers of James Boswell. New Haven: Yale UP, 1950. 1–37.

Powell, Hickman. *The Last Paradise: An American's "Discovery" of Bali in the 1920s.* 1930. New York: Oxford UP, 1986.

———. *Ninety Times Guilty: Lucky Luciano, His Amazing Trial and Wild Witnesses.* Intro. Charles Grutzner. 1939. Secaucus, NJ: Citadel, 1975.

Powers, Thomas. "Cry Wolfe." *Commonweal* 102 (1975): 497–99.

Raleigh, Walter. *The History of the World.* 1614. Ed. C. A. Patridas. Philadelphia: Temple UP, 1971.

Ralph, Julian. *People We Pass: Stories of Life among the Masses of New York City.* New York: Harper, 1896.

Reed, John. *Adventures of a Young Man: Short Stories from Life.* San Francisco: City of Lights Books, 1985.

———. *Ten Days that Shook the World.* 1919. New York: Modern Library, 1935.

Rhodes, Richard. *The Inland Ground: An Evocation of the American Middle West.* New York: Atheneum, 1970.

Riis, Jacob. *The Making of an American.* New York: Grosset and Dunlap, 1901.

Riley, Sam G. Email to the author. 6 Mar. 2000.

———, ed. *American Magazine Journalists, 1900–1960.* First ser. Detroit: Gale, 1990.

———, ed. *American Magazine Journalists, 1900–1960.* Second ser. Detroit: Gale, 1990.

Rischin, Moses. Introduction. *Grandma Never Lived in America: The New Journalism of Abraham Cahan.* Ed. Moses Rischin. Bloomington: Indiana UP, 1985. xviii–xliv.

Roberts, Nancy. "Dorothy Day." *A Sourcebook of American Literary Journalism: Representative Writers in an Emerging Genre.* Ed. Thomas B. Connery. New York: Greenwood, 1992. 179–85.

Robertson, Michael. "Stephen Crane." *A Sourcebook of American Literary Journalism: Representative Writers in an Emerging Genre.* Ed. Thomas B. Connery. New York: Greenwood Press, 1992. 69–80.

Rogers, Agnes. "The Gibson Girl." *American Heritage* Dec. 1957. Rpt. in *A Treasury of American Heritage.* New York: Simon, 1960. 320–37.

Rogers, Everett. *A History of Communication Study: A Biographical Approach.* New York: Free, 1997.

Rogers, Everett M., and Steven Chaffee. "Communication and Journalism from 'Daddy' Bleyer to Wilbur Schramm: A Palimpsest." *Journalism Monographs* 148 (Dec. 1994).

Ross, Lillian. *Portrait of Hemingway.* 1961. New York: Modern Library, 1999.

———. *Reporting.* 1964. New York: Dodd, 1981.

———. *Vertical and Horizontal.* New York: Simon, 1963.

Rowlandson, Mary. *A Narrative of the Captivity and Restauration of Mrs. Mary Rowlandson.* 1682. *Narratives of the Indian Wars, 1675–1699.* Ed. Charles H.

Lincoln. *Original Narratives of Early American History*. Gen. ed. J. Franklin Jameson. New York: Scribner's, 1913. 118–67.

Royko, Mike. *Slats Grobnik and Some Other Friends*. New York: Dutton, 1973.

Ruland, Richard, and Malcolm Bradbury. *From Puritanism to Postmodernism: A History of American Literature*. New York: Viking Penguin, 1991.

Runyon, Damon. *The Best of Damon Runyon*. New York: Hart, 1966.

——. *The Damon Runyon Omnibus*. Garden City, NY: Sun Dial, 1944.

——. *A Treasury of Damon Runyon*. New York: Modern Library, 1958.

Ryan, Maureen. "Green Visors and Ivory Towers: Jean Stafford and the New Journalism." *Kenyon Review* 16.4 (1994): 102–19.

Rygiel, Dennis. "Style in Twentieth-Century Literary Nonfiction in English: An Annotated Bibliography of Criticism, 1980–1988." *Style* 23 (1989): 566–617.

——. "Stylistics and the Study of Twentieth-Century Literary Nonfiction." *Literary Nonfiction: Theory, Criticism, Pedagogy*. Ed. Chris Anderson. Carbondale: Southern Illinois UP, 1989. 3–28.

Sanford, George. "One in Four UFO Pilots Is Drunk!" *Weekly World News* 4 Jan. 2000: 13.

Sartre, Jean Paul. *Nausea*. 1938. Trans. Lloyd Alexander. New York: New Directions, 1964.

Sauerberg, Lars Ole. *Fact into Fiction: Documentary Realism in the Contemporary Novel*. New York: St. Martin's, 1991.

Sayre, Robert F. Notes. *Walden*. Henry David Thoreau. 1854. New York: Vintage-Library of America, 1991. 285–91.

Schlesinger, Arthur Meier. *Political and Social Growth of the United States, 1852–1933*. Rev. ed. New York: Macmillan, 1934.

——. *The Rise of the City, 1878–1898*. New York: Macmillan, 1933. Vol. 10 in *A History of American Life*. New York: Macmillan, 1933.

Schudson, Michael. *Discovering the News: A Social History of American Newspapers*. New York: Basic, 1978.

Schuster, Charles I. "The Nonfictional Prose of Richard Selzer: An Aesthetic Analysis." *Literary Nonfiction: Theory, Criticism, Pedagogy*. Ed. Chris Anderson. Carbondale: Southern Illinois UP, 1989. 3–28.

Settle, Elkanah. *The Life and Death of Major Clancie, the Grandest Cheat of This Age*. London: 1680. *Early English Books, 1641–1700* 1158 (1981): 12.

Shaaber, M. A. *Some Forerunners of the Newspaper in England, 1476–1622*. New York: Octagon Books, 1966.

Sheehan, Neil. *A Bright Shining Lie*. New York: Random, 1988.

Sims, Norman. "Joseph Mitchell and the *New Yorker* Nonfiction Writers." *Literary Journalism in the Twentieth Century*. Ed. Norman Sims. New York: Oxford UP, 1990. 82–109.

——. "The Literary Journalists." *The Literary Journalists*. Ed. Norman Sims. New York: Ballantine, 1984. 3–25.

——, ed. *Literary Journalism in the Twentieth Century*. New York: Oxford UP, 1990.

————, ed. *The Literary Journalists.* New York: Ballantine, 1984.

Sims, Norman, and Mark Kramer, eds. *Literary Journalism.* New York: Ballantine, 1995.

Skinner, Constance Lindsay. "Rivers and American Folk." *Suwannee River: Strange Green Land.* By Cecile Hulse Matschat. Ed. Constance Lindsay Skinner. New York: Farrar, 1938. N. pag.

Sloan, William David, comp. *American Journalism History: An Annotated Bibliography. Bibliographies and Indexes in Mass Media and Communications 1.* New York: Greenwood, 1989.

Smith, John. *The Generall Historie of Virginia, New-England, and the Summer Isles.* . . . 1624. Ed. Philip L. Barbour. Chapel Hill: U of North Carolina P, 1986. Vol. 2 of *The Complete Works of Captain John Smith.*

Smith, Kathy. "John McPhee Balances the Act." *Literary Journalism in the Twentieth Century.* Ed. Norman Sims. New York: Oxford UP, 1990. 206–27.

Smith's Currant Intelligence, or an Impartial Account of Transactions both Foraign and Domestick. 10–13 Apr. 1680: 1. Research Publications (n.d.): 1173. Charles Burney Collection of Early English Newspapers from the British Library.

Snyder, Louis L., and Richard B. Morris, eds. "A Reporter for the *London Spy* Finds Bedlam 'an Almshouse for Madmen, a Showing Room for Whores, and a Sure Market for Lechers.'" *A Treasury of Great Reporting: "Literature under Pressure" from the Sixteenth Century to Our Own Time.* Pref. Herbert Bayard Swope. 2d rev. ed. New York: Simon, 1962. 5–6, 10.

Solotaroff, Theodore. "Introduction to Writers and Issues." *The Reporter as Artist: A Look at the New Journalism Controversy.* Ed. Ronald Weber. New York: Hastings House, 1974. 161–66.

Stallman, R. W., and E. R. Hagemann, eds. *The New York City Sketches of Stephen Crane and Related Pieces.* New York: New York UP, 1966.

————. *The War Dispatches of Stephen Crane.* New York: New York UP, 1964.

Stark, Freya. *Baghdad Sketches.* New York: Dutton, 1938.

————. *A Winter in Arabia.* New York: Dutton, 1940.

Steffens, Lincoln. *The Autobiography of Lincoln Steffens.* New York: Harcourt, 1931.

————. "The Shame of Minneapolis: The Rescue and Redemption of a City That Was Sold Out." *McClure's Magazine* (1903). Rpt. in *The Shame of the Cities.* 1904. Intro. Louis Joughin. New York: Sagamore, 1957. 42–68.

Stephens, Mitchell. *A History of News: From the Drum to the Satellite.* New York: Viking, 1988.

Stevenson, Elizabeth. *Lafcadio Hearn.* New York: Macmillan, 1961.

Stott, William. *Documentary Expression and Thirties America.* New York: Oxford UP, 1973.

Sutherland, James. *English Literature of the Late Seventeenth Century.* New York: Oxford UP, 1969.

Talese, Gay. *Fame and Obscurity.* New York: Ivy Books, 1993.

————. *The Kingdom and the Power.* New York: World, 1969.

Tarbell, Ida. "The History of the Standard Oil Company." *McClure's Magazine* (1902). Rpt. *The History of the Standard Oil Company.* New York: P. Smith, 1950.

Taylor, John. *All the Workes: Being Sixty and Three in Number.* London: Printed by J.B. for J. Boler, 1630.

Tebbel, John William. *The Media in America.* New York: Thomas Y. Crowell, 1974.

Theroux, Paul. Introduction. *Cape Cod.* By Henry David Thoreau. New York: Penguin, 1987.

Thomas, Lowell. *With Lawrence In Arabia.* Garden City, NY: Garden City, 1924.

Thompson, Maurice. "The Prospect of Fiction." *Independent* 52 (1900): 1182–83.

Thoreau, Henry David. *Cape Cod.* 1865. New York: Penguin, 1987.

———. *Walden.* 1854. New York: Vintage-Library of America, 1991.

"Titanic Sinks Four Hours after Hitting Iceberg . . . Col. Astor and Bride . . . Aboard." *New York Times* 16 Apr. 1912: 1–2.

Trachtenberg, Alan. "Experiments in Another Country: Stephen Crane's City Sketches." *Southern Review* 10: 265–85.

———. *The Incorporation of America: Culture and Society in the Gilded Age.* New York: Hill and Wang, 1982.

Troyer, Howard William. *Ned Ward of Grubstreet: A Study of Sub-Literary London in the Eighteenth Century.* Cambridge, MA: Harvard UP, 1946.

Twain, Mark. *Life on the Mississippi.* 1883. New York: Bantam, 1945.

"2,000 Reds Attack Police at City Hall." *New York Times* 20 Jan. 1931: 1.

"Violet." *Rodale's Illustrated Encyclopedia of Herbs.* Allentown, PA: Rodale, 1987.

Vitalis, Oderic. *The Ecclesiastical History of Oderic Vitalis.* Ed. and trans. Marjorie Chibnall. Vol. 4. Oxford: Clarendon, 1973.

Wakefield, Dan. "Harold Hayes and the New Journalism." *Nieman Reports* (summer 1992): 32–35.

———. "The Personal Voice and the Impersonal Eye." *The Reporter as Artist: A Look at the New Journalism Controversy.* Ed. Ronald Weber. New York: Hastings House, 1974. 39–48.

Walker, Stanley. *City Editor.* New York: Frederick A. Stokes, 1934.

[Ward, Edward "Ned."] *London Spy.* Apr. 1699. 3d ed. *English Literary Periodical Series* (1954) 62E.

———. *London Spy.* Apr. 1700. Vol. 2. *English Literary Periodical Series* (1954) 62E.

Warner, Langdon. "The Editor's Clearing-House: Need Journalism Destroy Literature?" *Critic* 48 (1906): 469–70.

"Washington Notes." *New Republic* 18 May 1927: 353–54.

Webb, Joseph. "Historical Perspective on the New Journalism." *Journalism History* 1.2 (1974): 38–42, 60.

Weber, Ronald. "Hemingway's Permanent Records." *Literary Journalism in the Twentieth Century.* Ed. Norman Sims. New York: Oxford UP, 1990. 21–52.

———. *The Literature of Fact: Literary Nonfiction in American Writing*. Athens: Ohio UP, 1980.

———. "Some Sort of Artistic Excitement." *The Reporter as Artist: A Look at the New Journalism Controversy*. Ed. Ronald Weber. New York: Hastings House, 1974. 13–23.

Webster's New Collegiate Dictionary. 1967 ed.

Wells, Linton. "Mexico's Bid for Supremacy in Central America." *New Republic* 18 May 1927: 348–50.

Whibley, Charles. "Writers of Burlesque and Translators." *The Cambridge History of English Literature*. Ed. A. W. Ward and A. R. Waller. Vol. 9. Cambridge: Cambridge UP, 1912. 255–78.

White, E. B. "Clear Days." *One Man's Meat*. New York: Harper, 1950. 18–22.

Wiles, R. M. *Freshest Advices: Early Provincial Newspapers in England*. N.p.: Ohio State UP, 1965.

Williamson, G. A. Introduction. *Foxe's Book of Martyrs*. By John Foxe. 1596–97. 5th ed. Ed. and abr. G. A. Williamson. Boston: Little, 1965.

Wilson, Edmund. *Axel's Castle: A Study in the Imaginative Literature of 1870–1930*. New York: Scribner's, 1943.

———. "Communists and Cops." *New Republic* 11 Feb. 1931: 344–47.

Wilson, Harold S. *McClure's Magazine and the Muckrakers*. Princeton: Princeton UP, 1970.

Winterowd, W. Ross. *The Rhetoric of the "Other" Literature*. Carbondale: Southern Illinois UP, 1990.

Wolfe, Tom. *The Electric Kool-Aid Acid Test*. New York: Bantam, 1969.

———. *The Kandy-Kolored Tangerine-Flake Streamline Baby*. New York: Farrar, 1965.

———. "The Kandy-Kolored Tangerine-Flake Streamline Baby." *The Kandy-Kolored Tangerine-Flake Streamline Baby*. New York: Farrar, 1965. 76–107.

———. "The Last American Hero." *The Kandy-Kolored Tangerine-Flake Streamline Baby*. New York: Farrar, 1965. 126–72.

———. "The New Journalism." *The New Journalism: With an Anthology*. Ed. Tom Wolfe and E. W. Johnson. New York: Harper, 1973.

———. *The Right Stuff*. New York: Farrar, 1979.

Wycherley, William. Dedication. *The Plain Dealer*. 1676. *The Complete Works of William Wycherley*. Ed. Montague Summers. Vol. 2. New York: Russell & Russell, 1964. 97–102.

Yagoda, Ben. Preface. *The Art of Fact: A Historical Anthology of Literary Journalism*. Ed. Kevin Kerrane and Ben Yagoda. New York: Scribner's, 1997.

Zalinski, E. L. "Destruction of War Ship Maine Was the Work of an Enemy." *New York Journal and Advertiser* 17 Feb. 1898, greater New York ed.: 1.

Zavarzadeh, Mas'ud. *The Mythopoeic Reality: The Postwar American Nonfiction Novel*. Urbana: U of Illinois P, 1976.

Ziff, Larzar. *The American 1890s: Life and Times of a Lost Generation*. Lincoln: U of Nebraska P, 1966.

Index